Eat Feed
Autumn Winter

30 ways to celebrate when the mercury drops

Anne Bramley

Photographs by Tina Rupp

Stewart, Tabori & Chang

NEW YORK

Published in 2008 by Stewart, Tabori & Chang
An imprint of Harry N. Abrams, Inc.

Text copyright © 2008 by Anne Bramley
Photographs copyright © 2008 by Tina Rupp

Library of Congress Cataloging-in-Publication Data

Bramley, Anne.
 Eat feed autumn winter : 30 ways to celebrate when the mercury drops / Anne Bramley ;
photographs by Tina Rupp.
 p. cm.
 Includes index.
 ISBN 978-1-58479-719-7
 1. Entertaining. 2. Cookery. 3. Menus. I. Title.

TX731.B6645 2008
641.5—dc22
 2007050726

Editor: Dervla Kelly
Designer: LeAnna Weller Smith
Production Manager: Tina Cameron

The text of this book was composed in Avenir, Berthold Akzidenz Grotesk, Linotype
Centennial, and Shelley Andante Script.

Printed and bound in China
10 9 8 7 6 5 4 3 2 1

HNA

harry n. abrams, inc.

a subsidiary of La Martinière Groupe

115 West 18th Street
New York, NY 10011
www.hnabooks.com

For Daniel, who is always willing to eat beans on toast
so that the world can have caviar toast points

contents

8 acknowledgements
10 introduction
14 secrets of the cold-weather pantry
44 the host's toolbox

autumn

52 season of mists and mellow fruitfulness
58 fresh from the field
64 bringing in the sheaves
70 raking in the leaves
74 an orchard buffet
80 all hallows' eve
86 guy fawkes
90 the politics of food
94 the hunting party

winter

102 the first snowfall
108 festival of light
114 winter solstice
120 gathering greenery
126 highlands hogmanay
132 sunday roast
136 happy hour
142 twelfth night
148 citrus in season
152 feast away the winter blues
156 a posh pub night
162 the frozen north
168 haggis and a hooley
174 traveling the spice route
178 food of the gods

184 fireside chat
188 breakfast in bed
192 party hearty
198 après ski at the swiss chalet
202 afternoon tea
206 the last of the comfort food

210 flurries
217 conversion chart
218 index

acknowledgments

Like a great dinner or cocktail party, there are many people who make a cookbook possible, and to produce a book from start to finish requires supernatural creative insights as well as superhuman capacities for patience and flexibility. I'm lucky enough to have a team of people who possess all these traits in great abundance. Many thanks first go to my agent, Danielle Svetcov, for her loyalty, enthusiasm, and generous support and guidance as we both gave birth and navigated new parenthood just as this book went into production. Her hard work has transformed my life in many ways that, even for a writer, elude mere words. My editor, Dervla Kelly, has been an absolute pleasure to work with, as much for her skill and creative insight as for her endless patience and thoughtful reassurances. In giving my culinary passion a home at Stewart, Tabori, and Chang and encouraging me with the idea that not everyone wants a cookie-cutter approach to food, publisher Leslie Stoker has given me an opportunity for which I am grateful. I am also thankful for how enticingly delicious Tina Rupp made my recipes in her photography, how clear and organized Karen Fraley made my writing in her copy editing, and how persuasively inviting LeAnna Weller Smith made the book feel in her design.

No cookbook can happen without a dedicated troupe of eaters and testers. At the top of that list is one of my dearest friends, Lissa McBurney, who has always been so much more than either of those categories express. In addition to her unwavering support for nearly two decades, I value her scientific approach to testing the recipes for this book, which was exactly what my analytical mind craved. The most generous person in the food world, Wisconsin food expert Terese Allen, has always been there to support the podcast and the book, which never would have been finished without her connections to eager testers across a state where the folks know how to eat well when the mercury drops. Thanks especially to Sarah Marx Feldman for her insights on baking, Sarah Brooks for her vegetable knowledge and dining stories, Debra Shapiro for her encouragement on many fronts at once, and Mary Bergin for her journalistic approach. Thanks also go to Jean and Joel Devore, Chris Odt, and Dorothy Davenport. I feel eccentrically compelled to thank the whole state of Wisconsin—a winter paradise on which I thrive even when far away—for introducing me to snow shoeing, cross-country skiing by candlelight, and outdoor fish boils even when it's only (or as much as) 5° in January.

All new writers depend on those who gave them an early boost. Novelist Katherine Weber made it possible for me to think of myself as a Writer, capital W. Diane Daniel was not only a willing taster but also an adventurous journalist willing to cover my unorthodox ideas about the Midwest and endure my cold-climate fanaticism in spite of her Southern doubts. BBC journalist Chris Valance gave me my first "big time" radio interview, inflating my ego enough to help me believe I could take on such a project. Many famous foodies blessed this project early on as well, and I'm grateful to people like Steven Raichlen, Rose Levy Beranbaum, and Harold McGee, who were willing to lend an endorsement to a brave new medium like podcasting.

Because this book was launched out of *Eat Feed*, I must thank the many people who have donated their time, talent, experience, and pure sweat equity to the podcast. First and foremost is Mia Littlejohn, who has always been a sounding board and a support whenever my eyes were bigger than my stomach for the too-many tasks I'd set myself. She's an absolute gusher when it comes to fountains of creativity. Sandy Oliver has shown me the way through the world of food history beyond academia and has enriched the program with her vast knowledge of American food history. Erika Janik's audio essays delight me every month on our Midwest series and inspire me with new ideas about cold-weather food culture. Many others, including Shane, Rachel, and Erica, have helped build the program over the years.

We couldn't live without the farmers, fishermen and fisherwomen, and food producers everywhere, who are so deeply invested in the turn of the seasons and the fateful cycles of plenty and want. I am grateful for their hard work that makes possible pleasures and rarities like smoked Great Lakes whitefish, artisanal British cheeses, and heirloom winter vegetables.

Grandma Dorothy, Aunt Sandy, and Aunt Sarah schooled me early on by bringing everyday food to life. Though she never really cooked much, my mother's endless hours at difficult jobs meant I learned to cook at a very early age. I'm grateful especially for her gift of a new gas stove in my first house, without which this book would never have been written. Thanks also to my father for the perfect kitchen floor to put under that stove and my first mixer, which launched a small home baking business at sixteen.

Chantal Wright makes the impossible possible and there is no one I'd rather queue with in the frantic madness of a Berlin grocery store at rush hour. She's continued my education in British culinary traditions and encouraged my enthusiasm for a much maligned cuisine by sharing her excitement about Christmas cakes and teaching me that some of the best chips go from freezer to table in 20 minutes.

Most importantly, my love and endless gratitude go to my husband, Daniel Foster, who is as much a part of this project as I am. He is the main reason *Eat Feed* began. He is always there more than any spouse has the energy to be. He reassures me when I'm afraid of success and reminds me I deserve it. And more practically, he's the one-stop recipe tester, number-one feedback guru, late-night lost-ingredient shopper, first-line-of-defense editor, and best-ever life coach. Without him, I couldn't thank Oona, who was there with me every long day in the kitchen, every morning at the computer, and who was kind enough to wait to be born until I delivered my manuscript first.

introduction

I was born in a blizzard. Which means that my earliest memories of celebrating are set against a backdrop of neck-high snow drifts you could lose a small child in (and sometimes did), windchill factors that leave you checking to make sure you are indeed wearing clothes, and welcoming rituals that center on finding a place for all those slushy boots and guests' coats. The privilege of picking my favorite birthday menu each year got me hooked at a young age on roasted meats, winter roots, and citrus desserts in January. There was more than one childhood slumber party that nearly became a week-long affair as the snow came down fast and heavy the next morning. And countless were the cups of hot chocolate and homemade cookies that fueled impromptu post-birthday entertainments during those adventures of sledding and igloo building afforded by the extra days off school.

For as long as I can remember, my passion for cold-weather cooking and entertaining has gone beyond cozy quaintness to something others might call frigidly obsessive. I wait impatiently for those early days of September to melt away in the final rays of a hot and lazy summer and for those often sudden winds to blow in from the north almost overnight as the first day of autumn falls into view toward the end of the month.

With this drop in temperature, I am revitalized and head back into the kitchen. I am the cook who came in from the cold, invigorated by the new crop of fruits and vegetables pouring forth from my local market stands: all those heirloom varieties of apples and pears that small farmers are lovingly bringing back to diners hungry for real food. I treasure those oddly colored and shaped squashes that multiply in size and kind each season, along with the precious seasonal rarities like cranberries that can't be had for love or money except for a few months each year.

And at the same time, I am in awe of how life seems to slow down as September fades into October, as the months grow colder and our Filofaxes shed appointments like trees their leaves. We no longer rush from work to beach to work, hopping into our cars for long-distance vacation marathons, trying to pack as much as possible into a sun-filled day. Instead, we seem to spend more time at home, with friends, with family, or indulging in the peaceful solitude that colder seasons bring. As twilight comes on earlier and transforms into night even more quickly, our attention shifts from the outdoor barbecue grill to the indoor oven, our modern hearth, a contemporary vestige of what was for so long the center of the home. We retreat inside to bake, braise, and stew with all the time and patience those cold-weather methods of cooking require. While the heat of the oven fills our home with those signature spicy and earthy autumnal scents of the season, and our Dutch ovens and other favorite workhorse pots and pans take their rightful place back on the stovetop, we cuddle up on the sofa to the new season of our favorite television shows and contemplate which of the many holiday book releases to dive into first.

Though we indulge in these retreats into the self, we also throw open our doors and update our guest lists, refresh our memories of our favorite holiday get-togethers, and re-imagine ourselves the consummate cold-weather hosts. There's something more than generous, almost culinarily poetic, definitely symbolic, in sharing with our favorite people the season's first batch of hot-from-the-oven cookies, a triumphantly perfect-crust chicken pot pie, or a wonderfully nostalgic stew, the recipe for which has morphed and transformed as it has moved from great-grandmother's custom to aunt's recipe box to the printout from our laptop.

Autumn and winter are the seasons for entertaining and we can't find enough excuses to pull out the cookbooks, crank up the oven, and lay out all those gorgeous plates hiding under the paper and plastic gear of summer. We let our imaginations run wild with whimsical adult updates for Halloween cuisine, contemplate globally infused Thanksgiving meals, and promise to put on the most dramatic spread for New Year's Eve. With visions of butternut squash and roasted chestnuts dancing in our heads, we eagerly flip through the November and December glossy food magazines looking for inspiration. Hence the reason for a book about eating well and entertaining in the coldest months, about inviting friends and strangers alike to your table, always extending a warm welcome, an extra plate, and endlessly delicious, seasonally inspired things to put on it. A drop in temperatures has me racing back to the kitchen to start entertaining. Rather than going into a hibernation cocoon, I look forward to the chance of having everyone back in town from their summer travels and knowing I can put a dinner party together in a flash.

But...

It's often made me much more than a little melancholy to notice how, as much as we love the candlelit tables, the vastly enlarged social sphere, the endless opportunities to wine, dine, and lose ourselves in good conversation and even better food, we aren't always sure how to really cook, or how to cook well, through the cold season. In summer hordes of cooks and noncooks alike flock to their local farmers' markets in ritual-like precision every Saturday morning or Wednesday afternoon to stock up on local, seasonal favorites. But after these markets pack up their tables in autumn and disappear for winter, I watch as eager eaters displace their enthusiasm for the seasonal with excuses about ease and throw out all concern for the local to return to the grocery store, where everything is always available no matter what the calendar says. We rush to buy out-of-season asparagus and strawberries pushed on us for the perfect Valentine's meal and green beans shipped in by the truckload for Thanksgiving and Christmas recipes

touted as seasonal menus while we too often overlook the gorgeous beets and cranberries from which to craft elegant and organic heart-red Valentines, as well as all the roots, game, greens, and preserves that should be gracing the holiday table in November and December.

Certainly some cooks have begun to recognize the need for truly cold-weather food, especially in the era of climate shifts when we find winter doesn't really come until January but still has its own peculiarities of intensity. But flip through so-called cold-season cooking guides and you'll still find them brimming with requests for chives, cherry tomatoes, okra, eggplant, and so many other foods I love—in summer that is, when they are at the peak of their season, not autumn and winter. Among the staples of recipes for butternut squash soups and apple pies, you'll find blueberry tarts and roasted zucchini in months when you cannot possibly get these sunshine-loving ingredients unless you extend your open hand southward and beg for imports from Chile or Mexico. There are so many great foods and flavors from September to March—and several that will surprise you as being in season in cold months—that there's simply no need to fall back on our hot-weather habits. The problem is not in being able to find enough in-season food but rather in making sure you get a chance to taste it all at least once before the pleasure of cold-weather food melts away in April and May.

Thus, for planting such heresies in your head and in your garden, I sometimes think I should have called this book *The Dangerous Book for Cooks*. But also because in an era of commercially prescribed gifts and fading rituals, it is perhaps hard to imagine young children with flaming candles on their head for St. Lucia Day (p. 212) or bonfires for Guy Fawkes (p. 86). There's good reason so many of these celebrations center on fire, whether from the fondue pot or a dessert flambéed tableside. Naturally with longer nights and shorter days, we crave the heat and fire as creative not only of literal warmth but also symbolic of spiritual warmth, of the roaring hearth for cooking or heating, of a cozy place by the fire, of the lighted inn for the weary traveler. I have looked around the world and reached into the past to uncover not only the tastes from far away and long ago but also the traditions, the many good reasons in the calendrical cycle for gathering together. And it is in these that I find the most fun—if you're willing to get a bit dangerous. There are so many reasons to bring everyone to the table, whether it's entertaining for 2 or 20. So unite your comrades, spark your imagination against the flint of these recipes, and warm your bellies with good food and good cheer as you eat and feed through my favorite seasons of autumn and winter.

secrets of the cold-weather pantry

Apples and Pears	Cheese	Dried Fruits	Roots
Beans and Grains	Chocolate	Game	Spices
Braising Cuts	Citrus	Nuts	Spirits
Canned Tomatoes	Cranberries	Pickles	Squash
Charcuterie	Crucifers	Preserves	More Staples

The reassuring plenty in the pantry and the necessary philosophy of stocking up is never more important than in colder months when you can't just step out onto the stoop and pluck a tomato from your urban garden or head to the farmers' market to pick up armfuls of fresh basil. Until relatively recently, humans—women usually—had to work hard during the summer months to "put up" for winter, whether in the root cellar, the larder, or the pantry. Today, for better or worse, refrigeration and shipping have transformed the way we eat. But we still need to keep our mind on being prepared for any entertaining opportunity that might come our way.

We have managed to overcome so much of the annual seasonal cycle that once dictated the lives of our not-too-distant ancestors, with central air conditioning, windowless cubicles, and Congressionally mandated clock time rather than the natural rhythm of the sun and the earth. But try as we might, one thing that still stops us, quite literally, in our tracks, is a good hard snow. I'm happiest when it's at least down to 20° outside, there's snow falling (the faster the better), and the hectic pace of life slows down just a little and we have to think a little more carefully about our food. What I find absolutely maddening is this irrational hording tendency that grips so many at the least whisper of a dusting and sends even McMansion denizens with deep freezers and survivalist-inspired walk-ins stocked with warehouse foods to rush to the grocery store and buy the last bottle of water, the last pint of skim milk, and the last loaf of preservative-laden bread. As if these three ingredients alone are going to get you through a flurry, let alone a blizzard. But with a little sense and decorum and just a bit of planning ahead, we can avoid the insanity of those rushes and instead be prepared to throw together a wonderfully inventive meal when any waylaid soul or cabin-fevered friend may turn up on our doorstep in desperate need of a warm meal, a place by the fire, and a good winter's tale.

Apples and Pears

Edward Behr originally made me fall in love with apples not just as a food but as a concept, a symbol, an object of desire, and a force to be reckoned with. It was both his lament, in *The Artful Eater*, for lost varieties and his story of the evolution and dispersion of the apple that did it. I found a kindred spirit in his confession that "I have nearly always had a cold-climate attitude toward apples. I associate them with the first cool days of later summer or with bracing days in autumn, when snow is a not-too-distant possibility."

Unfortunately, at some point the variety of apples available commercially dwindled and we were left with the misnamed Greenland of the fruit world, that ubiquitous bred-for-shipping Red Delicious, which while certainly red is anything but delicious. Happily, though, we've seen renewed interest in more unusual apple varieties that are valued for their taste and historical importance. One of the things I really love about heirloom apples and pears is all the delicious, whimsical, incomprehensible, and even obscene names growers have bestowed on these autumn fruits over the centuries. I've been lucky enough to talk on *Eat Feed* with some delightfully fanatical heirloom fruit revivalists, including Charles Martell in Gloucestershire, England, who is not only bringing back some truly intriguing varieties but also is known for being the maker of the infamous Stinking Bishop cheese that revives the dead in Wallace and Gromit's *Curse of the Were-Rabbit*. It might be difficult to find his apple varieties like Hens' Turds, Hagloe Crab, Pretty Beds, and Leathercoat at your local farm market or grocery store. But there are plenty of others beyond the typical three or four varieties that grocery store chains carry year-round that will become your own local favorite if you taste and experiment.

Stock Up on Apples and Pears

It would take volumes and volumes to try to catalogue and detail every variety of apple and pear available in North America alone. But here a few suggestions for what you're more likely to find in the store that will get you started in investigating the endless colors, flavors, and profiles of these autumn orchard fruits.

Apples

Arkansas Black: An apple variety I discovered after moving south; it's the gorgeous near-purple skin that first catches your eye. Arkansas Black is a great keeper and good cider apple and is just as good in cooking as eating fresh.

Braeburn: From New Zealand, one of those varieties that has diversified commercially available apples and done a lot to get us thinking beyond the 2 or 3 choices of industrial production. Good, all-purpose fruit for lunch boxes that stores well for many months.

Gala: Another prize from New Zealand that, like the Braeburn, has done a lot to get us to try new apples. Mild flavor that appeals to a range of apple lovers.

Lady Apples: Though perfectly edible with a good crispness, these apples are often used to grace the punch bowl, adorn wreaths, or garnish holiday cakes. Hence their nickname of "Christmas apples."

Macoun: As one of the many apples that can trace its lineage to the McIntosh, the Macoun is a firm and delicious apple perfect to eat right off the tree.

Nonesuch: More formally known as the *Hubbardston Nonesuch,* this apple wins my prize for favorite name, so while it is harder to come by, I couldn't resist including it as a good example of something fun to keep an eye open for. But its rich-tasting flesh and bright red skin make it a good choice for eating as well.

Northern Spy: This perfect specimen, often found in New York and the Upper Midwest, is my number one North American favorite both for its tart taste and its keeping qualities. In one of the best Marches I have ever baked through, one Michigan grower presented me with 3 perfect Northern Spy that had kept beautifully since the autumn harvest. They became the inspiration for Maple Apple Tartlets (p. 72). For Northern Spy and other select apple varieties in season, see www.seedlingfruit.com.

Pears

Bartlett: The classic Bartlett, which turns a lovely autumn yellow when ripe, is excellent for cooking and baking. The red Bartlett, one of my favorites, has all the same great taste and culinary qualities but with the benefit of adding a bit more color to the autumn table. It's also beautiful and tasty when put up in glass jars with cinnamon sticks during canning season.

Bosc: With a yellow-brown papery skin, these pears have a wonderfully rustic appearance. Their flesh is ideal for culinary uses, which is why along with the Bartlett, they are recommended for the rigors of making Pears in Nightshirts (p. 99), which undergo both poaching and baking.

Comice: Favored for their sweetness as well as their juiciness, these pears make a great addition to a fruit and cheese plate.

Seckle Pears: Like Lady Apples, good for small hands and even better for decorating holiday cakes and tables.

Cooking with Apples and Pears

* Maple Apple Tartlets (p. 72)
* Pork Chops with Apples and Brandy (p. 75)
* Lincoln's Inaugural Chicken Salad and Lobster Salad (p. 92)
* Watercress and Apple Salad with Honey Vinaigrette (p. 98)
* Pears in Nightshirts (p. 99)
* Lambswool Punch (p. 115)
* Whisky Trifle (p. 129)
* Roast Beef Sandwiches with Pear Spread and Stilton (p. 138)

Beans and Grains

Although really two categories with countless variations, we speak of beans and grains in the same breath for many reasons. They are both such basic, ancient foods—some of the first cultivated by humans—that they have become strong cultural symbols of elemental life. They are worshipped around the world in rice festivals and rituals of the wheat harvest. With "ancient grains" like quinoa and amaranth as well as heirloom bean varieties like Christmas lima, Jacob's Cattle, and Cranberry beans, they also connect us to a long culinary lineage and remind us of great foods we may have lost touch with over the years.

Beans and grains both store easily so that you can keep them around in your favorite Mason jars all season or stock up on canned beans to always have at the ready. When there's nothing else in the house, you've just returned from holiday travel, and guests threaten to stop by, you can do a lot with just a fistful of grain or a hill of beans. Store both beans and grains through the winter, but replenish each season. Maybe that jar of beans that has been in the back of your cupboard for 4 years isn't growing mold or rotting, but it has gone bad in ways you can't see. For starters, it will take much longer to cook. Old beans are tough.

When you tire of hearty meat dishes, beans and grains provide that uplifting alternative packed with all kinds of health benefits, from the high fiber content of beans to all those "superfood" qualities that are renewing interest in the likes of the humble oat. Some of my favorite cold-weather bean dishes are built from the simple and simply elegant white bean. Many wintry Italian soups start with this building block, but my favorite way to cook up something perfect for the incoming cold is white beans, garlic, sage, and a splash of olive oil. Cover it all with water and simmer for 2 to 3 hours until the beans are soft. Salt and pepper to taste and serve with your favorite crusty bread. And don't forget the transformation of white beans to something altogether different in a good dish of Canadian baked beans with maple syrup and mustard powder.

There are so many beans and grains to choose from that I'm tempted just to point you in the direction of your nearest bulk aisle and let you run wild. But here are a few ideas to get you started. To uncover more, tune into sources like www.seedsavers.org and www.ranchogordo.com, both of which sell a selection of heirloom beans. Also check out your favorite health food store for new directions in whole grains.

Stock Up on Beans and Grains

Ancient Grains: This includes foods like quinoa, teff, millet, and amaranth that remind us of treasures from the so-called New World that often provide a more healthful alternative to overprocessed staples. Keep in mind that amaranth and quinoa are both technically fruits rather than grains but you'll never find them in the produce aisle.

Brown Rice: Brown rice offers a nutty flavor that works well with so many cold-weather foods. Though brown rice requires a cooking time twice that of white rice, you can make them separately, mix them together, and then toss in dried fruits, nuts, onions, garlic, and other favorite tidbits to make an easy pilaf that has a lot more going for it than plain white rice.

Couscous: This North African grain is a form of wheat. It cooks incredibly quickly and is the perfect pairing for slow-cooked lamb dishes and sweet-hot stews.

Lentils: A good source of iron, protein, and selenium, this is another of those large categories that includes really distinct foods from many parts of the globe. There are the small French lentils or *lentils de Puy*, cooked al dente and often used in lentil salads mixed with cold-weather vegetables like carrots or celery roots and livened up with a nice vinaigrette. And then there are just your versatile everyday brown lentils that are perfect for a wintry vegetarian soup.

Split Peas: In yellow or green, they're both an absolute winter necessity. When the holiday table is cleared and the leftovers all gone, you'll find yourself staring at the lonely hambone, grateful for a jar of split peas to make a smoky winter soup that lets the memories of the meal live on through the marrow of the bone.

Oats: This is one of those much talked about foods that has recovered from Samuel Johnson's eighteenth-century slight, which defined them as "a grain, which in England is generally given to horses, but in Scotland supports the people." In fact, they've more than recovered to find their way into the pantheon of superfoods that are revered at present for doing everything from lowering your cholesterol to enhancing your mood. No longer are oats just a bowl of porridge to be disparaged.

White Rice: This includes a range of diverse flavors and varieties. It's a good idea to at least keep on hand one all-purpose long-grain white rice. I also have at the ready basmati rice for impromptu Indian curries to warm the winter palate and a short-grain style like sushi rice for a simple dinner of miso-glazed fish over rice.

Wild Rice: Another one of those culinary misnomers, wild rice is not really a rice but an aquatic grass. It really is worth it to try to get your hands on some truly wild rice rather than the cultivated rice available in most grocery stores. You will never go back. For more on wild rice, see p. 76.

Cooking with Beans and Grains

* Wheat Berry and Fig Salad (p. 68)
* Wild Rice Pilaf with Cherries and Pecans (p. 76)
* Chicken Breasts with Pumpkin Seed Filling and Butternut Sauce (p. 82)
* Thai Coconut Rice Twists (p. 103)
* Whisky Trifle (p. 129)
* Double Oatmeal Cookies (p. 135)
* Coconut Black Beans (p. 149)
* Dollars and Coins (p. 153)
* Lamb Meat Loaf with Marmalade Glaze (p. 169)
* Lamb Stew with Figs and Apricots (p. 177)
* Chocolate Beef Stew with Butternut Squash and Amaranth (p. 179)
* Quick and Easy Italian Soup (p. 196)

Braising Cuts

Instead of pricey tenderloins or chops for the summer grill, turn to braising cuts at a fraction of the price and indulge in the season by warming the house while your wonderfully fragrant dinner cooks slowly. So-called "low cuts" do equally well on the stovetop or in the oven. The two key ingredients for making the most of braising cuts are heat and moisture. They require long, slow cooking times and a little liquid to help tenderize tough connective tissues. One of the greatest benefits to entertaining with such foods is that you can let them do their thing all day while you attend to other things. Even better, you can start the prep, let the dish cook, and take your time getting ready so that you and the meal are finished simultaneously, rather than greeting your guests half-dressed with wet hair as you just start to put the steak on the grill.

One caveat: never waste your money on a cut of meat intended for grilling or roasting and then subject it to a braise. Another caveat: when purchasing anything labeled "stew meat" be sure to ask what exactly it is. These are often the odds and ends of various cuts and the cooking time can vary widely. For example, pork stew can be anything from country ribs to pork loin, depending on what the butcher has left over.

Stock Up on Braising Cuts

Beef Chuck: Chuck is one big category describing a lot of different shoulder cuts. You might find it as blade roast, bottom chuck, or plain old chuck shoulder roast, among other guises. Because the shoulder is a hard worker, it contains a lot of connective tissue, which means that you need that magic combination of hot and wet for a long period to make those tissues mouthwateringly melty.

Pork Shoulder: You'll find pork shoulder as either ham ("fresh" or "picnic") or, in one of those culinary in jokes, "Boston butt." They can be used pretty much interchangeably, though the hams tend to be a bit leaner than the "butt." Like beef chuck from the shoulder, pork shoulder requires a long slow braising treatment.

Lamb Shoulder: And from a third beast, we find the perfect braising cut in the shoulder again. You can find lamb shoulder as a bone-in or boneless roast or as chops. Because cubed lamb labeled "stew meat" is often but not always from the shoulder, it's better to buy the shoulder roast and cut it to your taste. Don't confuse shoulder chops with rib chops, a far more expensive cut that is best grilled or broiled.

Lamb Shanks: Nothing says winter comfort food quite like these hardy and hearty bits at the end of the leg. Because of the wonderful sinews, lamb shanks produce rich gelatinous broths as they cook. Better still, they look gorgeous on the plate and are possibly one of the least expensive lamb cuts.

Cooking with Braising Cuts

* French Onion Pot Roast (p. 133)
* Beef and Brown Ale Pie (p. 158)
* Lamb Stew with Figs and Apricots (p. 177)
* Chocolate Beef Stew with Butternut Squash and Amaranth (p. 179)
* Rustic Winter Stew (p. 195)
* Stout-Glazed Lamb Chops (p. 207)

Canned Tomatoes

Almost all vegetables taste best fresh. A few, like peas and corn, do pretty well frozen and make a great addition to winter soups. But there is only one vegetable—and technically it's really a fruit—that I would say is fair game for eating from a can: tomatoes. There are many instances when heartier, richer, and more intense canned tomatoes are preferred to the vine-ripened delicacies that glut farmers' markets in summer when you're craving the perfect BLT or salsa fresca. This is especially true in braises and stews, which demand long cooking times and often have other intense flavors like spices, meats, and greens with which the tomatoes must blend.

One of the best things about canned tomatoes is they don't require rocket science to prepare. If you like the taste of tomatoes, you can toss in a can anywhere you want. Even if you don't like them, by adding them to any slow-cooked dish they often disappear into the soup, as they say, leaving you with the benefits of vitamins and antioxidants. So stock your pantry with diced tomatoes and you'll always have the perfect style for almost any recipe you clip from a magazine or print from the web.

Stock Up on Canned Tomatoes

Tomato Sauce: A good base for making your own customized pizza sauce with things like garlic, onions, olives, or intensely flavored dried mushrooms such as porcini. Of course, these same embellishments work for pasta as well. Tomato sauce comes in 14.5-ounce cans or smaller 8-ounce cans. One 14.5-ounce can is perfect for two 12-inch pizzas.

Diced Tomatoes: This is the real workhorse of the quick and easy kitchen. If there's one kind of canned tomato you see most often in recipes, it's this one.

Whole Tomatoes: Not as popular as diced because, in the end, you wind up cutting them up anyway. But if you want control over the size of the tomato chunks, start with whole rather than diced or crushed.

Crushed Tomatoes: Somewhere between diced and sauce, crushed tomatoes can be used to make a deliciously thick sauce for pizza or pasta.

Tomato Juice: Perfect for winter cocktail parties and an absolute necessity for the classic Bloody Mary or the transformed Bloody Sigrid (p. 141). Start with a good quality organic tomato juice and then let your imagination run wild with variations on the drink.

Cooking with Canned Tomatoes

* Spanish Pizza with Chorizo and Peppers (p. 61)
* Lamb Stew with Figs and Apricots (p. 177)
* Rustic Winter Stew (p. 195)
* Quick and Easy Italian Soup (p. 196)

Charcuterie

Preserving is a key word in stocking the cold-weather pantry—preserving food for preserving life for the long, cold winter. Preserving meat was once a part of the seasonal cycle and marked the turn toward the cold months as our ancestors put up what they could to survive outside the growing season. Preserving can be accomplished by salt, air, smoke, or sugar, with drying being one of the oldest forms practiced by humans—as early as the sixth century BCE. Today, thanks to the wizardry of freezers and the globalization of foodstuffs, we aren't dependent on food preservation and can enjoy the ancient arts of smoking and curing simply for the tastes they create. Of course charcuterie also includes cooked meats like pâté, but it's long-preserving techniques like smoking and curing we really care about for stocking the cold-weather pantry. When it comes to meat and fish, smoking and dry-air curing produce flavors that just aren't possible with fresh meat. Consider the difference between prosciutto and a pork chop or poached salmon and lox.

In terms of cooking and entertaining, what is so marvelous about these kinds of meats is that you get a lot of bang for your buck. As with dried fruit, in which water is removed to concentrate flavor, so too with smoked and cured meats: a little goes a long way. Instead of wallowing in fat-laden meats, use flavor-packed meats sparingly in dishes that focus on seasonal vegetables and grains. Think collards with a bit of bacon, slivers of prosciutto added to a pizza after it comes from the oven, Spanish chorizo tossed with potatoes, or smoked salmon stirred into scrambled eggs.

Stock Up on Smoked and Cured Meat and Fish

Bacon: This should top your charcuterie list. It's easy to find, affordable, comes in many styles, and the uses for bacon in winter cooking are endless. I tend to favor applewood smoked bacon in my cooking, and among applewood smoked bacons, to particularly seek out Nueske's from Wisconsin.

Smoked Salmon: Another classic in the smoked category, you'll find it cold-smoked or hot-smoked. Hot-smoked salmon is processed between 120°F and 180°F and can often be kept on the shelf rather than the refrigerator. It's a bit heartier and more rugged than cold-smoked, is often sold in large chunks and it is as good on a cracker as it is flaked and crafted into smoked fish salads. Cold-smoked salmon undergoes far lower temperatures in processing, is thinly sliced, and is often labeled with geographical markers such as "Irish smoked salmon" or "Scottish smoked salmon," although they vary little in style. Lox is a popular form of cold-smoked salmon that is brined first, sometimes with the addition of sugar.

Prosciutto: A classic Italian salt-cured and air-dried ham found in specialty markets and good delis, usually served in paper-thin slices. Prosciutto de Parma and Prosciutto San Daniele are two of the most common regional appellations you'll find. Jamón Serrano is Spain's answer to prosciutto. And in the past few years, a domestic prosciutto from La Quercia in Iowa has been giving this imported pig a run for its money. You will find recipes that call for cooking prosciutto, but I think that ruins an expensive delicacy when something more appropriate like pancetta would do. Instead, save prosciutto for topping, garnishing, and finishing off cooked dishes or just adding to the perfect charcuterie platter.

Salami: A broad category that includes several different kinds of air-cured sausages (including the standard pepperoni pizza topping). Great for sandwiches and a favorite on the antipasta platter, it's easy to locate and comes in a lot of different varieties.

Smoked Haddock: Sometimes labeled "finnan haddie," smoked haddock is harder to find on this side of the Atlantic, but it's a real treat you'll want to hunt down. Use in Scottish dishes like Cullen Skink or add to Welsh Rarebit (p. 71) with a poached egg for a very hearty savory dish.

Smoked Whitefish: Usually by the time this versatile smoked fish gets to the consumer it's already been done up into salad. If you don't see it out in the fish or deli section, ask for it. Often it's hiding in the back waiting to be mixed with mayonnaise. If you can't find smoked whitefish at your local grocer or fishmonger, have some of the best delivered right from the source to your table through Charlie's smokehouse in northeastern Wisconsin (www.charliessmokehouse.com).

Spanish Chorizo: A cured sausage not to be confused with raw pork Mexican chorizo. For more on chorizo, see p. 62.

Cooking with Smoked and Cured Meat and Fish

* Spanish Pizza with Chorizo and Peppers (p. 61)
* Oat Cakes with Smoked Salmon and Salmon Caviar (p. 127)
* Citrus Bacon Brussels Sprouts (p. 145)
* Dollars and Coins (p. 153)
* Ham and Hot Pepper Jelly Biscuits (p. 153)
* Smoked Fish Cakes with Spicy Hmong Slaw (p. 167)
* Whitefish Chowder (p. 193)

Cheese

Perhaps second only to bread, the staff of life, no other food has so shaped cultures as much as cheese. It has even spawned a language of its own. Things radically different from one another are said to be as "chalk and cheese." At picture time, photographers push up the corners of our mouths by urging us to say "cheese." In nineteenth-century slang, *cheese* was a term for something high quality, and we still talk about important people as "the big cheese." I think we all agree when it comes to negative images of cheese, though, we'd all rather be somewhere else when someone is cutting it. "To be cheesed" is to be fed up, and fans of British underworld tales are familiar with the order to "cheese it," or shut up or cut it out, made polite by Jeeves in P. G. Wodehouse's famous novels in passages like "He had been clearing away the breakfast things, but at the sound of the young master's voice cheesed it courteously."

Having saturated our language, cheese has shaped great literature over the centuries as well. In Shakespeare's *All's Well That Ends Well*, we hear the lament "Virginity breeds mites, much like a cheese." In Robert Louis Stevenson's *Treasure Island*, isolated Benn Gunn hungrily remembers, "Many's the long night I've dreamed of cheese." And the twentieth-century poet W. H Auden argued that a poet's hope was "to be, like some valley cheese, local, but prized elsewhere." Several contemporary novels like *The Mammoth Cheese* and *Edward Trencom's Nose: A Novel of History, Dark Intrigue and Cheese* have turned cheese into a key plot device and personified it into a character. In Jasper Fforde's Thursday Next detective series there is even a cheese black market supplying addictions to the strong stuff as well as serving up some deadly supercheeses.

Autumn and winter are definitely the time for delightfully odorific cheeses and part of me wants to put cheese not in "Secrets of the Cold-Weather Pantry" but over in "The Host's Toolbox". If you've got cheese, you've got a party.

People just love it. A big plate of hot melted cheese is probably the last thing you'd want on a hot summer day but is warmly welcomed as the ideal winter meal. Which is why we turn to places like Switzerland, Germany, and Britain when looking for some cheesy inspiration at this time of year. So save your mild mozzarellas and tame Monterey Jacks for summer and go for the big, bold flavors when the snow starts falling. Choose from my favorites here or consult a cheese expert like one of *Eat Feed*'s previous guests, Laura Werlin: www.laurawerlin.com.

Stock Up on Seasonal Cheese

Blues like Stilton, Gorgonzola, Roquefort: These chesses add zip to almost anything and pair particularly well with other seasonal foods like pears and port.

Nutty and fruity Gruyère, Comte, Beaufort: As at home in fondue mixes as that thoroughly Swiss treat, raclette.

Grating cheese like Parmesan and Pecorino: For a bit of salty intensity, add these cheeses to pasta dishes as well as hearty soufflés, creamed soups, and winter vegetable dishes.

Scandinavian cheeses like Gjetost: Not on everyone's radar screen, this nutty brown cheese definitely should be. It's a great snack cheese or breakfast cheese.

Cooking with Cheese

* Spanish Pizza with Chorizo and Peppers (p. 61)
* Phyllo Cigars: Lamb-Mint and Feta-Olive (p. 67)
* Welsh Rarebit (p. 71)
* Chicken Breasts with Pumpkin Seed Filling and Butternut Sauce (p. 82)
* Chicken with Barley and Green Sauce (p. 123)
* French Onion Pot Roast (p. 133)
* Chicken, Sage, and Cheddar Tart (p. 137)
* Roast Beef Sandwiches with Pear Spread and Stilton (p. 138)
* Parsnip Fries with Two Sauces (p. 140)
* Parsnip Soufflés (p. 157)
* Beet Fries with Blue Cheese Sauce (p. 166)
* Cheese Fondue (p. 199)
* Walnut, Fig, and Goat Cheese Sandwiches (p. 205)

Chocolate

When Cortez first arrived in the New World and demanded gold, he was led instead to mountains of cocoa beans. Or so the story goes. But true or not, it's a testament to the value we've always invested in chocolate. For thousands of years before Cortez, Mayans used this black gold as currency. More importantly for us twenty-first-century hot cocoa fans, these "coins" were converted into deep brown potables held sacred as ceremonial drinks for royal banquets and religious rites.

Spanish colonists originally found the dark liquor bitter and unpalatable. But they eventually adopted and transformed it, serving this ritual drink hot rather than cold, adding sugar, and even creating a prototype for today's hot cocoa mixes—a solid chocolate tablet to dissolve in water. Early in its history, chocolate fortified colonial ladies who took cocoa breaks in the middle of Mass.

Once this New World delight made its debut in the Spanish court, it went on to become the signature drink of bull fights and the Spanish Inquisition.

This colonial draft, however, would be as unrecognizable to us as its indigenous ancestor, and not only because we no longer idly sip frothy cups of steaming cocoa at public tortures. Its descendants, though, have evolved into sweet drinks synonymous with cold-weather coziness. Much like the earliest imbibers of this hypnotic potion, we enjoy chocolate as much for the drinking ritual as for the taste. Thus we still have our equally powerful chocolate moments—from cozy après ski nights by the fire to holiday caroling, sledding, and snowman-building. We've discovered ways to enjoy chocolate in the kinds of cakes and cookies that became popular in the nineteenth century, as well as in savory dishes like moles that remind us of the ancient origins of this treasured taste.

Even though chocolate is a product of tropical climates, it seems as if it really does have a season: it is most revered, worshipped, and indulged in during the colder months of the year. Plastic pumpkins and pillowcases full of Halloween candy kick off the chocolate season in October. By Christmas and Hanukkah, with cookies, cakes, and tortes, we're in full swing. We get another big chocolate chance in February with Valentine's Day. I also wait until the temperature drops to do a lot of my chocolate cooking because it's easier to work with in a cool kitchen than a warm one. You can keep chocolate in the pantry rather than the refrigerator without fearing it will immediately melt in your hands as you work with complex desserts October through March.

Stock Up on Chocolate

Cocoa Powder: Chocolate with most of the cocoa butter extracted, cocoa powder has a much lower fat content than solid chocolate. It comes in two forms: natural and "Dutched." Dutch-processed cocoa powder has been subjected to an alkalization process that removes some of the bitterness, which makes it the preferred choice for eating raw: sprinkled on lattes, as a dusting on cookies, for coating truffles, and in making chocolate sauces. Natural cocoa requires cooking and works best when a recipe also calls for greater amounts of sugar.

Milk Chocolate: This form of solid chocolate gets much of its bulk from milk, obviously, and sugar. In the United States, milk chocolate must contain at least 12% whole milk, which is usually added in as dry milk in the manufacturing process.

Semisweet and Bittersweet Chocolate: These solid chocolates come in chips, bars, and blocks. Although there is some conventional wisdom about what falls into each of these categories, there are no hard and fast rules. Generally, bittersweet chocolate is that labeled 70% or higher, referring to the percentage of cocoa solids. Semisweet chocolate usually comes in at 35% to 70%. When cooking with large amounts of solid chocolate, you can save a few pennies by avoiding armfuls of individually wrapped bars and buying in bulk from gourmet shops (and even some higher-end grocery stores). Many carry brands like Valrhona, El Rey, and Callebaut, which can be purchased by the pound (usually $6 to $18 per pound) and are often already broken up and packaged for you.

Unsweetened Chocolate: Once a favorite for baking, and hence its alternate label of "baking chocolate," this 100% cacao content form of chocolate has fallen out of favor in the past decade as more and more recipes call for starting with a bittersweet chocolate.

Cooking with Chocolate

* Yule Log Cake (p. 118)
* Mississippi Mud Parfaits (p. 155)
* Chocolate Beef Stew with Butternut Squash and Amaranth (p. 179)
* Triple Chocolate Stuffed Mocha Cupcakes (p. 180)
* Hot Chocolate (p. 182)
* Sipping Chocolate (p. 183)
* Chocolate Chip Steamed Pudding (p. 197)
* S'mores (p. 201)

Citrus

In spite of the fact that we often associate these fruits with summery thirst-quenching lemonade, lime-drenched margarita mix, and countless citrusy marinades for grilling, these tangy, tart surprises are best in winter. It's that time of year that some of the more unusual varieties begin to appear among the garden variety oranges and tangerines, like the many-fingered Buddha's hand, a kind of citron; the Meyer lemon, a kinder, gentle version of its more quotidian cousin; and the kumquat, not technically citrus but used in many of the same ways. We also find giant pomelos, oddly named ugli fruits, and hybrids like tangelos.

Citrus fruits are of course an important source of vitamin C. Ask any scurvy-plagued eighteenth-century sailor about the importance of C during the deprived days on board a long sea journey and you'll soon find out about its life-saving benefits. Though we mostly consume our citrus in juice form year-round, it's time to take a step back and think about exploring beyond "with or without pulp" and learn how to cook with citrus as well as try less familiar varieties out of hand.

Don't forget the fruit-in-three benefit, a sort of culinary trifecta. You get the flesh, juice, and zest, all of which can be easily separated and used to different ends—whether to eat fresh, create a sauce, or add a bit of zing to your baking. With a genealogy that goes back 20 million years, citrus fruits deserve any and all praise we may give them in the dark days of winter.

Stock Up on Citrus

Citron: Because of its thick, sweet rind, this citrus fruit is mainly used as a candied peel in holiday fruit cakes.

Clementine: Perhaps the most popular variety of tangerine, Clementines do a brisk business in winter as devotees buy them by the crate.

Lemon: Though the lemon came originally from Asia, we owe thanks to the Arabs who propagated the fruit around the Mediterranean, as well as to the European Crusaders, who brought a taste for lemons back to their homes. Thin-skinned Meyer lemons offer a gentler flavor that reveals their cross between a lemon and an orange.

Lime: A popular garnish for cocktails, this essential ingredient for a gin and tonic originated in Malaysia. Our everyday sort of limes are known as Persian limes, while Key limes are a specialty variety and a bit harder to come by, though absolutely necessary for the traditional Key Lime Pie.

Orange: Our most popular citrus fruit, found fresh as well as in juice form and in many types of prepared foods. Seedless navel oranges dominate the fresh market. Varieties like blood oranges from the Mediterranean, with their telltale deep red coloring, have become favored in the last decade in both fresh and juice forms. Turn to juicy Valencias during winter months to produce some great breakfast drinks. And though you won't find them in the produce section because they are too bitter to eat out of hand, sour oranges or Seville oranges show up on the breakfast table in marmalades.

Tangelos: Like many citrus fruits, tangelos are a hybrid of others, in this case the marriage between a sweet orange and a grapefruit. Though they are delicious as a fresh fruit, tangelos aren't as good in cooking as some of the other choices in the citrus family.

Yuzu: Very resistant to cold, this hybrid fruit looks like a yellow mandarin orange and smells like a lime. In Asia it is reserved for cooking rather than eaten raw, and in the West we tend to favor the rind for enhancing food flavors as well as to scent cosmetics and toiletries.

Cooking with Citrus

* Watercress and Apple Salad with Honey Vinaigrette (p. 98)
* Wassail Bowl (p. 115)
* Whisky Trifle (p. 129)
* Bloody Sigrid (p. 141)
* Citrus Bacon Brussels Sprouts (p. 145)
* Twelfth Night Cake (p. 147)
* Chili Lime Shrimp with Rice (p. 149)
* Orange Almond Cake (p. 150)
* Lamb Meat Loaf with Marmalade Glaze (p. 169)
* Orange and Rose Water Ice Cream (p. 177)
* A Good Morning Squeeze (p. 189)
* Meyer Lemon Tea Bread (p. 203)

Cranberries

Cranberries are one of my favorite food topics, and here's the really great thing about them: you simply cannot get them year-round. You can't import them from the Southern Hemisphere. You won't find them on any black market of out-of-season fruits. There is no cranberry underground. The only thing you can do is wait until they are harvested in October and enjoy them while you can until they disappear from grocery store shelves around February. They are amazing, longed-for gems whose occasional existence makes them all the more desirable. Of course, market demands for altering the seasonality are changing this, and cranberries are starting to be grown in—where else—Chile. But these are used primarily in the production of juice rather than reaching us in the form of those bright red orbs we love for autumn cooking.

Cranberries are another of those wonderful foods indigenous to North America. Related berries are important to the cuisines and cultures of Northern Europe, like lingonberries in Scandinavia. You can find a similar small berry known as a wild cranberry in Germany as well. But you have to go to North America for *vaccinium macrocarpon,* those big red jewels for stringing around a Christmas tree and the large, tart fruit that is the signature side dish of Thanksgiving dinner in the United States. In our national cultural mythology, cranberries are also very much a colonial fruit. They are part of the story we tell about the so-called first Thanksgiving meal in 1621

when English settlers feasted with New England Indians. We often think of cranberries as still very much a part of Massachusetts. However, two other states are significant cranberry producers: New Jersey and Wisconsin. In fact, Wisconsin now produces more cranberries than any other state.

Like other wonderful cold-weather foods, cranberries thrive on adversity: acid soil and low temperatures. One of the most intriguing things about cranberries is how they are harvested by flooding, giving them a biblical sense of reverence. Another interesting thing is that they grow in cranberry bogs or marshes created by glacial deposits. So-called wet-harvested cranberries are usually processed into juice and other prepared foods and dry-harvested cranberries make their way into our kitchens as fresh fruit ready for seasonal recipes.

Cooking with Cranberries

* Franklin's True American Original Turkey and
  Cranberry Sandwiches (p. 91)
* Venison with Cranberry-Port Relish (p. 97)
* Double Oatmeal Cookies (p. 135)
* Cranberry Tarts (p. 167)

Crucifers

Unfortunately, this ill-sounding word for things like greens and cabbages makes us feel they are more a cross to bear than a seasonal treat to look forward to. This label has done little to help in the marketing of the most health-filled bunch of cold-weather foods going. Parents who have made sprout eating a condition for not slowly aging at the dining table and the open presidential dislike of broccoli haven't done much to boost their profile either. But once you have the opportunity to taste them cooked with a bit of style and imagination, rather than just boiled until their smell fills the house, you will be absolutely saddened by all those wasted hours of despising them. Braise your sprouts in a bit of stout or orange juice and zest, taste greens with spicy Italian sausage, or experience kale lightly tossed with thick organic cream or dressed Asian style with soy sauce and sesame oil. Let yourself be inspired by global traditions like Indian mustard greens, Korean bok choi, and the collards of soul food.

You might be wondering why crucifers are so prolific in winter and such a part of cold-climate cuisines like those of Germany and Britain. One of the great things about this crop of veggies is that they do well in cold weather and many thrive long after the first frost.

Stock Up on Crucifers

Bok Choi: Also known under a variety of other spellings, including bok choy, bak choy, and pak choy, this is a Chinese cabbage, though not to be confused with another vegetable actually called "Chinese Cabbage." It cooks up quickly, so don't leave the stove unattended for too long if you're a bok choi novice.

Brussels Sprouts: Why this geographical designation? No one is quite sure, except that they have been popular in Belgium for some time. In France, they are known as *choux de Bruxelles* or Brussels cabbages.

Cabbage: Cabbage comes in many forms: red, green, Savoy, Chinese, among them.

Cauliflower: Mark Twain once claimed that this vegetable—as good raw as it is cooked—was "nothing but cabbage with a college education." Though most commonly white, cauliflower also comes in green and purple varieties.

Collard Greens: This soul food staple often begs for salt pork. Sometimes confused with kale, collards have their own particular taste that means you should use collards specifically when a recipe calls for them.

Kale: Though in Scotland the word *kale* might be applied to any form of cabbage or leafy greens, in the United States, kale means a specific curly-leafed green. It's one of the hardiest and thrives on frost. It is a great source of folates, an essential vitamin for pregnant women.

Cooking with Crucifers

* Indian Spiced Cauliflower (p. 56)
* Watercress and Apple Salad with Honey Vinaigrette (p. 98)
* Renaissance Winter Greens Tart (p. 121)
* Chicken with Barley and Green Sauce (p. 123)
* Citrus Bacon Brussels Sprouts (p. 145)
* Dollars and Coins (p. 153)
* Smoked Fish Cakes with Spicy Hmong Slaw (p. 167)
* Quick and Easy Italian Soup (p. 196)
* Colcannon (p. 207)

Dried Fruits

Perhaps even more ancient than any other form of food preservation is the super basic and totally low-tech method of drying to preserve foods long past their pick-by date. Drying is elemental and so unlike pickling, which produces a completely different result than the fresh food with which you began. Indeed, the purpose of drying is to intensify the natural flavors already present by removing water from the taste equation. With this form of concentrated fruit you get a lot out of each one, and I don't have to mention the importance of certain varieties in a more, shall we say, relaxed diet, even beyond the cliché prune.

Dried fruits are my favorite winter food accessory because they really go with anything and there are so many from which to choose. Make sure you always have on hand traditional raisins, currants, and cranberries; splurge on cherries, strawberries, and blueberries; or experiment with mango, pineapple, and papaya. If you tour the bulk aisle of a health food store, you'll find many surprises to spark your culinary imagination.

Of course, you can always add dried fruits to cookies, like oatmeal drops, as well as to cakes, muffins, and scones. But also think about adding a few raisins to a chicken pie or some currants to your sautéed spinach. This is an ancient method of flavor combination borrowed from an era when possessing such items was a sign of privilege: the space to store them, the staff to preserve them, and the money to buy fruit in the first place. Though this medieval habit of dried fruits in meat dishes isn't as popular in Western cooking anymore, you still readily find them in the cuisines of other cultures, such as India and North Africa.

Stock Up on Dried Fruit

Raisins, Golden Raisins, and Currants: Basically different versions of the same thing: dried grapes.

Cranberries: Dried cranberries usually have added sugar, which is sometimes overpowering. When you can find them, look for those sweetened with juice so that the cranberry essence comes through in your dish. You'll sometimes find them marketed as "craisins." These dried fruits are especially wonderful tossed into the dough of buttermilk scones, and, as with fresh cranberries, their flavor profile is a perfect match for orange.

Dates: An ancient fruit and one packed with intense sweetness. For cooking, I advise purchasing dates in the produce section, where you can find them whole and of a higher quality than in the baking aisle, where they are too often chopped and processed and already too far on the dry side. This is especially key when making Let's Make a Date Muffins (p. 190), when you need to have enough moisture for these knock-offs of sticky toffee pudding. Dates are a good foundation for a lot of cocktail party finger foods. You can stuff them, wrap them, or enjoy them perfectly naked.

Figs: Another ancient fruit, found in literature from the fig leaves of Genesis to the fig symbolism in Shakespeare's *Antony and Cleopatra*. Dried figs include lighter colored varieties such as Turkish or Calimyrna as well as the deep purple to black Black Mission or Mission figs.

Citrus Peel: Though not strictly dried, citrus peel is important "candied" fruit for the baking season. Make your own or keep packs on hand for tossing into muffins and cakes just as you might do with dried fruits. Orange peel especially can give a sweetly intense citrus essence to many baked goods that can't be achieved with minced zest.

Cooking with Dried Fruit
* Wheat Berry and Fig Salad (p. 68)
* Wild Rice Pilaf with Cherries and Pecans (p. 76)
* Venison with Cranberry-Port Relish (p. 97)
* Renaissance Winter Greens Tart (p. 121)
* Whisky Trifle (p. 129)
* Double Oatmeal Cookies (p. 135)
* Twelfth Night Cake (p. 147)
* Bread Pudding (p. 160)
* Fruited Gingerbread with Butterscotch Sauce (p. 172)
* Lamb Stew with Figs and Apricots (p. 177)
* Let's Make a Date Muffins (p. 190)
* Walnut, Fig, and Goat Cheese Sandwiches (p. 205)

Game

There is something really wonderfully antique about game in autumn. Even if you aren't a hunter, you can enjoy these autumn flavors on seasonal restaurant menus or through mail-order. If you have a shop nearby, all the better. Sourcing is easier overseas where small butchers even carry bits and bobs in season. Though you are much more likely to find game recipes in European cookbooks, American palates are catching on. During game season in the Scottish Highlands, U.S. online provider D'Artagnan (www.dartagnan. com) provides access to a range of birds, like pheasant, partridge, grouse, and wood pigeon, that come straight from wild fields of heather to your table.

Cooking with Game
* Duck Breasts with Grapes (p. 54)
* Venison with Cranberry-Port Relish (p. 97)

Nuts

Nuts make it into the winter pantry for two reasons. First, they have all those great storage qualities of dried fruits, pickles, and smoked meats without needing any kind of preservative technique applied to them. They are natural keepers right off the tree. Second, so many of our favorite nuts come into season when the leaves start to fall.

Stock Up on Nuts

Almonds: First mentioned in the Bible, the almond's origins actually go back much further than recorded history. In addition to the nut proper, we enjoy many other products from this ancient food that actually was born into the same family as cherries and apricots: almond milk, once a medieval staple and now a health food alternative to cow's milk; almond paste, the basis for marzipan; and almond oil, as good for making a delicate salad dressing as for a bit of massage therapy after a long day in the kitchen.

Peanuts: Technically a legume rather than a nut, the peanut is superversatile, super American. Without it we wouldn't have peanut oil, ideal for frying with its high smoking point, and peanut butter, which after ketchup seems to be the country's national condiment.

Pecans: Native to North America, pecans are actually a subset of the hickory family. Thriving in temperate climates, pecans and hickory have taken on a reputation as particularly Southern nuts in signature foods like pecan pie and hickory-smoked ham and bacon. Of course, whether you put the stress on the first or second syllable is a dead giveaway about your geographical origins.

Walnuts: An equal opportunity nut, walnuts were originally found in Asia, Europe, and North America. European walnuts go back as far as ancient Greece and Rome, and specifically American nuts like the black walnut developed on this side of the Atlantic. Black walnuts are particularly sweet and delicious in baking, but buy them already shelled because they are frustratingly difficult to crack open.

Cooking with Nuts

* Cheesecake with Sherry Sauce (p. 62)
* Almond Cookies (p. 69)
* Wild Rice Pilaf with Cherries and Pecans (p. 76)
* Lincoln's Inaugural Chicken Salad and Lobster Salad (p. 92)
* Jefferson's Peanut Sundaes (p. 92)
* Orange Almond Cake (p. 150)
* Smoked Fish Cakes with Spicy Hmong Slaw (p. 163)
* Let's Make a Date Muffins (p. 190)
* Walnut, Fig, and Goat Cheese Sandwiches (p. 205)

Pickles

There's more than one way to put up summer's harvest, and though we usually turn to canned and frozen vegetables in the off season, don't forget about the brilliant transformation you get with one of the oldest forms of preserving: pickling. You might not be able to get local cucumbers or okra fresh in winter, but you can get them stored in brine or vinegar, and often further enhanced with sugar, dill, or hot peppers and mustard seeds.

Beyond vegetables in brine or vinegar, think also about sauerkraut, which isn't actually pickled but salted and fermented—a technique that goes back to the Romans. Push yourself beyond the hot dog and even classic French *choucroute garnie* (sausages on a bed of wine-soaked sauerkraut) and experiment by adding rinsed and drained sauerkraut to winter soups and stews for an extra tang. Sauerkraut is another of those great winter foods that have been catching the headlines lately with promises of greater health because of its antioxidant properties, which some scientists say are actually greater in cabbage fermented than fresh.

Though the sort of German-inspired sauerkraut we associate with Oktoberfest and backyard brats might be the most familiar (and the best served with almost any pork dish), the hottest fermented cabbage these days is *kimchi*. While you're exploring the endless varieties of *kimchi* at your local Asian market, don't just stop when you get acclimated to the most common cabbage form but experiment with radish, leeks, cucumbers, and other mixtures. Keep scanning the aisles for Japanese, Chinese, Indian, and other pickles in jars, cans, and the refrigerator section, including another popular favorite, Japanese pickled daikon radish.

Add pickles to any sandwich for a vitamin boost (sauerkraut with corned beef, dills with cheddar cheese or turkey, daikon radish pickles with a vegetarian special) or help fight off winter ills with a virtuous snack that keeps all day as you tote it from home to office.

Stock Up on Pickles

Bread and Butter Chips: The sugar-sweetened version of a traditional cucumber pickle.

Dill Pickles: Classic spears, slices, and whole cucumbers brined and packed with the herb dill that need little by way of introduction.

Japanese Daikon Radish Pickles: You'll recognize this pickled form by its bright yellow color. It is usually sold in one large piece from which you can slice the portion you want. Makes a great accompaniment to your next sushi spread.

Kimchi: Comes in countless varieties. One great way to experiment with Korean pickled vegetables is not in the kitchen but in a restaurant. Seek out a Korean restaurant near you and enjoy the customary spread of *banchan* (side dishes) they put out for every diner.

Sauerkraut: For one episode of *Eat Feed* I asked guests at a sauerkraut party what they think it's made of and they all replied cabbage and vinegar, but actually sauerkraut is made just by packing cabbage with lots and lots of salt and allowing it to ferment. Sauerkrauts labeled "Bavarian style" are usually created with the addition of sugar and caraway.

Cooking with Pickles

∗ Rustic Winter Stew (p. 195)

Preserves

In addition to pickles, which are mainly vegetables, or dried fruits with their particular texture, sugared fruit preserves carry the flavors of summer fruit into colder months without all the environmental problems of trucking in out-of-season raspberries from Chile and strawberries from Mexico.

Nothing is so wonderful as a slice of hot buttered toast with heaps of strawberry jam, unless perhaps it's an afternoon tea scone with heaps of clotted cream and strawberry jam (p. 203). But there's far more to be done with jam in our winter cooking for entertaining. Use a pastry bag to fill cupcakes or cream puffs with jam you've pureed in the food processor, or use the chunkiest, fruit-filled preserve to frost between cake layers. For a quick dinner-party dessert, buy a pound cake from the bakery, slice lengthwise into 5 even layers and fill with up to 3 kinds of fruit-packed jam. Or heat jam with just a splash of water over low heat and create a sauce to drizzle over bread pudding.

Stock Up on Preserves

Jelly: Jellies are made by cooking fruit with sugar and allowing just the juice to strain off, leaving the chunky fruit behind. Jelly is also the term in Britain for what we call Jell-O.

Jam: Preserves made from fruit, pectin, and some kind of sweetener—typically sugar or fruit juice. The texture and quality of spreads labeled as "jam" varies widely, but luckily they come in clear glass jars so you can choose a good chunky one just by looking. If you want to try your hand at preserving, jam is a good place to start since it's the easiest for the novice to tackle. You can simply cook down your favorite fruit with a bit of sweetener, pack into freezerproof Tupperware, and enjoy the taste of summer all winter long.

Marmalade: Best described as the citrus versions of jam. Although orange marmalade is standard, you'll also find marmalades of lemon and lime.

Curd: This is where the citrus grove meets the barnyard. Curds are creamy, almost custardlike preserves made from eggs, butter, and citrus juice—typically lemon.

Cooking with Preserves

* Sufganiyot (Hanukkah Donuts) (p. 112)
* Lamb Meat Loaf with Marmalade Glaze (p. 169)
* Scones with Jam and Clotted Cream (p. 203)

Roots

Let's get back to our roots and celebrate these basic, diverse, flexible, and—when it comes to even novice cooks—forgiving foods. And let's not forget to throw "earthy" into the adjective love fest. With their name they tell us they come straight out of the earth. This very feature allowed roots like potatoes to play a revolutionary role in the European diet, since they could stay in the ground until needed, unlike previous staple crops such as wheat and barley. Moreover, they provided a lot of calories in a small food and radically altered the face of poverty and dearth when they were brought from their New World home and adopted across Europe from the sixteenth to nineteenth centuries.

From milky white and sharp-tasting turnips and rutabagas to sweet orange carrots and deep burgundy beets, roots are the perfect foundation for any winter meal—and you need do nothing more than peel, boil, and mash (or toss in the food processor) with whatever quantity of butter and salt suits you. Try individual flavor profiles and then experiment with combinations to create a mixed root mash that easily and quickly accompanies everything from a weeknight cheeseburger to a full Thanksgiving spread. If you dig a little deeper, you'll unearth many other intriguing roots like cassava, burdock, jicama, salsify, and taro.

When you have the time to roast, the high heat of the oven brings out the best in almost every root but especially in my favorite trilogy of parsnips, beets, and sweet potatoes. Even if you are cooking for a strictly meat-and-potatoes crowd, try substituting roots like rutabagas, beets, or sweet potatoes with high vitamin profiles for plain old white potatoes in complexly flavored dishes that can mask the taste people think they don't like. You'll provide your guests with an often much needed nutritional boost on a cold winter night and chances are they won't even notice it in the rich broths and sauces of winter soups, stews, and braises if you're good at the ¼-inch dice.

There's more than one way to skin a potato and more than one way to create what I like to call a "mix and mash." When making a custom mash, remember that different roots have different water content. If you have a high proportion of white potatoes, you'll need to add more milk, butter, or cream. If turnips play a bigger role, you can do a really smooth puree in the food processor and go with just a bit of butter and omit the milk or cream altogether. Keep in mind also that high-starch roots like potatoes don't do well in the food processor where they turn to glue. Give them a light hand with a manual masher or a quick fluff with the whisk attachment of the electric mixer. For kicks, try the following proportions, or invent your own:
- equal parts white potatoes, carrots, and rutabagas
- two parts potatoes, one part carrots, one part turnips
- equal parts carrots and parsnips

Stock Up on Roots

Beets: Both sweet and earthy, they pair well with tangy citrus or intense flavors like blue cheese or horseradish, and of course sour cream, as in Borscht or pickled beet salads. If you absolutely swear off those big purple orbs because they stain your hands, do at least give newer entrants like golden beets and striped Chioggia beets a try.

Carrots: After the white potato, perhaps our most loved winter root and a good source of vitamin A. As a substitute for the everyday orange carrot, you might try the golden carrots showing up more frequently in the produce aisle.

Celery Root: Along with other foods not endowed with the quality of pulchritude we often seek for entertaining menus, add celery root to the list with lobster and oysters. It's scrubby, nubby, and a bit ratty. But like other foods in this category, beneath that rough exterior is a delicious root with a sharp aroma of, well, celery, without the stringiness of the rib. It works well both raw, such as shredded in a winter salad, or cooked, often mashed with other roots.

Parsnips: Parsnips are best after a good hard frost, when their sweetness really comes through. They will do fine boiled and mashed with butter, but in roasting you really bring out the signature sugars of this root. Parsnips pair well with sweet flavors like honey or brown sugar and with spices like ginger. They also make a good match for carrots.

Sweet Potatoes: Considered an aphrodisiac by Henry VIII, sweet potatoes were some of the first potatoes adapted to Old World cooking when they first arrived from South America. Today sweet potatoes are often associated with the cuisine of the southeastern United States and are put to use equally indulgently in savories like sweet potato cakes and sweets like sweet potato pie.

White Potatoes: I think potatoes are just about the perfect food, and when you tire of potatoes, you have tired of life. Like eggs before them in the 1980s, white potatoes are taking a bad rap for all kinds of health ills because we have begun to take them for granted by making them the single most popular vegetable, usually in the form of French fries, where it's more the preparation method than the raw material itself that is the culprit. Also, like eggs, I predict they will be redeemed if we get a little smarter about how we use them. If you make this all-purpose, totally flexible vegetable just a part of your root repertoire rather than the default, that's a start. It is a bit of a misnomer to use the term *white potatoes* since it's a huge category that encompasses specimens diverse in color as well as shape like Red Bliss, Peruvian blue, and Russian fingerling.

Cooking with Roots

❋ Autumn Carrot Salad (p. 71)

❋ Turnip "Carpaccio" (p. 81)

❋ Pasty Pie (p. 87)

❋ Roasted Root Vegetables (p. 98)

❋ Curried Potato and Pumpkin Latkes with Yogurt Sauce (p. 109)

❋ Honey-Ginger Carrot and Parsnip Latkes with Crème Fraîche (p. 111)

❋ Caramelized Onion Mashed Potatoes (p. 128)

❋ Potatoes and Carrots for a Sunday Roast (p. 135)

❋ Parsnip Fries with Two Sauces (p. 140)

❋ Parsnip Soufflés (p. 157)

❋ Smoked Fish Cakes with Spicy Hmong Slaw (p. 163)

❋ Beet Fries with Blue Cheese Sauce (p. 166)

❋ Potatoes and Turnips with Bacon and Cream (p. 170)

❋ North African Potato Salad (p. 175)

❋ Lamb Stew with Figs and Apricots (p. 177)

❋ Whitefish Chowder (p. 193)

❋ Ancho Chili Soup with Sweet Potatoes and Chorizo (p. 196)

❋ Onion Rösti (p. 199)

❋ Colcannon (p. 207)

Spices

Save your love of delicate basil for summer when it's in season and turn to earthy, hot, and pungent spices for winter. Spices and slow cooking go hand in hand since the process allows the flavors to really get a chance to develop and steep into the food.

Just like a spring cleaning, I believe in autumn cleaning. You must get ready for the coming baking season, and part of that is purging your kitchen of old spices and restocking with new. Don't think that 3-year-old cinnamon is going to have the same punch as one you buy tomorrow to replace it. The best way to get the freshest, most intense spices is to buy them whole and grind them yourself, but that's not always practical. The recipes in this book are designed with spices that are as fresh as you can get ground.

Stock Up on Spices

Cardamom: This is a key Scandinavian spice for cookies and breads. Make sure each holiday baking season to have it on hand in both ground and pod form. It turns up in a lot of Indian cooking as well.

Cinnamon, Cloves, and Nutmeg: This is the magic autumn triumvirate. Think beyond pumpkin pie and mulled wine, though, and consider what these spices can do for savory dishes like North African stews and Indian curries.

Ginger: Sometimes the magic autumn triumvirate expands to embrace ginger as well. Ginger really is one of those truly flexible spices that works as well in sweet as in savory dishes.

Juniper: Don't start game cooking season without this deep purple berry that is the basis of gin as well as a great addition to venison, grouse, and other hearty game meats. Buy the whole berry and crush as needed in a mortar and pestle or just with the back of a spoon.

Pepper: The best accompaniment for a hearty chowder.

Cooking with Spices

* Indian Spiced Cauliflower (p. 56)
* Cinnamon Cream Puffs (p. 57)
* Cream Cheese Pumpkin Squares (p. 84)
* Ginger Rum Bonfire Pudding (p. 89)
* Snowball (p. 107)
* Curried Potato and Pumpkin Latkes with Yogurt Sauce (p. 109)
* Honey-Ginger Carrot and Parsnip Latkes with Crème Fraîche (p. 111)
* Wassail Bowl (p. 115)
* Lambswool Punch (p. 116)
* Twelfth Night Cake (p. 147)
* Fruited Gingerbread with Butterscotch Sauce (p. 172)
* Red Pepper Harissa and Yogurt with Pita Bread (p. 175)
* Lamb Stew with Figs and Apricots (p. 177)
* Cinnamon Cookies (p. 187)

Spirits

Spirits, of course, warm the spirit, but they also add flavor where you'd least expect it. Though you can't get the smoky taste of a grilled rib-eye in the middle of January because charcoal and a blizzard don't mix, pan fry your steak and then deglaze the pan with a bit of whisky and cream. Mix in some brandy with pork and apples. Or add a dash of aquavit to tomato juice for a pungent Bloody Mary.

Stock Up on Spirits

Brandy: This is my number one spirit friend in the kitchen. It's super flexible for sparking up a soup like a creamy chestnut puree and for deglazing after almost any kind of meat.

Gin and Vodka: Gin is great in game sauces, vodka with the tang of citrus or tomatoes. Either or both are absolutely essential for sparkling clear winter cocktails that catch the light of a low-slung sun as it goes down in the evening cocktail hour.

Port: Not officially a spirit, but a fortified wine, port can be used in the same way you use spirits: to clean out the frying pan after a steak and, in a seasonal favorite, shaped into a solid wobbly block of port gelatin that makes easy work for a last-minute dessert.

Rum: Born of colonial sugracane plantations, rum is naturally the spirit of choice for dishes inspired by the Caribbean and plays nicely with winter citrus fruits. The recent proliferation of artisanal rums means you're never without a sophisticated drink as perfect for sipping as for adding a little heat to cold-weather desserts.

Whisky: After brandy, whisky is the second most important spirit to have on hand in terms of flexibility. Transform almost any dessert with a sauce of whisky and cream or use it in meat sauces to bump up the Scottish quotient of the meal.

Cooking with Spirits

* Pork Chops with Apples and Brandy (p. 75)
* Poire William Ice Cream (p. 76)
* Ginger Rum Bonfire Pudding (p. 89)
* Venison with Cranberry-Port Relish (p. 97)
* Snowball (p. 103)
* Wassail Bowl (p. 115)
* Beef Rib-eyes with Whisky Sauce (p. 127)
* Whisky Trifle (p. 129)
* Bloody Sigrid (p. 141)
* Hazelnut Milk Punch (p. 141)
* Orange Almond Cake (p. 150)
* Bread Pudding (p. 160)
* Fruited Gingerbread with Butterscotch Sauce (p. 172)
* Cheese Fondue (p. 199)
* Maple Custards with Whisky Cream (p. 208)

Squash

I love the many varieties of squash because they do everything. They're beautiful, delicious, hearty, and useful. Consider the pumpkin, perhaps the most useful produce. It's great in sweets like pumpkin pie and pumpkin muffins, and in savories like pumpkin soup and roasted pumpkin. You can toast the seeds and use them for a snack. You can hollow out a pumpkin to make a Halloween lamp. In addition to *being* great food, they're pretty handy for *serving* great food. Use a medium one as a container for a baked squash custard or several mini pumpkins as individual soup bowls for serving squash soup. You can even turn it into a vase for an organic centerpiece filled with autumn-hued flowers. Or you can just put it as is on your front stoop and no one will look askance as they might if you put out, say, a summer squash like a giant zucchini.

Even though they are plentiful in grocery stores and farm stands for so many months, one of the best things about winter squash is just how well they keep. When stored properly and kept cool and dry, several varieties keep well into January, and some even will last a year.

Stock Up on Squash

Butternut: A cook's perennial favorite, butternut is usually the squash of choice for soup but is just as happy to be roasted and slathered in butter or substituted for pumpkin in pie.

Delicata: A smallish, oblong squash that, unlike other larger squash, often comes in just the right size for one person. One of my favorite quick autumn sides is a delicata sliced lengthwise, roasted cut side down, and then served with crumbled blue cheese on top. Like a lot of other squashes, delicata begs for the firm grip of a strong cheese.

Pumpkin: We couldn't have Halloween and Thanksgiving without this workhorse of the squash world. For cooking, look for smaller pie pumpkins or sugar pumpkins.

Spaghetti Squash: Because of its size and shape, this squash is sometimes confused from the outside with yellow skinned melons. Its signature trick and namesake is that you can run a fork across its cooked inner surface and the squash pulls up into pastalike strands that can be served in a tidy mound with a dollop of butter or, what else, pasta sauce.

Cooking with Squash

* Chicken Breasts with Pumpkin Seed Filling and Butternut Sauce (p. 82)
* Cream Cheese Pumpkin Squares (p. 84)
* Curried Potato and Pumpkin Latkes with Yogurt Sauce (p. 109)
* Butternut Squash Soup (p. 133)
* Chocolate Beef Stew with Butternut Squash and Amaranth (p. 179)

More Staples

Maple Syrup and Maple Sugar: If you can get your hands on granulated maple sugar, try substituting it here and there to add a maple component to your baking. It's rare and expensive, but if you're on a road trip, you can often find it by stopping at farms or farm stands in maple-growing regions like Ontario, the Upper Midwest, and the Northeast.

Dark Breads: Dense and intense Germanic and Eastern European breads like pumpernickel and rye stand up to hearty winter dishes and give you a little more oomph than more neutral tastes like a white Italian loaf.

Horseradish: This staple goes with roast beef in any guise, but don't forget to use it also as an embellishment to give some zing to roast meats, root vegetables, or anything else you think needs a little pick-me-up. Stir into mashed potatoes, spread on any sandwich, add it to a dip for chips, fries, or pretzels. It's easiest to buy prepared horseradish in a jar, but also consider experimenting by buying the whole root, which looks a little like a daikon radish, and grating your own.

Spicy Mustard: Like horseradish, any kind of spicy mustard is perfect for beef but necessary for so much else. Slather on a brat, add to a vinaigrette, or stir into a cream sauce for root vegetables.

Dried Chilies: These hot-climate natives are great for getting some heat into your cold-climate cooking. Stock a gorgeous array of ancho, guajillo, and cayenne whole dried peppers in clear glass jars to brighten up your kitchen and your cooking during the icy blue months.

Butter: This may seem obvious, but when baking season rolls around, make sure you have really good butter on hand. You want the perfect high-fat content for making flaky crusts, chewy cookies, and airy cakes.

the host's toolbox

My grandmother taught me to cut biscuits with an ordinary drinking glass and that Cool-Whip containers are perfect for food storage, so I'm not one of those cooks who thinks you need endless specialized gadgets to turn out the perfect meal. In fact, there are so many gadgets out there I just can't even fathom the purpose of—beyond something to keep the Home Shopping Network from having to fade to black. But I do think that when it comes to entertaining, there are a few nifty things to have around the kitchen to make your work quick and the outcome more uniform, easier to serve, a little more fun, and a lot more gorgeous. These ideas run the gamut from actual gadgets to ingredients and foods that should be a part of every host's toolbox.

Stainless Steel Scoops

Start with the standard 1⅜-inch scoop that will serve you well for almost everything, including perfectly shaped cookies, fritters, meatballs, mini ice cream sundaes, and tiny bites of palate-cleansing sorbets between courses. Then build up your collection with other sizes and venture out with more ideas for making round food easy.

Baking Pans with Removable Bottoms and Sides

Make sure to have at least one standard 9-inch tart pan with a removable bottom and one 9-inch springform pan with removable sides. With just these two, you can turn out a variety of sweet and savory tarts as nibbles for a cocktail party, a centerpiece quiche for a French buffet, and desserts for sit-down dinners from simply elegant apple tarts to stunning cheesecakes and multilayer chocolate tortes. Digging and scooping with whatever serving spoon is on hand is all well and good for everyday cooking, but entertaining requires just a bit more elegance, so have on hand pans that make serving up beauty easy. One thing to remember: when taking a tart to someone else's potluck, don't leave your bottom behind!

Ice Cream Maker

This might be one of those things that has long ago been entered into your column of totally useless and space-hogging kitchen gadgets, but I beg you to reconsider. Like a good stockpot into which you can put almost any assortment of meat and vegetable and get a delicious winter stew, an ice cream maker allows you to endlessly invent your own flavor combinations that will beat the pants off even the most creative Ben and Jerry's flavors. Moreover, it's so quick and easy to make a fast dessert in advance and then be assured that all your burners and the oven is reserved for the rest of the meal. The bottom line: homemade ice cream is one of those things that people just ooh and ahh over. For $40 to $60 you can pick up the model that works basically like a frozen mixer, with an inner sleeve you keep in the freezer until that perfect idea for churning pops into your head.

Fondue Pot

Nothing is easier than entertaining with fondue. It's last minute, communal, fun, and Swiss. Enough said.

Ovenproof Coffee Cups

Yes, you can invest in all sizes of the most enticingly sexy French ramekins of the most pristine porcelain, but there's no need to. I must confess that I have a set of 12 old Crate and Barrel basic white coffee cups from eons ago that I use for everything from individual savory soufflés to molten brownies. For the kinds of temperatures called for in such delicate work, you'd be surprised just how many everyday pieces of crockery in your kitchen can double as ovenware.

Pudding Bowls

Pudding, as in that odd British portmanteau word for many different kinds of desserts, not as in Jell-O instant. What we're really talking about here are mixing bowls, but like the coffee cups, they go into the oven just as well. That's not to say go ahead and put any old mixing bowl into your oven. The pudding bowls we are talking about are actually designed for oven and stove, for both baking dome-shaped cakes and steaming puddings (like traditional Christmas plum pudding). But because they come in sizes from 1 to 10 cups, I use them for any mixing task. My favorites are the simple white "pudding basins" manufactured by the British company Mason Cash, which you can find at www.amazon.com, www.surlatable.com, or other good cookware sources.

Ordinary Wine Glasses

In addition to the obvious use of serving that great bottle your favorite guest always lavishly bestows on you, such all-purpose pieces are great for serving small sundaes and parfaits and for more whimsical treats like champagne gelatins and historically inspired syllabubs. They also double as serving dishes for cocktail munchies like nuts and pretzel sticks, so put out a couple in different places around the room.

Large Roasting Pan

Of course a 13 by 9-inch pan is great for a small roast chicken or roasted potatoes for you and your beloved, but for feeding 6, 10, or 14 people for larger celebrations, this all-purpose bit of kitchen rigor is more in demand. Naturally, it's perfectly good for making heaps of roasted vegetables or getting a large bird into the oven, but it's ideal for filling with ice for laying out scads of fresh oysters at once and gathering together lots of ramekins or coffee cups for individual soufflés or mini dessert cups.

Teapot

Even among all the cappafrappagrande hoo-ha, tea is making a big comeback and is one of those great new culinary fixations that is attracting that curious sort called the connoisseur. Whether you want to join the ranks of these aficionados by tasting and studying national styles, origins, plantations, and first and second flushes is up to you, but my basic contention is to get a teapot because, as any 5-year-old girl will tell you, a tea party is simply the easiest way to entertain. (See "Afternoon Tea" on p. 202.) If you're on a budget or find yourself hosting teetotalers of any variety, it's one of the least expensive and most appropriate gatherings. An afternoon tea is also a favorite for bakers who want to strut their stuff without having to think about complicated things like entrées. Just have a lovely pot on hand to take the main course to the table, and let your romantic notions of English gardens and finger sandwiches run wild. Pinkies in the air are optional.

Bamboo Hors d'Oeuvre Forks

Much better and hipper than those toothpicks with red, blue and yellow plastic curlicues on the end. Ideal for serving small bites of this and that like Cornmeal Catfish Bites (p. 155), small fritters, or even a single elegantly presented heirloom grape. Think beyond the ubiquitous and now hackneyed Chinese soup spoon not just for your soupcons but also your *quelquechoses*. We cannot all have treasure chests of Ming heirlooms at our disposal, but most of us can afford these nifty little forks in the 50-count package.

Small Dip Cups

Though officially they go by many names, we all know I'm talking about those things you get at the supermarket when someone is giving a free taste. You can pick them up in any color that suits your fancy when you find yourself drawn to a party supply warehouse. They are perfect for preventing double-dipping by giving everyone their own cup of sauce for finger foods like Beet Fries with Blue Cheese Sauce (p. 166), Parsnip Fries with Two Sauces (p. 140), and Fried Cod Fingers (p. 109).

Puff Pastry and Phyllo Dough

Like bamboo forks and small dip cups, they let you serve small bites in countless creative ways, but in this case the containers are also edible. Win-win. With puff pastry, create spur-of-the-moment fruit or chocolate turnovers for an unexpected dinner party or breakfast in bed. Use it in place of a tart crust or to make a deep-dish pot pie topping, as with Beef and Brown Ale Pie (p. 87). Start with puff pastry rounds or squares for individual savory or dessert tarts like Maple Apple Tartlets (p. 72). Make phyllo cups, wraps, or rolls like Phyllo Cigars for a Greek buffet (p. 67). Both puff pastry and phyllo dough look gorgeous and allow you to produce amazingly complex finger foods with very little effort.

Lavash

I like to purposely misname this flatbread *lavish*. Every wrap is based on this bread and you can create indulgent little bits of almost anything with lavash and a very basic foodstuff. For a quick party snack, spread on whatever fillings you like, roll up tight, and cut into sushi-sized bites, as with Thai Coconut Rice Twists (p. 103).

Tubes of Savory Pastes

I know you will accuse me of having taken the retro aesthetic too far by allowing it into the culinary realm and not just leaving it at sofa cushions and dinner plates in the other room, but trust me. Far from being kitschy, tubes of creamed cod roe and anchovy paste reveal that indeed the Europeans know something we don't about hospitality beyond the welcoming cheek kiss. Look for fun Italian, British, or Scandinavian spreads in the refrigerator section of your favorite gourmet outlet or even in the food section of Ikea for instant finger sandwiches you didn't have to lift a finger for.

Affordable Caviar

Do not be intimidated by osetra, beluga, and sevruga. For entertaining in a manner most of us have become accustomed to, there are plenty of exciting and tasty caviars, with more becoming available every day. The larger orange orbs of salmon caviar make a great accompaniment to smoked salmon and range from $12 for 2 ounces to $24 for 8 ounces. Tiny golden whitefish caviar put a sparkle on things like Golden Caviar Toasts (p. 103), costing between $5 for 3 ounces and $60 for 4 ounces. Icelandic red, black, and flavored tobiko caviars run about $15 for 4 ounces. Best of all, these caviars don't carry the complicated political issues that surround more expensive caviars, so have your caviar and keep your social conscience, too.

A Well-Stocked Bar

Of course, hospitable entertainers are always ready with their guests' favorite potable. But I also rely on the bar in the kitchen for deglazing, making quick dessert sauces, and soaking dried fruits in to give a little zip before adding to cakes or cookies. Slice a store-bought pound cake into multiple layers, brush each layer with your favorite fruit-flavored liqueur, spread with jam, and repeat for the other layers. Pour your favorite rum over the best vanilla ice cream or layer espresso-soaked Italian lady fingers with whipped cream and brandy and you have a modified tiramisu in a fraction of the time.

Candles in Bulk Quantities

It pretty much goes without saying that when it comes to entertaining through the long dark nights, you can do a lot with a little by offering your guests the basic comfort of candlelit meals.

iPod Speakers

Instead of limiting yourself to the CD collection or having to pass the earbuds round the table, you can project the best mood music to the whole room with even the most basic setup.

The Address of a Good Bakery

People just love good bread. Even if you don't have time for anything else, start with getting the bread right by buying it from an expert. Add cheese. You're done.

autumn

1

season of mists and mellow fruitfulness

the first day of autumn

✦

MENU

Number in Party: 4 Guests

Duck Breasts with Grapes
Indian Spiced Cauliflower
Cinnamon Cream Puffs

✦

For me autumn is a homecoming and a housewarming after a summer of quick and cool meals that are often eaten *al fresco*. What felt like an oppressively hot kitchen in August transforms into a cozy, warm kitchen in September. That is the enchantment of autumn—the many transformations of the season and the endless possibilities for renewal. It is not the death of the year but the beginning of a whole new way of eating and entertaining.

I couldn't be happier than when autumn officially begins in late September and the cool weather moves in with a double bonus: the last of the summer bounty and several early autumn surprises. This get-together celebrates the vineyard with a menu that makes the most of the grape as a fruit and as a drink, both of which pair perfectly with an autumn classic of game fowl, like duck breasts cooked to medium-rare perfection. Add in the last of the farmers' market cauliflower and kick off the baking season with that signature autumn spice, cinnamon.

To Autumn

Almost two centuries ago on the eve of the season, September 19, John Keats penned some pretty sexy words about autumn. They remind us that this isn't a time of dearth and want but one of the most fruitful and abundant periods of the whole year. I always usher in the season by bestowing a poetic "blessing" on the first autumn meal. So, raise a glass of your favorite harvest and grace the table with a famous poem before tucking into the meal.

Season of mists and mellow fruitfulness,
Close bosom-friend of the maturing sun;
Conspiring with him how to load and bless
With fruit the vines that round the thatch-eves run;
To bend with apples the moss'd cottage-trees,
And fill all fruit with ripeness to the core;
To swell the gourd, and plump the hazel shells
With a sweet kernel; to set budding more,
And still more, later flowers for the bees,
Until they think warm days will never cease,
For Summer has o'er-brimm'd their clammy cells.

Who hath not seen thee oft amid thy store?
Sometimes whoever seeks abroad may find
Thee sitting careless on a granary floor,
Thy hair soft-lifted by the winnowing wind;
Or on a half-reap'd furrow sound asleep,
Drows'd with the fume of poppies, while thy hook
Spares the next swath and all its twined flowers:
And sometimes like a gleaner thou dost keep
Steady thy laden head across a brook;
Or by a cyder-press, with patient look,
Thou watchest the last oozings hours by hours.

Where are the songs of Spring? Ay, where are they?
Think not of them, thou hast thy music too—
While barred clouds bloom the soft-dying day,
And touch the stubble plains with rosy hue;

Then in a wailful choir the small gnats mourn
Among the river sallows, borne aloft
Or sinking as the light wind lives or dies;
And full-grown lambs loud bleat from hilly bourn;
Hedge-crickets sing; and now with treble soft
The red-breast whistles from a garden-croft;
And gathering swallows twitter in the skies.

From Vine to Wine

Quite often when we think about cooking with the fruit of the vine, we're talking about deglazing with a bit of port, braising with a splash of Pinot, or creating a quick sauce with whatever white wine is at hand. But there are delicious ways to use the grape in cooking before it takes that immortal leap toward wine. On one of *Eat Feed*'s September shows, Maria Helm Sinskey, who writes about using a good vintage in the kitchen as well as the perfect fresh grape, shared some of her favorite varieties for cooking.

· **Muscat:** encompasses many styles and tastes from pale white grapes used primarily for golden raisins to deep reddish-blue globes that can be eaten out of hand or cooked with lamb and pork dishes

· **Concord:** a favorite of Northeasterners, best known as a juice and jelly grape whose sweet pulpy center is excellent in a range of autumn dishes

· **Ribier:** black grapes with a slightly bitter skin and sweet flesh, the two of which play nicely together in almost any hearty meat dish

duck breasts with grapes

Long before American Prohibition stomped out viniculture, long before Christian Eucharist traditions were shaped around bread and wine, and even long before Homer's *Iliad* poetically captured death in "the winedark sea," the liquid grape has been right there at the center of the big stuff going on in humans' lives. This recipe celebrates the grape in a glass as well as on the vine by pairing two favorite reds together in a sauce for game.

2 cups red grapes (about 12 ounces)
1 tablespoon unsalted butter
2 teaspoons sugar
1 teaspoons flour
½ cup plus 2 tablespoons fruity red wine
4 boneless duck breast halves with skin
   (5 to 6 ounces each)
Salt
Freshly ground black pepper

Cut the grapes in half and set aside. Preheat the oven to 450°F.

Melt the butter in a large skillet over medium-high heat. Add the grapes. Sprinkle with the sugar and sauté a bit to melt the sugar and warm the grapes. Sprinkle with the flour and continue to cook and stir to thoroughly coat the grapes and to cook the flour slightly, about 3 minutes. Slowly pour in ½ cup of the wine, about 2 tablespoons at a time, stirring to thoroughly incorporate the liquid into the sauce and prevent lumps. If you prefer a thinner sauce, add an additional 2 tablespoons wine. Set aside while you prepare the duck breasts.

Place duck breasts, skin side up, on a cutting board. With a sharp knife, score the skin in a crisscross pattern, being careful not to cut through to the meat. Generously season the breasts with salt and pepper on both sides. Heat a heavy large ovenproof skillet over high heat. Add the duck breasts, skin side down, to the skillet. Reduce the heat to medium and cook about 5 minutes until the skin is golden brown, checking occasionally to make sure it isn't burning. Turn the breasts over and transfer the skillet to the oven for another 4 to 6 minutes (5 minutes should get you a good medium-rare). Remove to a plate and tent with foil to rest 5 to 10 minutes.

While the duck breasts are resting, reheat the grape sauce and Indian Spiced Cauliflower (recipe follows) for just a few minutes each. Serve each breast on a bed of cauliflower. Spoon the grape sauce over all.

Serves 4

Extra! Extra! Grapes usually come in much larger quantities than this menu calls for. Of course, you can always eat the leftovers right out of hand, but if you want to keep enjoying them in your cooking, try tossing halved grapes into a salad, use as a topping on a white pizza with red onions, or throw some into a savory Indian dish.

Duck, Duck, Breast

In a world where the ubiquitous and bland boneless, skinless chicken breast has become the default poultry option upon which we too often unsuccessfully map our desires for a quick and easy dinner, it's time you got game. If you find yourself hunting in the meat department rather than on the moors, brush up on your duck breast varieties before taking aim.

· Pekin, aka Long Island, are the most common commercially available duck breasts. They have a thick layer of fat that crisps up nicely and are milder than either Moulard or Muscovy.

· Moulard, not to be confused with Mallard, is a species known for much larger breasts that weigh in at a full pound or more.

· Muscovy, aka Barbarie, is a South American breed that needs less fat than a Long Island duck to stay warm. Some producers even make claims that these ducks are 30 to 40 percent leaner. Moreover, they offer a real red-meat alternative with a strong flavor.

duck breasts with grapes & indian spiced cauliflower

Ancient Mustard

Mustard is the perfect spice to insert into this celebration of the grape since, like wine, its story is that of human development and its history is of biblical proportions: "The kingdom of heaven is like to a grain of mustard seed, which a man took, and sowed in his field: Which indeed is the least of all seeds: but when it is grown, it is the greatest among herbs, and becometh a tree…" (Matthew 13:31–32). Archaeological evidence of mustard seeds turns up in the prehistoric Swiss village Morigin. In the Middle Ages, many European courts had a mustardarius on staff who oversaw the cultivation and preparation of mustards. Mustard seeds are labeled yellow, brown, or black. The yellow, which actually appears more white, is used to make some of the most common ballpark and sandwich mustards we know. Brown mustard seeds are the basis for Dijon mustard, and black mustard seeds have the strongest and spiciest taste and are the most difficult to harvest and thus the most expensive. Both brown and black are used in Indian cooking to lend a bit of sharp nuttiness rather than the chili-like fire you get by mixing mustard seeds with vinegar or water to make the condiment.

indian spiced cauliflower

The gentle heat of the spices plays nicely against the fat of the duck and the sweetness of the grapes. It's a great way to combine the traditions of northern European game, southern European vineyards, and the valuable commodities of the spice trade with more distant lands.

1 large head cauliflower (about 2 pounds)
2 tablespoons unsalted butter
1 teaspoon ground coriander
½ teaspoon ground ginger
½ teaspoon ground cumin
¼ teaspoon turmeric
¾ teaspoon brown mustard seeds
⅛ teaspoon cinnamon
1 cup chicken broth
¼ teaspoon salt
¼ teaspoon freshly ground black pepper

Remove the outer leaves of the cauliflower. Cut the cauliflower in half, remove the core, and break into small-to-medium florets. Melt the butter in a large skillet over medium heat. Add the florets and stir to coat with butter. Sprinkle with the coriander, ginger, cumin, turmeric, mustard seeds, and cinnamon; stir to coat with spices. Pour the chicken broth over the cauliflower and bring to a boil. Reduce heat to a simmer, cover, and cook for 10 minutes, stirring halfway through. Remove the lid and continue to cook at a simmer, stirring frequently, until all liquid is evaporated and cauliflower is fork-tender, about another 10 minutes. In two batches, coarsely chop in a food processor by using "pulse" just a few times; don't puree it into a mash. It should look a little like popcorn when you're done. Return to the skillet. Stir in the salt and pepper. Reheat when the meat is ready and serve topped with the duck breasts.

Serves 4

cinnamon cream puffs

This recipe makes more than you need for four guests, but making pastry in small amounts is sometimes difficult. The plus side is leftovers.

DOUGH

1 cup water

½ cup (1 stick) unsalted butter, cut into 4 equal pieces

⅛ teaspoon salt

2 teaspoons sugar

1 cup plus 1 tablespoon flour

½ teaspoon vanilla

4 large eggs

FILLING

1 cup whipping cream

1 teaspoon cinnamon

2 tablespoons sugar

Honey or maple syrup to drizzle

Preheat the oven to 400°F. Line a baking sheet with parchment paper.

To make the dough: Combine the water, butter, salt, and sugar in a medium saucepan. Cook over high heat until the butter melts. Bring to a boil. Reduce the heat to medium, add the flour and stir constantly for 2 to 3 minutes until the dough forms a ball. Remove from the heat and cool slightly.

Transfer the dough to the bowl of an electric mixer. Add the vanilla and beat slightly. Add eggs, one at a time, beating well after each addition.

Use a pastry bag to pipe dough onto the prepared baking sheets or drop by heaping tablespoonfuls and gently mound each into a ball. Bake for 30 minutes until dry and golden. Cool completely.

To make the filling: Whip the cream with the cinnamon and sugar until soft peaks form. Use a pastry bag to fill the cream puffs. (See "Filling Station" sidebar, p. 113.) Arrange 3 puffs on each plate and drizzle with honey or maple syrup before serving.

Makes 24 cream puffs

Cinnamon's Bark and Bite

Much of the cinnamon available in the United States is actually cassia bark, whose bite varies from a very mild Indonesian Korintje cassia to a super-intense Vietnamese cassia. Even more distinct is true cinnamon, or *Cinnamomum zeylanicum*, whose lower volatile oil content lends a far more subtle flavor to delicate dishes. In autumn when we're all clamoring for our favorite baking spices, the Spice House in Chicago freshly grinds over 100 pounds of cinnamon a week, from the Vietnamese cassia that arrives as thick as a baseball bat to the Ceylon cinnamon in 5-foot fragile lengths. Co-owner Patty Erd reminds us that such precious foods should be kept airtight and stored away from heat that can damage them rather than next to the oven. They should be used and then replaced on a regular basis. Her husband Tom jokes, "Even though spices are expensive, they shouldn't be bequeathed to your grandchildren." Cinnamon and other autumn spices can be found at www.thespicehouse.com.

Variations on a Theme

Later in the season, when winter citrus is on the table, replace the cinnamon cream filling with orange or lemon curd. Instead of a drizzle of maple syrup or honey, serve with a dollop of whipped cream on the side. Any of the fillings for Sufganiyot (Hanukkah Donuts, p. 112) make great stuffing for cream puffs.

2

fresh from the field

the bounty of september

MENU
Number in Party: 4 to 6 Guests

Tomato Salad
Spanish Pizza with Chorizo and Peppers
Cheesecake with Sherry Sauce

As you usher in great autumn tastes, don't forget that depending on where you live and the whims of the weather, the early days of autumn are really the last days of summer. This meal is a homage to the highlights of summer's twilight: the plumpest, reddest tomatoes and most fragrant, ripest peppers. Celebrate these abundant ingredients fresh from the field in a Spanish-inspired menu that's comfortable as a weeknight family meal or a weekend dinner party.

tomato salad

This is one of those recipes that is more an idea or a hint than a detailed set of instructions. By September you will be knee-deep in tomatoes, either from an overzealous morning at the farmers' market or an overeager gardener neighbor looking for someone to help support his habit. Make the most of them with a simple, flexible salad that you can personalize to suit your taste.

Tomatoes
Olive oil
Balsamic vinegar
Salt
Freshly ground black pepper

Thinly slice the tomatoes. Lay in overlapping circles. Drizzle with however much olive oil (Spanish, of course, if you want to keep up the theme) and balsamic vinegar suits you. Sprinkle with salt and pepper. You're done! Save your energy to make the pizza.

You Say Tomato

Tomatoes are really leading the way in directing our attention toward the importance of botanical diversity and culinary quality. As a backlash against an industrial tomato bred not for taste or culinary desire but instead for ease of transport and shelf life, home gardeners and farmers are working to keep alive memories of tomatoes we have known. There are far too many to name here, but some more popular varieties popping up in market stands across the country include German Johnson, Pink Girl, Mortgage Lifter, Cherokee Purple, and Brandywine. Talk to farmers in your area about what you're really looking for in a tomato—small and pasty or large and juicy; yellow, orange, red, or pink; sweet and mild; or high acid with a lot of tang—and they will be happy to recommend the perfect one to suit your taste.

Pick a Pepper

In early autumn, choices for peppers abound, ranging from very mild sweet red bell peppers to super-hot Scotch bonnets—all of which have been maturing under a long, summer sun and are at their peak in so many places in September. The poblanos used in this menu are a medium-hot pepper. They look like a pointy bell pepper and are deep, dark green. If allowed to ripen, they turn reddish-brown and in their dried form are known as *ancho chilies*.

spanish pizza with chorizo and peppers

spanish pizza with chorizo and peppers

Sometimes I like to call this migration pizza or Old World–New World pizza. It combines that signature Spanish ingredient, chorizo, with peppers native to North America, especially the poblano that is a definitive part of Mexican cooking. If you want a bit more spice on your pizza, you can add a few seeds from the poblano and use chorizo labeled "picante."

DOUGH
2 packages active dry yeast

2 teaspoons sugar

1½ cups warm water (110° to 115°F)

2 teaspoons salt

2 tablespoons olive oil, plus more for bowl

4 cups flour

SAUCE AND TOPPINGS
2 tablespoons olive oil

6 to 8 garlic cloves, minced

One 14-ounce can tomato sauce

8 ounces mozzarella cheese, grated (about 2 cups)

8 ounces Spanish chorizo, thinly sliced

3 medium poblano chilies, thinly sliced

1 large red bell pepper, thinly sliced

4 ounces Manchego cheese, grated (about 1 cup)

To make the dough: In a small bowl, sprinkle the yeast and sugar over the warm water. Stir. Let sit for 5 minutes until the yeast starts to foam. Transfer the mixture to an electric mixer. Add the salt and olive oil. Turn the mixer to the lowest speed and gradually add in 1 cup of the flour, mixing until most of the lumps disappear, about 30 seconds. Slowly add in ¾ cup flour and mix until just combined. Sprinkle ¼ cup flour on pastry board or countertop. Turn out the pizza dough and knead in the remaining 2 cups flour. Continue kneading for a total of 5 minutes.

Coat a clean mixing bowl with olive oil. Transfer the dough to the bowl and turn to coat with oil. Cover with a towel, then place a plate on top to hold it in place. Let the dough rise in a warm place until double in size, about 1 hour.

While the dough rises, make the sauce: In a medium saucepan, heat the olive oil over medium-low heat. Add the garlic and sauté for 2 minutes, until fragrant. Add the tomato sauce, bring to a simmer, and cook for another 5 minutes, until the sauce begins to thicken. Set aside to cool until the dough finishes rising.

Preheat the oven to 450°F. After the dough has risen, punch it down and divide in half. Roll one half into a 12-inch round and place on a heavy baking sheet. Spread half of the tomato sauce over the dough, leaving a ½-inch border. Sprinkle with half of the mozzarella cheese. Top with half each of the chorizo, poblanos, and bell pepper. Bake for 15 to 20 minutes until the crust is lightly browned. While the first pizza is baking, prepare the second with the remaining ingredients. As each pizza comes from the oven, top with half of the Manchego cheese. Slice and serve.

Makes two 12-inch pizzas; serves 4 to 6

Extra! Extra! Chances are you're going to have to buy the chorizo in a larger quantity than the pizza recipe demands. Of course, any kind of cured sausage makes a nice snack. If you want something else, consider a grilled cheese sandwich with Manchego (which you'll also probably have left over) and thin slices of chorizo. Throw on any tomato going wanting as well, or add some diced chorizo to scrambled *huevos* or tuck them into an omelet.

A Sausage by Any Other Name

In the confusing culinary world of things that seem to be the same but aren't, you'll find Spanish chorizo and Mexican chorizo—two totally different culinary beasts that should not be used interchangeably. Spanish chorizo is made from smoked pork, and you'll find it in the deli section of the market looking a lot like salami and other cured and smoked sausages that can be eaten without cooking. Mexican chorizo is a raw pork sausage stocked in the meat department or refrigerator section of Mexican specialty markets and some grocery stores and should always be cooked like other raw pork products. When choosing a Spanish chorizo for your pizza, you'll likely find everything from presliced, prepackaged large rounds from San Daniele to thick chunky lengths from Palacios, and countless others. Choose whatever suits you. Just like with the more pedestrian pepperoni pizza, it isn't rocket science, just sausage, so go with your gut feeling.

cheesecake with sherry sauce

The sweetness in the crust and the filling is kept to a minimum, first, to allow the real nuttiness of pecans to come through; second, to not inhibit the wonderful tang of the cream cheese; and third, because the really wonderful sweetness is in the accompanying sherry sauce that makes this a dessert and a drink in one. Because a water bath often stands between the home cook and a cheesecake, this recipe doesn't call for one (though it's still important to follow the directions for letting the cake cool in the oven). This produces a thick dense texture that stands up to an intense sauce.

CRUST

1½ cups pecans (about 6 ounces)

1 tablespoon flour

3 tablespoons packed brown sugar

3 tablespoons unsalted butter, melted

FILLING

2 pounds (four 8-ounce packages) cream cheese, softened to room temperature

1 cup granulated sugar

3 eggs

¼ cup whipping cream

2 teaspoons vanilla

½ teaspoon salt

SAUCE

1 cup sweet sherry

¼ cup sugar

¼ cup whipping cream

Butter the sides and bottom of a 9-inch springform pan. Preheat the oven to 350°F.

To make the crust: Spread the pecans on a heavy baking sheet. Bake for 10 minutes, stirring halfway through. Cool for 5 minutes.

In a food processor, finely grind the toasted pecans with the flour and brown sugar. Add the melted butter and pulse a few times until mixture just holds together. Pat into the prepared pan, smoothing across the bottom and ½ to 1 inch up the sides. Place on a baking sheet and bake for 10 minutes. Remove from the oven and cool on a wire rack while you prepare the filling. Reduce the oven temperature to 325°F.

To make the filling: In the bowl of an electric mixer (preferably with the whisk attachment), combine the cream cheese and sugar. Beat on medium speed until completely smooth, scraping down the sides occasionally, 2 to 3 minutes. Mix in the eggs, one at a time. Make sure each one is thoroughly combined before adding the next and scrape down the sides in between additions to maintain a smooth texture and prevent lumps from forming. Add the cream, vanilla, and salt. Mix again until you achieve a completely smooth consistency, 1 to 2 minutes more. Pour the batter into the cooled crust. Place on a baking sheet and bake at 325°F until the middle is set but still slightly wobbly. Check after 1 hour. Add another 10 minutes if necessary. The middle will still be slightly wobbly. Turn off the oven and leave the cheesecake inside for another hour to slowly cool. Remove from the oven and continue to cool on a wire rack until room temperature. Refrigerate at least 4 hours.

To make the sauce: Combine the sherry and sugar in a small saucepan. Bring to a gentle boil over medium heat. Gently boil until it is reduced to ½ cup, about 7 minutes. Stir in the whipping cream, bring to a simmer, and simmer for another 5 minutes until thickened and syrupy. Remove from the heat and cool. Drizzle over individual slices of cheesecake or spread over the top of the whole cake. (The sauce can be refrigerated overnight and reheated for a few seconds in the microwave.)

Makes one 9-inch cake and ¾ cup sauce; serves 10

Sherry Hour

Too often sherry gets a bad rap as the beverage equivalent of the rubber chicken dinner. But sherry is a complex and diverse fortified wine that comes in many guises for many occasions. Get to know the range of sherries, including bone-dry Fino, medium Amontillado, and dessert-sweet Pedro Ximenez.

3
bringing in the sheaves
a greek harvest celebration

✦

MENU
Number in Party: 8 to 10 Guests,
depending on how you fill out the
menu with Greek cheeses, sausage,
and other embellishments

Phyllo Cigars: Lamb-Mint and Feta-Olive
Wheat Berry and Fig Salad
Almond Cookies

✦

Of all the symbols of the harvest season, none is perhaps so widespread as wheat—a symbol of life and prosperity. Sheaves of wheat are so powerful an icon that they have become a religious metaphor and a traditional hymn that has us all rejoicing as we bring in the sheaves. But long before that, wheat was central to the early religions and stories of ancient Greece and Rome, whose flavors and ingredients inspired this harvest menu.

Ceres is the Roman goddess of the harvest and wheat, and the myth of seasonal change from summer to winter centers on her daughter, Proserpina. In one version of the myth, Proserpina was gathering flowers in a field when the god of death, Pluto, suddenly appeared and spirited her away to the underworld. Her mother, desperate with grief, searched for her everywhere above ground. Unable to find her, she let the Roman fields of wheat and grains grow barren. At last, through the help of the sun and other gods, Proserpina was found among the world of the dead. Jupiter, through his divine messenger, Mercury, was eventually able to convince Pluto to release her. Before she left, though, Pluto tricked Proserpina into eating 6 seeds of a pomegranate, an act which guaranteed that she would return each year to the underworld for 6 months, splitting the year into summer and winter. In the Greek version, the characters of this seasonal drama are Demeter, Persephone, Hades, Zeus, and Hermes.

It's All Greek to Me

Brush up on your Greek food terms before putting on this spread.

- **Baklava:** A traditional Greek dessert crafted from layers of phyllo dough and nuts (usually pistachios or walnuts). Hot from the oven, these layers are drenched in a honey syrup.

- **Saganaki:** Thick slices of kasseri cheese soaked in alcohol and then flambéed tableside in Greek restaurants; the fire is extinguished with a generous squeeze of lemon juice.

- **Spanakopita:** Another good idea that starts with phyllo dough into which is stuffed spinach, onions, and feta cheese. Usually made into phyllo triangles.

- **Taramasalata:** It starts with *tarama*, or tiny orange carp roe, and is mixed with olive oil and lemon juice. This spread, usually found in the refrigerator section of the store or in Greek specialty shops, is the perfect quick topping for a cracker.

- **Tsatsiki:** A sauce of yogurt, cucumbers, garlic, and olive oil used on many Greek foods, from souvlaki to gyros.

phyllo cigars

phyllo cigars

Wheat unbelievably transforms into the thinnest sheets of pastry. Phyllo, or filo, can be harder to make from scratch than to pronounce. But luckily, for this recipe all you need to do is go to the grocery freezer section and ask for it by name: "Where is your phyllo (FEE-lo) dough, please?"

LAMB-MINT FILLING
2 tablespoons olive oil
½ cup finely diced onion
1 garlic clove, minced
½ pound ground lamb
½ teaspoon dried rosemary
½ teaspoon dried thyme
Salt, to taste
Freshly ground black pepper, to taste

FETA-OLIVE FILLING
8 ounces feta cheese
½ cup finely chopped mixed green and black Greek olives (such as kalamata; about ½ pound)
1 egg, beaten
¾ teaspoon dried oregano
Freshly ground black pepper, to taste

PHYLLO CIGARS
6 to 8 sheets phyllo dough, thawed according to manufacturer's directions
5 tablespoons unsalted butter, melted

To make the lamb-mint filling: Heat the oil in a medium skillet over medium heat. Add the onion and cook until soft and translucent, about 5 minutes. Add the garlic and cook 1 minute more. Add the lamb and cook until browned, about 8 minutes, breaking up the meat as it cooks. Stir in the rosemary, thyme, salt, and pepper. Remove from the heat and cool. Put the mixture in a food processor and pulse until you get an evenly fine texture, being careful not to grind it to a paste.

To make the feta-olive filling: Place the feta in a medium bowl and crumble with a fork. Add the olives, egg, oregano, and pepper. Mix to combine.

Preheat the oven to 375°F. Line 2 baking sheets with parchment paper.

To make the phyllo cigars: Lay 1 sheet of phyllo dough on a work surface with the long side toward you. Brush lightly with the melted butter. Lay another sheet of phyllo on top. Keep the remaining sheets covered with a damp towel. Brush the second layer with butter. Cut the phyllo in half lengthwise so that you have 2 half-sheets, one above the other. Cut each half into fourths so you have

8 equal-size wrappers. With the short side facing you lay 1 scant tablespoon of filling at the bottom of the wrapper. Roll up the filling in the phyllo dough partway. Fold in the sides and continue to roll into a cigar shape. Place, seam side down, on the prepared baking sheet. Repeat with the remaining filling and sheets of dough.

Brush the cigars with butter and bake for 25 to 30 minutes until crisp and golden brown.

Makes 24 to 32 phyllo cigars

Illusive Eleusis

The Greek god Demeter was worshiped in the city of Eleusis, which gave its name to some of the most well-guarded mysteries of the ancient world, the Eleusinian Mysteries. Although we do not know much about these rites, we do know the name of one of its most important figures, the primordial, Adam-like figure of Triptolemos, the "apostle of grain," a kind of Johnny Appleseed responsible for the spreading of cultivation throughout the ancient world. And lest we think these names and ideas have disappeared, think about the following twisted connections: the Norse version of Triptolemos, the son of Gaius and Okeanus, is named Baldar. Mythopoetically mixing these names together to come up with something entirely new out of something utterly old, the television series *Battlestar Gallactica* has given us Gaius Baltar. This questionably human revolutionary/traitor hails from the colony of Aerelon, the agricultural seat of *Battlestar*'s fictitious universe and known as the "food basket for the twelve worlds."

My Big Fat Greek Party

This menu easily expands to serve any number of unexpected guests with just a simple trip to the cheese shop or grocer. Fill out the home-made buffet with store-bought extras like

· **Dolmades:** stuffed grape leaves

· **Greek olives:** When you buy olives in a jar, you often get only two choices: green or black. But styles vary from country to country and region to region, and you'll find more choices if you head to a Greek market or even the olive bar of your local grocery store. For specifically Greek olives, look for the vinegar-soaked kalamata or the dark green Naphilion. Keep an eye out for Greek "oil-cured" black olives as well. These are intense and earthy.

· **Greek cheeses:** Try feta, Manouri, Myzithra, or kasseri.

Separating the Sheep from the Goats

Feta was traditionally made with sheep milk or a mixture of sheep and goat milk, but today we often find cow milk feta.

A Peloponnesian Potable

More good-quality Greek wines have been coming to the United States lately. Choose your favorites to pair with your buffet. But even before the fun begins, if you're looking for an aperitif to make your guests shout "opa!" try ouzo, an anise-flavored liqueur that, much like pastis, turns cloudy when mixed with water.

> The corn was orient and immortal wheat, which never should be reaped, nor was ever sown. I thought it had stood from everlasting to everlasting.
>
> —Thomas Traherne, *Centuries of Meditations*

wheat berry and fig salad

The wheat berry is what's left after you "separate the wheat from the chaff." And, like its signature adage, this tasty, nutty kernel can separate the adventurous eaters from the timid.

1½ cups wheat berries
1 tablespoon olive oil
1 medium onion, halved and thinly sliced
3 garlic cloves, minced
2 cups chicken or vegetable stock
1 teaspoon salt
4 dried figs, diced
½ cup cranberry juice
¼ cup balsamic vinegar
⅓ cup kalamata olives, pitted and halved
½ cup quartered canned artichoke hearts
4 ounces feta cheese

Soak the wheat berries in water for 1 hour while you prepare the other ingredients.

Heat the olive oil in a 2½-quart saucepan. Add the onion and cook over medium heat, stirring occasionally, for 8 minutes. Add the garlic and cook 2 minutes more or until softened. Remove the onions and garlic to a bowl and refrigerate.

Drain the wheat berries and put in the same saucepan with the chicken or vegetable stock and salt. Bring to a boil. Cover, reduce heat to a simmer, and cook for 45 to 50 minutes. When the wheat berries are tender but still slightly chewy, remove them from the heat and drain off any excess liquid.

Meanwhile, in another saucepan combine the figs, cranberry juice, and balsamic vinegar. Simmer on low heat for 20 minutes until the figs are soft and the liquid has become thick and syrupy. Set aside to cool.

Gently combine the wheat berries with the onions and garlic, olives, artichoke hearts, and fig compote. Toss with crumbled feta cheese just before serving.

Serves 6

almond cookies

Yet another honor is bestowed upon wheat in the ever-present, ever-ready form of the flour that forms the basis of so many desserts. Topped with glittering almonds, these cookies are one more acknowledgment of the pleasures of the seasonal table. If you'd like a shortcut, you can substitute toasted salted almonds for the raw ones and skip the steps for toasting, with the caveat that you won't have as wonderfully buttery and salty a taste.

TOASTED ALMONDS

2 teaspoons butter
40 whole raw almonds
Pinch of salt

COOKIES

1½ cups flour
1 teaspoon baking soda
½ teaspoon salt
¾ cup almond butter, at room temperature
½ cup (1 stick) unsalted butter, softened
⅓ cup granulated sugar, plus more for coating
⅓ cup packed light brown sugar
1 egg
2 tablespoons milk
1 teaspoon vanilla
¼ teaspoon almond extract

Preheat the oven to 375°F. Line 2 large cookie sheets with parchment paper.

To toast the almonds: In a large skillet over medium heat, melt the butter. Add the almonds and stir to coat. Sprinkle with the salt and continue stirring and cooking for another minute. Transfer the almonds to a plate, sprinkle with salt again, and spread in a single layer to cool.

To make the cookies: Combine the flour, baking soda, and salt in a medium bowl and set aside. Place the almond butter, butter, and sugars in the bowl of an electric mixer. Cream together on medium speed for 3 minutes. Add the egg and thoroughly beat. Add the milk, vanilla, and almond extract and beat to incorporate, about 1 minute. With the mixer running, add the flour mixture by heaping spoonfuls. Mix until just incorporated, but don't overbeat or the dough will be tough.

Roll the dough into 1½-inch balls. Roll in granulated sugar to coat. Place 2 inches apart on the prepared cookie sheets. Using the bottom of a glass, press down slightly to create 2½-inch cookies. (It helps to coat the glass bottom with a bit of nonstick spray and dust with more sugar every 3 to 4 cookies.) Press 1 toasted almond into the center of each cookie. Bake for 10 to 12 minutes until golden. Cool on wire racks.

Makes 40 cookies

Extra! Extra! Many natural food stores and outlets of the Whole Foods chain will let you freshly grind just as much almond butter as you like. But if you don't have access to such a privilege and end up buying a whole jar of almond butter, you can use the leftovers as a dip for apple slices or other snacks where you'd normally use peanut butter. How about an almond butter and fig jelly sandwich for lunch?

Almond Origins

Almonds were first cultivated in Jordan, and since then Jordan has lent its name to those candy-coated almonds we use for celebrations of all kinds, regardless of the origin of the almond inside. Greece, too, has a notable link to the almond, which is prevalent throughout the country's cookery. Almonds were some of the first trees to be domesticated in Greece and since early days have been served in desserts at Greek banquets.

A Pantheon of Harvest Deities

- **Baldar:** Norse god of grain
- **Chicomecoat:** Aztec goddess of maize
- **Inari:** Shinto god of rice
- **Lakan Pati:** Philippine goddess of the fields and fertility
- **Mama Allpa:** Incan earth and harvest goddess
- **Mbaba Mwana Waresa:** Zulu goddess of the harvest and agriculture, revered for giving the gift of beer
- **Mokos:** pagan Slavic goddess of fertility and the harvest
- **Peko:** Estonian god of grain crops and brewing
- **Renenoulet:** Egyptian harvest goddess
- **Min:** Egyptian god of cultivation
- **Rosmerta:** Celtic goddess of fertility and plenty
- **Sri:** Javanese rice mother

4
raking in the leaves
easy seasonal entertaining

❧

MENU

Number in Party: 6 Guests
(Easy to double for 12)

Autumn Carrot Salad

Welsh Rarebit

Maple Apple Tartlets

❧

There's a part of me that still really loves raking leaves, if for no other reason than that memory of so many autumn plunges into the pile. Double hands make for faster work, so entice others to turn this autumn chore into some childish fun and reward yourselves with a simple but sophisticated meal made up of do-aheads and last-minute group cooking.

autumn carrot salad

Like a lot of salads, this one can expand or contract to feed just the right number of people.

> Shredded carrots (about 1½ average-size carrots per person)
> Salt
> Freshly ground black pepper
> Pumpkin seed oil

Toss shredded carrots with salt and pepper to suit your taste. Arrange on salad plates and drizzle with pumpkin seed oil.

Kürbiskernöl

The German word for pumpkin seed oil is *kürbiskernöl*, a deep green-gold liquid that doesn't get much play in North America but is revered in Austria and parts of eastern Europe, where it originates. It's one of the top nutritional oils, delivering vitamins A and E as well as omega-3 fatty acids. Its rich nutty flavor isn't duplicated by anything else, so accept no substitutes. Drizzle it on salads of any kind, swirl atop a pumpkin soup, or just use it as a dipping oil for your favorite crusty bread.

Rabbit or Rarebit?

There's some disagreement about how the term *rarebit* came about and myths persist. Did it originate in some slander against the Welsh, did it come from anti-poaching laws which left poor cottages settling for cheese instead of meat, or was it just a trick of the dialect? Like the Victorian savory Scotch woodcock (scrambled eggs on toast with anchovies), there's no clear reason why we should call it as we do. Whatever the story behind rarebit, though, the fact that we still love it today attests to the timeless good taste of the Welsh. Add a poached egg on top, and you can contemplate yet more oddities of nomenclature with your new creation of Buck Rarebit.

Worcestershire Sauce

Often this comes tripping off American tongues more like "Woos-chester-shire" sauce. But instead, think "Bertie…" or "Earl of…" and abbreviate your syllables to a simple "Wooster" sauce.

welsh rarebit

This hearty dish mirrors the colors of the season with deep-yellow mustard, nut brown ale, and golden cheddar cheese. It's super easy; if you have a group, assign bread toasting to one person and cheese grating to another, and then marshal your ingredients to pull it all together in less than 10 minutes.

> 2 tablespoons unsalted butter
> 2 tablespoons flour
> 2 teaspoons dry mustard powder
> 1 cup dark beer
> 12 ounces sharp cheddar cheese, grated (3 cups)
> 2 teaspoons Worcestershire sauce
> 12 large slices of white bread, toasted

Melt the butter in a medium saucepan over medium heat. Whisk in the flour and continue to whisk while cooking, until the mixture begins to brown slightly, 3 to 5 minutes. Whisk in the dry mustard. Pour in the beer very slowly while continuously whisking so as to create a smooth sauce without lumps. Whisk in the cheese by handfuls, allowing it to melt between additions. Remove from the heat. Stir in the Worcestershire sauce.

Pour the rarebit over toast slices and serve.

Serves 6

> A Welsh rabbit, in the speech of the humorless, who point out that it is not a rabbit. To whom it may be solemnly explained that the comestible known as toad-in-a-hole is really not a toad, and that riz-de-veau à la financière is not the smile of a calf prepared after the recipe of a she banker.
>
> —Ambrose Bierce, *The Devil's Dictionary*

The Apple of Your Eye

When it comes to choosing apples for baking, select varieties that still hold their shape under the heat and don't go mushy after cooking. Try:

· Cortland
· Golden Delicious
· Granny Smith
· Ida Red
· Jonathan
· Spartan

A Thousand Leaves

The French call puff pastry *mille-feuille*, or a thousand leaves, for the way it is made by the constant turning and folding of dough around butter. According to Julia Child, a thousand is just a slight exaggeration. A finished puff pastry has 994 layers of dough and 993 of butter.

Bring the Outdoors Inside

Decorating the table for this meal is as simple as scattering a few handfuls of your autumnal harvest down the center as an organic table runner.

The nut-brown ale, the nut-brown ale,
Puts down all drink when it is stale!
The toast, the nutmeg, and the ginger
Will make a sighing man a singer.
Ale gives a buffet in the head,
But ginger under-props the brain;
When ale would strike a strong man dead
Then nutmeg tempers it again.
The nut-brown ale, the nut-brown ale,
Puts down all drink when it is stale!

—John Marston

maple apple tartlets

These tartlets are the ideal quick and easy end to an autumn meal. The key to perfection is making sure to keep the puff pastry cold. If using frozen puff pastry, start preparing the oven, baking sheet, and apples in advance of the time the pastry will be completely thawed. If it thaws too quickly, cut out the rectangle pastries, place on a baking sheet, and keep chilled in the fridge while you finish up. You can make them the morning of your leaf-raking chores, but they are best eaten within a few hours.

> 1 sheet puff pastry
> ½ teaspoon ground cinnamon
> 2 tablespoons sugar
> 3 small to medium baking apples
> 2 tablespoons unsalted butter, melted
> 2 tablespoons maple syrup

Preheat the oven to 400°F. Line a heavy baking sheet with parchment paper. Thaw puff pastry, if frozen.

In a small bowl, mix the cinnamon and sugar. Peel, core, and cut the apples in half. Place one half, cut side down, on a cutting board. With a small sharp knife, thinly slice the apple half into about 12 slices. Do not move or separate the slices. Repeat with the remaining 5 halves. Leave cut side down.

Place the puff pastry on a cold surface. Cut into 6 rectangles and place on the baking sheet. Pick up one apple half without disturbing the slices. Place on a pastry rectangle and apply slight pressure on the diagonal to fan out the apple slices until they nearly fill the length of the pastry rectangle. Leave a border of ¼ inch all the way around. Repeat with remaining rectangles of puff pastry and apple halves.

Sprinkle each tartlet with the cinnamon and sugar mixture. Drizzle with the melted butter. Bake for 25 minutes, until the pastry is golden around the edges and the apples are softened. Drizzle each with 1 teaspoon maple syrup. Serve warm or at room temperature. These are best served the day they are made.

Makes 6 tartlets

Extra! Extra! Most store-bought puff pastry comes in two sheets and you only need one for this recipe. To make use of the other, you could, of course, make another batch of Maple Apple Tartlets. But also think about cutting out small rounds and sprinkling with your favorite melting cheese or whipping up some quick breakfast treats by fashioning turnovers out of canned pie filling and squares of puff pastry.

5
an orchard buffet
—— comfort me with apples and pears ——

✣

MENU
Number in Party: 8 Guests

Pork Chops with Apples and Brandy
Wild Rice Pilaf with Cherries and Pecans
Poire William Ice Cream
Assorted varieties of apples, pears, and
quince with paired cheeses

✣

In an era when we often feel disconnected from the source of our food, autumn comes along with the pleasures of u-pick groves, hayrides, and corn mazes to give us a good reason to head out to the countryside and spend a day doing the work to get our food to the table.

pork chops with apples and brandy

Pork and apples are a classic autumn pairing, the kind of dish that everyone has some version of in their home cooking repertoire. Perhaps it's gilding the lily, or rather larding the pig, but anytime I pair pork and apples, I just have to have a bit of brandy and cream to bring out the flavors of both.

    8 boneless center-cut pork loin chops
        (4 to 5 ounces each)
    Salt
    Freshly ground black pepper
    4 to 5 tablespoons unsalted butter
    4 sweet apples, such as Golden Delicious, peeled,
        cored, and sliced
    ½ cup brandy
    ½ cup nonalcoholic apple cider
    ½ cup whipping cream

Using a meat mallet, pound the pork chops until they are ½ inch thick. Generously salt and pepper.

Melt 3 tablespoons of the butter in a large skillet over medium-high heat. Add the apples and sauté until golden brown, about 5 minutes. Remove to a separate bowl.

Melt another tablespoon of butter in the same skillet. Brown the chops on both sides, 3 to 4 minutes per side. Do it in two batches if necessary, adding another tablespoon of butter for the second batch. Remove to a separate plate.

Deglaze the pan with the brandy and cider. Bring to a boil and cook until reduced by half, 7 to 8 minutes. Stir in the cream. Reduce heat to low. Stir in the apples and any accumulated juices. Return the pork chops to the pan, cover, and cook until chops are cooked through, about 4 more minutes.

Serve with Wild Rice Pilaf with Cherries and Pecans (recipe follows). Divide rice among 8 plates. Place chops on top of rice. Mound apples on top of chops and pour sauce over all.

Serves 8

Extra! Extra! I can't imagine many leftovers from this menu, but if you have enough cheese and apples, make an autumnal grilled cheese sandwich and pair it with your favorite bowl of soup for a weeknight dinner after the party is over.

Taste Test

Follow this meal with a tasting tour of the orchard that highlights all your favorite varieties of apples and pears. Even if you didn't spend the day out among the trees, make sure to get together a wide array of apples and pears from your favorite vendor. Or, better yet, have each guest bring a couple of his or her favorites, and turn it into a contest or a guessing game, like a wine party from the orchard. For more on apples, see p. 16 in "Secrets of the Cold-Weather Pantry."

Load Your iPod with Apple and Pear Songs

Don't Sit under the Apple Tree by Glenn Miller

Little Green Apples by Roger Miller

Jenny Pluck Pears Traditional folk tune

Apple Suckling Tree by Bob Dylan

Apples by Buddy Rich

Sweet Pear by Elvis Costello

An Apple a Day

Of all the foods to pair with an apple in the savory world, nothing seems so perfect as pork. But there are many other great pairings to show off your great taste in apples. Try one of these each day of the week:

1. **maple syrup** (as in Maple Apple Tartlets, p. 72)
2. **smoked trout** (as in smoked trout and apple finger sandwiches)
3. **watercress** (as in Watercress and Apple Salad with Honey Vinaigrette, p. 98)
4. **raisins** (stirred into applesauce or stuffed into a baked apple)
5. **toasted walnuts or pecans** (ditto)
6. **nut butters** like peanut, almond, or cashew (just dip and eat)
7. **parsnips** (make a mash of the two and add lots of good butter)

wild rice pilaf with cherries and pecans

In an effort to get as much of the orchard into this menu but still stay with our dedication to the season, this pilaf reminisces about fruits of past seasons and brings them back to life in the form of dried cherries.

> 1 cup wild rice
> 2 tablespoons butter
> ½ cup minced shallots
> 1 cup long-grain brown rice
> 2 cups unsalted chicken broth
> ½ teaspoon salt
> ¼ teaspoon freshly ground black pepper
> ¼ teaspoon ground coriander
> Pinch of ground ginger
> ½ cup dried cherries
> ¾ cup coarsely chopped, toasted, salted pecans
> (about 3 ounces)

Cook the wild rice according to package directions.

While the wild rice cooks, prepare the brown rice. In a large skillet, melt the butter over medium heat. Add the shallots and cook, stirring constantly until softened, about 2 minutes. Add the brown rice and stir to coat with butter. Add the chicken broth, salt, pepper, coriander, and ginger. Bring to a boil. Reduce heat to low, cover, and simmer for 40 minutes until the rice is tender. Stir in the dried cherries, cover, and set aside for 10 minutes. Add the wild rice to the brown rice mixture. Stir in the pecans just before serving.

Serves 8

poire william ice cream

Poire William is a liqueur baptized after the French name for the pear that is its essence: William's *Bon Chretien*. In English, that's "Good Christian" for what we call in America a plain old Bartlett pear. And what does this many-named pear taste like? To be even more homey about it, as the *Magazine of Horticulture, Botany, and All Useful Discoveries and Improvements in Rural Affairs* put it in 1868, it has a "yellar" taste. On this point, I concur with the author of that long ago article: I couldn't have put it better myself.

> Vanilla ice cream
> Poire William or other pear-flavored liqueur

Serve single scoops of ice cream splashed with a shot of Poire William. How you interpret a "scoop" and a "shot" is up to the tastes and whims of you and your guests. I recommend pulling out that stainless steel scoop from "The Host's Toolbox" (p. 45) and mounding 3 to 5 small balls of ice cream into a wine glass before adding a jigger of Poire William.

Wild Rice and Tame Rice

Wild rice, the official state grain of Minnesota, isn't really rice at all but rather an aquatic grass. And most wild rice found in grocery stores isn't really wild but is instead cultivated in flooded plains, usually in California, and is harvested with combines. This "paddy rice" is usually dark brown to black in color and takes at least 40 minutes to cook. Truly wild rice grows naturally in lakes and rivers of Minnesota, Wisconsin, Michigan, and Canada and is a delicacy indeed worth its dear price. It cooks in half the time as cultivated "wild" rice and the bold nutty taste blends perfectly with other autumn foods like wild mushrooms, winter squash, dried fruits, and wild game. With earthy hues from smoky sage to light brown to warm sienna, truly wild rice from the Great Lakes region not only tastes great but aesthetically enhances the rich tones with which we adorn our table this time of year. It is beauty—not to mention history and tradition—on a plate. It is harvested by hand, by two people in a canoe who work together to collect the rice by beating the grains into the boat. Buying and cooking with natural rice from Indian tribes like the Minnesota Ojibwa helps supports traditional cultures for whom wild rice is part of their very existence. In the prophesies of the Ojibwa people of the Great Lakes region, in their migration from the East Coast westward, they were told they'd find their homeland when they came to "the place where the food grew on the water." Find out more and buy this rare food at www.savewildrice.org.

pork chops with apples and brandy & wild rice pilaf with cherries and pecans

assorted varieties of apples, pears, and quince with paired cheeses

Lay out apples and pears along with a variety of cheeses whose flavor profile plays off the fruit. Some quick and easy suggestions:
· Apples: farmhouse cheddars, Manchego, Comté
· Pears: anything blue, but my vote especially goes to Stilton
For more on choosing a cheese, see "Stock Up on Seasonal Cheese," p. 25.

Extra! Extra! Apples and pears are of course delicious eaten straight out of hand but some people prefer theirs as a drink. You may find gorgeous bottles of these apple and pear brandies, often marinating fruit inside the bottle thanks to the bizarre technique of glass-laden trees on which the fruit is actually grown inside the bottle. But the point is that they taste magnificent. Make the perfect quick after-dinner toast, or pour it over ice cream. Soak your favorite cake in one as well. Delish!

Liquid Gold

Apples are lovely eaten fresh and crisp from the tree and are wonderful in savory or sweet dishes, but one of my favorite ways to enjoy an apple in autumn is in a glass. Though commercial ciders often rely on apple concentrate bought by the lowest bidder, artisanal cider makers who craft an intensely different drink by monitoring every step of the process are springing up around the country. My favorite is J. K. Scrumpy, hailing from Almar Orchards in Michigan; see www.organicscrumpy.com.

Separated by a Common Language

Cockney rhyming slang, or a method of coding words into often humorous and sometimes quite rude phrases far divorced from their original meaning, gives a kind of poetry to everyday language. "Apples and pears" is Cockney rhyming slang for "stairs."

Precious Fruits

In addition to being a word for expensive gems, *perry* is a drink made from pears, just as cider is from apples. Though it has been a popular drink in England since the Middle Ages, perry has only recently made its way to the United States. You can now get Tom Oliver's Blackeney Red medium perry at select grocery stores and wine shops. Find out more at www.theolivers.org.uk.

In addition to the Blackeney Red, the UK National Fruit Collection contains nineteen other delightfully named pears specifically for perry making:

1. Barland
2. Barnet
3. Brandy
4. Butt
5. Gelbmostter
6. Gin
7. Green Horse
8. Hellen's Early
9. Hendre Huffcap
10. Judge Amphlett
11. Moorcroft
12. Oldfield
13. Parsonage
14. Sweet Huffcap
15. Taynton Squash
16. Thorn
17. Wassenbirne
18. Winnal's Longdon
19. Yellow Huffcap

6
all hallows' eve
—— *it's the great pumpkin* ——

❧

MENU
Number in Party: 4 Guests
(8 if you double the entrée)

Turnip "Carpaccio"
Chicken Breasts with Pumpkin Seed Filling and Butternut Sauce
Cream Cheese Pumpkin Squares

❧

Halloween has long been my favorite holiday because perhaps more than any other it really is about hospitality. Unlike the family-centered holidays of Thanksgiving, Christmas, and Hannukah or the couple-focused holiday of Valentine's Day, Halloween is about giving good food to total strangers who happen to make their way to your door once night falls—and about the trick that befalls those who are lacking in good hospitality.

turnip "carpaccio"

As much as I'm against the proliferation of applying some rather specific culinary style to just about everything, I honestly couldn't think of a better way to entice you to try something mundane like turnips. Eerie black seeds against the spooky whiteness of the turnips make the perfect Halloween starter. They look gorgeous on the plate and taste super-fresh on a cool night.

    3 medium turnips
    3 tablespoons coarse salt
    Nigella seeds or black sesame seeds

Thinly slice the turnips. Layer with salt and set in a mesh colander to drain for 30 minutes. Thoroughly rinse off the salt. Arrange in a concentric circle on each plate. Garnish with the nigella seeds.

Serves 4 to 6

> Nigella seed is a remedy for
> every disease except death.
>
> —Arab proverb

Turnip O'Lantern

Long before craft stores started selling home carving kits for pumpkins, there were all sorts of other vegetables used as lanterns as the days grew shorter and the nights longer. Katie Hill, historical interpreter at Old Sturbridge Village in Massachusetts, once explained on *Eat Feed* that the jack o'lantern is actually a pretty recent cultural import that came with nineteenth-century Irish immigrants who had already merged ancient pagan Celtic traditions with Catholic ritual. Back in Ireland, it was more common to carve a turnip or a kind of beet often used for animal feed known as a mangel-wurzel. Having carved a lot of mangel-wurzels herself, she points out a great Halloween benefit over the pumpkin: they dry up and start to resemble rather scary shrunken heads. When immigrants from the Old Sod discovered that pumpkins were far more plentiful in their new home in the United States, the tradition and the aesthetic changed.

Give Early and Often

Halloween has embedded in it so many traditions that focus on the importance of hospitality. Take the ritual whereby total strangers come to your door and beg for candy and you actually give it to them—unlike every other day of the year. I like to treat my guests to a ballad that is at once a ghost story and a medieval reminder of the importance of flinging wide our doors and putting on a good spread. "The Lyke Wake Dirge," which reminds us to be generous in this life—whether with your hosen and shoon (hose and shoes) or a good hot meal—for comfort in the next:

> This ae night, this ae night,
> Every night and all;
> Fire and sleet, and candle light
> And Christ receive thy saul.
>
> When thou from hence away art past,
> Every night and all;
> To Whinny-muir thou comest at last;
> And Christ receive thy saul.
>
> If ever thou gavest hosen and shoon,
> Every night and all;
> Sit thee down, and put them on;
> And Christ receive thy saul.
>
> If hosen and shoon thou ne'er gavest nane,
> Every night and all;
> The whins shall prick thee to the bare bane;
> And Christ receive thy saul.
>
> From Whinny-muir when thou mayst pass,
> Every night and all;
> To Brigg o' Dread thou comest at last;
> And Christ receive thy saul.
>
> From Brigg o' Dread when thou mayst pass,
> Every night and all;
> To Purgatory fire thou comest at last;
> And Christ receive thy saul.
>
> If ever thou gavest meat or drink,
> Every night and all;
> The fire shall never make thee shrink;
> And Christ receive thy saul.
>
> If meat or drink thou never gavest nane,
> Every night and all;
> The fire will burn thee to the bare bane;
> And Christ receive thy saul.
>
> This ae night, this ae night,
> Every night and all;
> Fire and sleet, and candle light,
> And Christ receive thy saul.

chicken breasts with pumpkin seed filling and butternut sauce

It's true that I've railed against the blandness of chicken breasts before. But sometimes they do have their place. Teamed with jalapeños, pumpkin seeds, and garlic, the chicken breast is transformed, like a kid in a Halloween costume. You won't even recognize it.

PUMPKIN SEED FILLING

1 cup raw pumpkin seeds
2 tablespoons olive oil
3 to 4 garlic cloves, minced
2 ripe jalapeño chilies, deseeded and coarsely chopped
¾ cup chicken broth

BUTTERNUT SAUCE

1 large leek
1 pound butternut squash
2 tablespoons olive oil
1 cup chicken broth
¼ teaspoon ground cumin
¼ teaspoon salt
¼ cup whipping cream

CHICKEN BREASTS

4 boneless, skinless chicken breast halves (about 1½ pounds total)
½ cup grated Dry Jack Cheese (or your favorite cheddar)
1 tablespoon olive oil
2 tablespoons unsalted butter
Flour for dredging
4 cups cooked long-grain white rice

To make the pumpkin seed filling: Heat a large skillet over medium heat. Add the pumpkin seeds. Cook, stirring and shaking the pan, until fragrant and slightly golden, about 4 minutes. They will pop as they cook, so stand back. Transfer toasted pumpkin seeds to a food processor to cool slightly.

In the same skillet, heat the olive oil over medium-low heat. Add the garlic and sauté until softened, about 4 minutes. Stir in the jalapeños and cook another minute. Stir in the chicken broth, turn heat to medium, and cook for another 3 minutes, until the stock is slightly reduced and the jalapeños are softened. Add the mixture to the pumpkin seeds in the processor. Blend until the mixture is a coarse but spreadable paste. Place in a medium bowl and cool while you prepare the butternut sauce.

To make the butternut sauce: Wash leeks thoroughly and then thinly slice the white and pale green parts only. Peel the butternut squash. Cut it in half, and scoop out and discard seeds and stringy flesh. Cut the squash into ¾-inch pieces. In a large skillet, heat the olive oil over medium heat. Add the leek and sauté until soft, about 3 minutes. Add the squash and chicken broth, increase the heat to high, and bring to a boil. When it reaches a boil, reduce the heat to a low simmer, cover, and cook until the squash is tender, 10 to 15 minutes. Transfer to a blender. Add the cumin, salt, and whipping cream. Puree until the sauce is completely smooth. Return to the skillet. If the sauce is too thick (possibly because you started with too heavy a squash), thin with a bit more chicken broth.

To make the chicken breasts: Lay each breast flat and pound until ⅛ to ¼ inch thick. Spread ¼ of the pumpkin seed filling across each breast. Sprinkle ¼ of the Dry Jack cheese over the filling. Fold each breast in half, short-end to short-end, to create a pocket.

Heat the olive oil and butter over medium heat. Place the flour in a shallow bowl and carefully dredge each chicken pocket in the flour. Add to the pan, one by one. Cook until all pink is gone, about 5 minutes per side. In the meantime, gently reheat the squash sauce. Divide the rice among 4 plates, top each with a stuffed chicken breast. Spoon the butternut sauce over all.

Serves 4

That's Ripe!

Choosing a good jalepeño is counterintuitive, but like plantains that are ready and sweetest when they have turned an unattractive black and brown all over, this Mexican chili is best when it looks a little more ropey than refined. Look for skin with brown ridged creases starting to form rather than a pristine smooth green. If you can't get a good ripe jalepeño, leave a few seeds behind in the mix if you like a little heat with the dish.

Pick a Pumpkin Seed

The kind of pumpkin seeds, or pepitas, you'll need for the filling can be found in health food stores, Mexican markets, or in the health section or international food aisle of the grocery store. Raw pumpkin seeds are pale green and unsalted. Avoid cleaning out your own pumpkin and using those seeds for this recipe. While they will make a nice snack, jack o'lantern seeds will be too wet and too tough for cooking.

chicken breasts with pumpkin seed filling and butternut sauce

cream cheese pumpkin squares

Not quite a cheesecake and not really a pumpkin pie, this creamy, tangy, pumpkiny treat is suitable for any autumn holiday.

SHORTBREAD CRUST
¾ cup flour
¼ cup yellow cornmeal
¼ teaspoon salt
½ cup (1 stick) unsalted butter, softened
¼ cup granulated sugar

FILLING
8 ounces cream cheese, softened
½ cup packed light brown sugar
¼ cup granulated sugar
2 large eggs
1 cup canned pumpkin
1 teaspoon ground cinnamon
½ teaspoon ground ginger
¼ teaspoon ground allspice
¼ teaspoon ground cloves
¼ teaspoon salt
½ cup whipping cream
1 teaspoon vanilla

Preheat the oven to 350°F. Butter a 9-inch square pan.

To make the shortbread crust: Place the bowl of the flour, cornmeal, and salt in a food processor. Process to combine and give the cornmeal a slightly finer texture. Add the butter and sugar and process briefly until you get a crumbly dough, about 30 seconds. Transfer the mixture to the prepared pan and use your fingertips to press the dough into a crust that covers the bottom of the pan. Bake for 10 minutes. Remove and cool slightly.

To make the filling: While the crust cools, prepare the filling. In the large bowl of an electric mixer, preferably with a whisk attachment, cream together the cream cheese and sugars on medium speed for about a minute. With the motor running, add the eggs, one at a time, blending well after each addition. Scrape down the sides. Mix in the pumpkin, cinnamon, ginger, allspice, cloves, and salt. Add in the whipping cream and vanilla and mix to blend. Scrape down the sides. Beat for 3 minutes until smooth and airy.

Pour the pumpkin mixture over the crust. Bake until set in the center, 40 to 50 minutes. Cool to room temperature and then refrigerate for at least 2 hours.

Makes nine 3-inch squares

Extra! Extra! Five things to do with leftover canned or cooked pumpkin:
1) add to a vanilla shake, along with pinches of your favorite autumn spices
2) infuse a hot milk drink by thoroughly pureeing pumpkin with cinnamon and sugar in a blender and adding warm milk—a splash of brandy wouldn't be amiss either
3) mix with a nice chèvre (goat cheese) and use as a filling for wonton wrappers to make your own ravioli
4) design your own autumnal burrito with black beans, your favorite chilies, a schmeer of pumpkin, and a dollop of sour cream
5) sauté garlic in olive oil, add in pumpkin and whipping cream, and puree for a pasta sauce

Peter Peter pumpkin eater,
Had a wife but couldn't keep her.
He put her in a pumpkin shell,
And there he kept her very well.

—Nursery rhyme

Pick a Pumpkin

Be careful in thinking that all pumpkins are alike. As different as butternut squash is from acorn squash, so too with different varieties of pumpkin. While it's an admirable idea not to waste your lantern by trying to cook it up, it simply won't work. Those pumpkins bred to be big and gorgeous for the front porch are virtually tasteless. For cooking and baking, be sure to look for smaller "pie pumpkins" or "cheese pumpkins."

Tricks and Treats

How do we get total strangers to just hand over candy? Experts have several different stories to tell on this front. In one lineage of the tradition, it looks a lot like Mexican Day of the Dead celebrations with the living laying out a feast for their ancestors. Others trace it back to more universal customs in which the poor might beg an indulgence of food at the landowner's gates, especially in times of dearth, as during the Irish potato famine.

What's in a Name?

Celebrated on October 31, Halloween is shorthand for All Hallows' Eve, the night before or the eve of All Hallows Day or All Saints Day. It's also known as Hallowmas-Eve, while November 1 is also called Hallow-tide.

Fortune-telling Foods

Many Halloween traditions center on using seasonal foods to predict the future. Scottish and Irish traditions include baked goods like a soul cake into which charms are buried. If you get the coin, you're bound for a life of wealth; receive a thimble and woe is the spinster. Pare an apple in one whole piece and toss the peel over your shoulder. The pattern it lands in reveals the initial of your future spouse. And lovers can test the state of their relationship by placing nuts next to each other on the fire to toast. If the nuts stay together, so too the couple. But if they pop and split, perhaps the pair should each start tossing those apple peels again.

7

guy fawkes

—————— *a very english coup* ——————

MENU

Number in Party: 6 Guests

Pasty Pie

Ginger Rum Bonfire Pudding

Festivities for Guy Fawkes night on November 5 take place outside, and that means portable food. Baked potatoes wrapped in foil to keep them warm are common at a homey gathering, as are carnival foods like candy floss and candied apples at more public-spirited events. One very long tradition lies with the greatest of all handheld British food: the pasty. Once the saving grace of Cornish miners who took a savory lunch in one end of the pasty and a sweet dessert in the other, the pasty is now just a great all-purpose bite on the go. This menu transforms the pasty into a pie for a sit-down dinner or an open-house buffet. Though bonfires are less common in the United States, there's a safe and theatrical way to make one at home with a flaming dessert.

pasty pie

Of all the things I learned while obtaining my Ph.D., I'm tempted to say that this is the most valuable. It's certainly the most delicious. This recipe comes from my one of my dissertation committee members, Sarah Beckwith, and her British family tradition of turning the individual pasties into a large pasty pie. Perhaps it is no coincidence, that in Sarah's courses I also learned the cultural importance of medieval rituals.

CRUST
1 large egg yolk (reserve the white)
1 tablespoon milk
3 cups flour
1 teaspoon salt
14 tablespoons (1¾ sticks) cold unsalted butter, cut into ¼-inch pieces
¼ cup ice water

FILLING
1 pound Russet potatoes, peeled and thinly sliced
Salt
Freshly ground black pepper
¾ pound rutabaga, peeled and thinly sliced
1 pound London broil or sirloin beef, thinly sliced
¾ cup packed chopped parsley
1 small onion or ½ large onion, thinly sliced
1 large egg white

To make the crust: Whisk together the egg yolk and milk in a small bowl. In à food processor, combine the flour and salt. Pulse to combine. Add the butter and pulse until the butter is marble size. Pulse in the ice water. Pulse in the egg and milk mixture until the dough forms large clumps. Turn onto a lightly floured pastry board or counter. Lightly knead the dough about 3 times to bring it together. Divide the dough in half, shape each into a disk, and wrap each in plastic wrap. Refrigerate at least 1 hour and up to 1 day.

Preheat the oven to 400°F. Line a large baking sheet with parchment paper.

To make the filling: Remove one dough disk from the refrigerator. On a lightly floured surface roll into a 13-inch circle. Keep lifting and turning as you go to prevent sticking, and flour your surface as necessary. Transfer the crust to a parchment-lined baking sheet.

On the bottom crust, create a layer with half of the potatoes, overlapping slightly, leaving a 1- to 2-inch border of crust. Generously sprinkle with salt and pepper. Next create a layer of half of the rutabaga, overlapping slightly. Repeat the first two layers, sprinkling with salt and pepper and a teaspoon of water. Layer half the London broil and sprinkle with salt, pepper, and water. Sprinkle with half the parsley. Add all the onion, salt, pepper, and water. Finish with the remaining beef; salt, pepper, water; the remaining parsley; salt, pepper, water.

Roll the second dough disk into a 14-inch circle on a lightly floured surface. Keep lifting and turning as you go to prevent sticking, and flour your surface as necessary. Lay the top crust over the pie. Seal the edges of the top and bottom crust and fold over all around, using your fingers to create a rope-like design. Make sure to leave no cracks. In a small bowl, whisk together the egg white and 1 teaspoon water. Brush the wash all over the crust. With a sharp knife, make a few cuts in the top crust to allow the steam to escape. Bake for 60 to 75 minutes, until golden brown. Cool for 5 minutes, cut into wedges, and serve.

Serves 6

Flame Wars

Guy Fawkes is burned in effigy every November 5, for it's on that day in 1605 that Fawkes planned the execution of the Gunpowder Plot but instead wound up being executed. A plot to blow up Parliament when all the members of both Houses were in it was designed by the Jesuits to destroy the Protestant reign of James I. Alas for Fawkes, he was caught the day before, and now bonfires and fireworks light the British sky in mock commemoration of this day.

Swedes and Neeps

Rutabagas are often called Swedes in Britain, for having been introduced into Scotland in the eighteenth century from Sweden as a new Swedish turnip. Neep is another local term for turnips, used mainly by the Scottish.

pasty pie

ginger rum bonfire pudding

The focus of the Guy Fawkes night is the bonfire, but short of the effort that takes, here's a more compact, tabletop bonfire inspired by flaming Christmas puddings.

1½ cups flour
1 tablespoon Dutch-processed cocoa powder
1½ teaspoons baking powder
1 teaspoon baking soda
1 tablespoon ground ginger
¼ teaspoon salt
4 tablespoons (½ stick) unsalted butter
½ cup packed brown sugar
1 egg
3 tablespoons whole milk
¼ cup rum

Butter a 4-cup pudding basin or pudding mold. Combine the flour, cocoa powder, baking powder, baking soda, ginger, and salt in a medium bowl. In the bowl of an electric mixer, cream together the butter and sugar. Beat in the egg. Add the flour mixture by heaping tablespoonfuls. Mix in the milk. Pour the mixture into the prepared pudding mold and seal the lid or pour into the pudding basin and cover with buttered foil, pleated in the middle to allow for expansion. Steam for 2 hours. (See "Steaming a Pudding," p. 197). Cool for 15 minutes. Invert the pudding onto a serving plate. Pour the rum over the pudding and carefully set alight at the table. The flame will extinguish itself when the alcohol burns off.

Serves 8

An Essential Spice

Ginger is one of those spices that seem to have been around forever. Mentioned in both the Koran and the writings of Confucius, this spice has helped humanity combat everything from nausea to colic.

Bonfire Night

Bonfire night is another name for Guy Fawkes Day. While a bonfire might seem out of place in the early days of November on this side of the Atlantic, I've devised another small commemoration in a bonfire dessert. Fawkes hailed from Yorkshire, where gingerbread and ginger parkin were popular desserts. This dessert draws on that gingery heritage.

8

the politics of food
—— an election night get-together ——

MENU
Number in Party: 8 to 10 Guests

Franklin's True American Original Turkey and Cranberry Sandwiches
Washington's Favorite Corn Cakes
Lincoln's Inaugural Chicken Salad and Lobster Salad
Jefferson's Peanut Sundaes

Long before "green washing" and "food miles" and all the dilemmas of omnivores and vegetarians alike, the politics of food were already brewing in our early nation. Every president has shaped the tastes of the country with his own tastes. From George Washington's sense of simple British frugality and Thomas Jefferson's penchant for elaborate French food to Ronald Reagan's obsession with jelly beans and Bill Clinton's passion for southern barbecue, we haven't just been what we eat but have eaten what we vote. This menu celebrates the favorites of many of our past politicians and the eras they helped shape.

franklin's true american original turkey and cranberry sandwiches

In addition to being the inventor of so many novelties, Benjamin Franklin was the number one fan of both turkey and cranberries. These simple sandwiches allow you to pay homage to the man, this classic American pairing, and a little bit of our nation's culinary history all at the same time. If you're really pressed for time, you can, of course, pick up a good-quality cranberry preserve in the jams and jellies aisle.

    2 cups fresh cranberries
    ½ cup packed brown sugar
    ¼ cup water
    1 French baguette
    ¾ pound sliced turkey

Combine the cranberries, brown sugar, and water in a medium saucepan. Bring to a simmer. Cook and stir until the cranberries pop and the sauce turns to a thick and chunky spread, about 8 minutes.

Slice the baguette in half lengthwise. Spread the bottom half with the cranberry relish. Layer the turkey over the cranberries. Place the baguette top on it and cut sandwiches into mini or medium lengths, depending on your taste.

Makes 6 to 10 sandwiches

A True Original Native of America

Benjamin Franklin baptized the turkey as our nation's unique treaure. He was so enamored of many "native" American foods that, while in England, he had large shipments of them—cranberries, corn, buckwheat, "Indian meal"—sent to him. "They will be a great refreshment to me this winter," he wrote, "for since I cannot be in America, everything that comes from thence comforts me a little, as being something like home."

You can tell a lot about a fellow
by his way of eating jelly beans.

—Ronald Reagan

washington's favorite corn cakes

Unlike Jefferson, who had a taste for French and Continental foods, our first head of state had rather homey desires. Corn cakes were one of his favorites.

    ½ cup flour
    ½ cup cornmeal
    ¾ teaspoon baking powder
    ½ teaspoon baking soda
    ¼ teaspoon salt
    Pinch of sugar
    1 large egg
    1 cup buttermilk
    Butter or nonstick cooking spray

In a medium bowl, combine the flour, cornmeal, baking powder, baking soda, salt, and sugar. In a small bowl, whisk together the egg and buttermilk. Whisk the egg mixture into the cornmeal mixture.

Heat a large skillet or griddle over medium heat. Coat with butter or nonstick cooking spray. Drop on the batter in circles, about 1 tablespoon each. Cook until golden brown on the underside and bubbling on top. Turn and cook until golden again. Serve with slices of your favorite cheeses or thick and hearty chutney or fruit preserve.

Serves 6 to 8

Little Orphan America

What is often considered the first truly American cookbook, *American Cookery*,—attributed to Amelia Simmons, self-named "an American Orphan"—first appeared in print in the early days of the American republic of 1796. In fact, the cookbook straddled two American ideologies to express a uniquely American food utopia: the fabled frugality of Franklin and the culinary abundance of Jefferson. It also plagiarized popular English recipes while promoting Native American ingredients. The book promised also to instruct young women in the art of domestic patriotism and to make women "useful members of society" by dedicating itself to "the improvement of the rising generation of Females in America."

lincoln's inaugural chicken salad and lobster salad

The bill of fare for Abraham Lincoln's second inauguration included many rather ordinary foods we still enjoy today. Dessert included grapes, almonds, and raisins as well as strawberry, orange, and lemon ices. There were four kinds of beer, four kinds of poultry, and three kinds of veal as well as pickled oysters, smoked hams, and chicken and lobster salads.

CHICKEN SALAD
Salt
Freshly ground black pepper
4 boneless, skinless chicken breast halves, cut into ¼-inch cubes (about 1½ pounds total)
1 tablespoon olive oil
2 tart apples
2 teaspoons lemon juice
¾ cup shredded celery root
¾ cup toasted walnuts, roughly chopped
¾ cup mayonnaise
Small dinner rolls or your favorite bread

LOBSTER SALAD
2 lobster tails (10 to 12 ounces each)
⅓ cup mayonnaise
1 tablespoon lemon juice
2 teaspoons paprika
Salt
Freshly ground black pepper

To make the chicken salad: Generously salt and pepper the chicken cubes. Heat the olive oil in a large skillet over medium heat. Sauté until the chicken is cooked through, about 8 minutes. Cool slightly.

Peel, core, and cut the apples into ¼-inch pieces. In a large bowl, toss with the lemon juice to prevent browning. Stir in the celery root, chicken, walnuts, and mayonnaise. Salt and pepper to taste. Serve piled on dinner rolls or your favorite bread.

To make the lobster salad: Cook the lobster tails in a medium pot of boiling salted water, for 5 to 8 minutes. Cool, remove from the shells, and dice the lobster meat. In a medium bowl, combine the lobster with the mayonnaise, lemon juice, and paprika. Salt and pepper to taste. This salad can be served with or without bread.

Serves 6 to 8 as hors d'ouevres

jefferson's peanut sundaes

Thomas Jefferson is one of two presidents known to be peanut farmers, Jimmy Carter being the other. Through his agricultural trials, he's credited with having helped popularize the ground nut in the United States. At the same time, one of the many food myths about Jefferson is that he introduced ice cream and ingredients like vanilla into the New Republic. While he didn't quite do that, his vanilla ice cream recipe is one of the treasures of Monticello. This recipe combines two great American flavors we still love today.

½ cup whipping cream
¼ cup sugar
½ cup chunky peanut butter
2 pints vanilla ice cream
1 cup salted peanuts, chopped (optional)

Gently heat the whipping cream and sugar in a medium saucepan over medium heat. Whisk in the peanut butter until the sauce is smooth. Serve over vanilla ice cream. Top with peanuts, if desired.

A President's Tastes

Jefferson is often praised as having introduced the United States to many new foods as well as cooking gadgets. Some of these stories have taken on a life of their own but many are grounded in solid archival research. Records at Monticello include invoices, account books, and letters that reveal a lot about what Thomas Jefferson loved to eat. Requests sent to Europe, for example, ask for wine, olive oil, pasta, anchovies, and Parmesan cheese. Letters and household books demonstrate the extent to which slaves who worked in the kitchen shaped the food of the nation's leader.

A Day of Thanks

We should thank Abraham Lincoln as much as Benjamin Franklin for our love of turkey, for it was the sixteenth president who officially gave us the Thanksgiving holiday. Several months after his more justly famous Emancipation Proclamation, in 1863 Honest Abe made another proclamation. On October 3 he proclaimed Thanksgiving to be a national holiday.

jefferson's peanut sundaes

9
the hunting party
game with games

―――――――― ❧✦❧ ――――――――

MENU
Number in Party: 4 to 6 Guests

Wild Mushroom Toasts
Venison with Cranberry-Port Relish
Roasted Root Vegetables
Watercress and Apple Salad with Honey Vinaigrette
Pears in Nightshirts

❧✦❧

For many centuries, one of the most important events that punctuated the calendar of the British gentry was an autumn country house weekend where the morning centered on hunting and the night on absolutely decadent food, drink, and entertainment. What you do with the entertainment is up to you, but this menu is chock-full of as many autumn treats as possible: venison, mushrooms, potatoes, parsnips, carrots, apples, pears, and cranberries.

wild mushroom toasts

If you're not much of a hunter, this starter allows you to show your talents off as a gatherer. But of course, if you don't have time to forage for wild mushrooms in the autumn woods, then you might do just as well to buy them from your favorite gourmet grocer.

1 ounce dried porcini mushrooms

1 cup boiling water

3 tablespoons unsalted butter

¼ cup diced onion

8 ounces mixed fresh wild mushrooms, such as oyster, chanterelle, trumpet, and hedgehog

8 ounces fresh cremini mushrooms

1 teaspoon cornstarch

⅓ cup dry sherry

Salt

Freshly ground black pepper

4 slices white or wheat bread

Place the porcini mushrooms in a small bowl. Cover with the boiling water. Soak for 30 minutes. Strain, reserving mushrooms and soaking liquid separately. Pour slowly as you drain and be careful to leave any sandy sediment in the bottom of the bowl and discard.

Clean the fresh mushrooms. Slice larger mushrooms and mince the stems. Melt the butter over medium heat in a large skillet. Add the onion and sauté until soft, 5 to 7 minutes. Add the fresh mushrooms and sauté until they begin to color and release their juices, 5 to 7 minutes more. Stir in porcini mushrooms. In a small bowl, stir the cornstarch with the sherry. Add the mixture to the cooked mushrooms, turn heat to high, and boil until the sauce thickens, about 2 minutes more. Season to taste with salt and pepper.

Toast the bread, then remove the crusts. Cut each slice crosswise into 4 triangles and place on salad plates. Top with the mushroom mixture.

Serves 4

Game On

Purchase an assortment of game terrines and pâtés for guests to nibble on and chat away while you finish up the roast. Look for pheasant or duck terrine or any pâté with "hunter" in the name.

Tally-ho

If you are lucky enough to know someone who hunts and likes you in a generous kind of way, you've already bagged dinner. But if you don't typically head to the Highlands for a bit of grouse in season, stalk your prey elsewhere. Even if venison isn't on display in the meat case at your local grocery store, chances are if they have a butcher on staff, it's the sort of store that can do a special order. Alternatively, there are great online sources for farmed venison: D'Artagnan (www.dartagnan.com) or Underhill Farms (www.underhillfarms.com).

> Unlike my predecessors I have devoted more of my life to shunting and hooting than to hunting and shooting.
>
> —Sir Fred Burrows

venison with cranberry-port relish

venison with cranberry-port relish

Venison is perhaps the most popular kind of game still enjoyed today, and with good reason. It's versatile, fairly easy to come by, and offers a leaner alternative to its barnyard cousin, beef. This recipe blends the earthiness of rare venison with a traditional accompaniment of tart cranberries spiked with a splash of another taste of delicious Olde England: port.

1 cup ruby port
¼ cup dried currants
4 juniper berries, crushed
2 teaspoons minced fresh thyme
1 teaspoon freshly ground black pepper
1 teaspoon salt
2 tablespoons olive oil
2 racks venison, 4 ribs per rack, trimmed between bones (1 to 1½ pounds each)
½ cup beef broth
1 cup fresh cranberries
2 tablespoons packed light brown sugar

Preheat the oven to 425°F. In a small saucepan, gently heat the port. Do not let it reach a simmer. Remove from the heat and add the currants. Set aside to soak.

Mix together the juniper berries, thyme, pepper, salt, and olive oil. Let steep for 10 minutes to meld flavors. Brush evenly over the venison. Arrange racks in a roasting pan facing each other so that the bones interlock and each rack has as much surface area exposed as possible. Roast until the internal temperature is 125°F for rare, 20 to 30 minutes, depending on the size of the racks. Remove from the oven and transfer the racks to a serving platter to rest for 15 minutes. Tent with foil.

Drain the currants, reserving the port. Set the roasting pan across 2 burners on the stovetop. Turn each burner to medium-high. Add the port and beef broth to deglaze the pan. Scrape up any brown bits as you stir. Bring to a boil. Cook until the liquid is reduced to ¾ cup, about 10 minutes. Reduce the heat to medium-low and add the cranberries and brown sugar. Cook, stirring occasionally, until the cranberries are soft and you have a relish consistency, about 7 minutes. Add the currants.

Carve the venison into chops by slicing between the ribs. Serve with the relish.

Serves 4

Extra! Extra! If you end up with any leftovers, make cold venison sandwiches. Many of the components of the meal make great sandwich toppings for venison: Stilton, cranberry sauce, watercress, and horseradish.

Revolution at the Table

In Renaissance England, aristocrats complained that commoners enjoyed too much venison and had degraded the status of the once noble food. When they were busy dismantling the class structure over dinner, pasties were one of the favorite celebration foods enjoyed by the proles. One seventeenth-century fictional shoemaker who trod the stage circa Shakespeare dreams of a party at which "venison pasties walk up and down piping hot like sergeants, beef and brewis comes marching in dry-fats, fritters and pancakes come trolling in in wheelbarrows."

Have a Hart

The hunted deer prances through the whole history of English love poetry, not to mention romantic banter of a more quotidian variety. *Hart* is another word for deer and is repeatedly deployed, for better or worse, as a pun for *heart*.

roasted root vegetables

What's better to serve with a traditional rack of roasted venison than a classic like roasted root vegetables? This particular mixture of roots blends the distinct flavors of three different vegetables with the perfect autumn herb and a smidge of onion.

1 pound potatoes
1 pound carrots
1 pound parsnips
2 large onions
3 tablespoons olive oil
2 tablespoons unsalted butter, melted
2 tablespoons chopped fresh sage
Salt
Freshly ground black pepper

Preheat the oven to 425°F. Peel the potatoes and cut into 1-inch cubes. Peel the carrots and parsnips and slice on the diagonal into 1-inch-thick slices. Quarter the onions. Place the prepared vegetables in a roasting pan. Pour the olive oil and melted butter over the vegetables and toss to coat. Add the sage, and salt and pepper to taste and toss again. Roast until tender, 45 to 50 minutes, stirring occasionally.

Serves 4

....

Three jolly gentlemen,
In coats of red,
Rode their horses
Up to bed

—Walter de la Mare, "The Huntsmen"

....

watercress and apple salad with honey vinaigrette

In traditional European fashion, serve this salad after the main course rather than at the start of the meal.

2 large bunches watercress (about 12 ounces)
1 tart green apple, such as Granny Smith
¼ cup plus 1 teaspoon apple cider vinegar
2 teaspoons Dijon mustard
4 teaspoons honey
¼ teaspoon salt
½ cup olive oil

Prepare the watercress by removing as much of the stem as you can. Rinse, dry, and place the leaves in a large salad bowl. (If you don't have a salad spinner, an easy way to remove excess water from salad greens is to place them in a mesh colander, cover with a plate, and shake over the sink.)

Peel and core the apple and cut into ¼-inch pieces. Toss with 1 teaspoon of the cider vinegar. Set aside while you prepare the vinaigrette.

In medium mixing bowl, whisk together the remaining ¼ cup cider vinegar, mustard, honey, and salt. Whisk in the olive oil. Toss the apples with the watercress. Toss the dressing with the salad to thoroughly coat the watercress leaves and apple cubes.

Serves 4

pears in nightshirts

This creation is reminiscent of a pear dumpling only it's much easier to make and far more interesting. No other dessert can possibly serve as the finale to such a meal.

PEARS
4 ripe baking pears, such as Bartlett or Bosc, with stems intact
2 cups pear juice
2 cups water
¼ cup sugar

MERINGUE
4 large egg whites
½ teaspoon cream of tartar
¾ cup sugar
4 large mint leaves (optional)

To make the pears: Peel the pears, leaving stems intact. Run the peeler a few times across the bottom of each pear to remove a bit of the papery end and to create a flat bottom for the pear to sit upright. In a Dutch oven or deep pan that can hold all the pears standing upright, combine the pear juice, water, and sugar. Bring to a boil. Stand the pears in the cooking liquid, reduce the heat to a simmer, cover, and cook until the pears are tender, about 20 minutes. (Cooking time may be longer if you have to use unripe pears.) Remove the pears from the pan with a slotted spoon, reserving the cooking liquid, and set on paper towels to soak up excess moisture. Cool for 10 minutes.

Preheat the oven to 375°F. Butter a glass or ceramic baking dish large enough to hold all the pears standing upright. Bring the reserved poaching liquid to a boil and boil until thick and syrupy, about 20 minutes.

While the sauce boils, prepare the meringue: In the large bowl of an electric mixer, beat the egg whites until foamy. Add the cream of tartar and beat until medium-stiff peaks form. With the motor running, slowly add the sugar, scraping down the sides when you've finished adding the final bit of sugar. Beat the meringue until stiff peaks form.

Blot the pears with paper towels to remove excess surface moisture and help the meringue to stick. Transfer the pears to a glass baking dish. Cover each pear in meringue, either by piping with a pastry bag or by frosting them with a silicone spatula. You can hold each pear up by the stem while you slather on the meringue, which allows you to cover the bottom as well. Bake for 15 minutes, until meringue is set and just beginning to turn golden.

Drizzle the pear syrup around the surface of 4 dessert plates. Place 1 pear on each plate on top of the sauce. Decorate the stem of each pear with a mint leaf, if you like.

Serves 4

Let the Games Begin

For centuries, one of the most popular games played by the hunting parties at country house weekends was, well, quite frankly, wife swapping. But if swinging isn't quite your thing, consider entertaining your guests with the other popular game played before the lights went out: charades. In old-style charades, the host provided props and makeshift costumes, and players put on short skits in which they acted out each syllable of the word in a series of acts that culminated in a final act of performing the whole word. When you clean out your closets in the fall to make way for your winter clothes, before you send your unwanteds off to charity, set them aside for the hunting party and offer your guests a chance to dress up and put on a show.

A Hodgepodge of Hunters

The hunt is the inspiration for many traditional European dishes. In a classic French repertoire, look for dishes with the word *chasseur*, as in the traditional dish *Chicken Chasseur*, or in Italian *Chicken Cacciatore*. *Hunter's Stew* is usually a mixture of the game the lucky shooter brought home that night.

winter

10
the first snowfall
banquet in white

MENU
Number in Party: 8 to 12 Guests

Snowball

Thai Coconut Rice Twists

Golden Caviar Toasts

Vanilla Cream

Meringues

T he tricky thing here is the timing. If you are lucky enough to live in a place where the snow sticks around long after it first falls, you've got some leeway. Or if you have a direct line to the local meteorologist, you can plan ahead. But then again, you've heard of a rain dance? Try this party on to evoke the divine powers of the snow gods even if there's nary a snowflake in sight.

snowball

This twist on a White Russian creates a truly white drink because the coffee flavor is infused into the drink by steeping coffee beans rather than through brewed coffee or coffee liqueur. Cinnamon offers the spicy undertone we expect of a proper winter drink. If you want a more elegant look, use martini glasses instead, and get the added bonus of stretching the recipe to serve a few extra guests.

1 cup cream
2 tablespoons granulated sugar
¼ cup coffee beans
3 cinnamon sticks
½ cup confectioners' sugar
1 lemon wedge
½ cup vodka
4 cups ice

Combine the cream, granulated sugar, coffee beans, and cinnamon sticks in a small saucepan and bring to a simmer over medium heat. Remove from the heat, cover, and let steep for 30 minutes. Strain through a fine-mesh strainer. Chill until ready to use (at least 30 minutes).

Sift the confectioners' sugar onto a small plate. Wet the mouths of 4 old-fashioned glasses with lemon and dip into the confectioners' sugar to create a "snowy" rim. In a blender, combine the cream mixture, vodka, and ice. Puree until you have a slush consistency. Pour into the prepared glasses and serve.

Serves 4

A Storm in a Blender Jar

There are a few things that really never go out of style for a good party; the blender is one of them. With the blender, you can actually make your own snow if the weather outside hasn't quite permitted. Pop in ice cubes. Puree. Voila! But then do something a little more interesting like drizzle with flavored syrups (the kind used in coffee drinks) for a sophisticated snow cone that allows you to have your snow and eat it too. For added winter warmth, sneak in a splash of alcohol, like gin, and follow with a drizzle of elderberry syrup. Some great gins to try: Plymouth, Hendricks, and Juniper Green Organic.

thai coconut rice twists

In other eras, these were called pinwheels, roll-ups, sushi, and wraps or roulades when you were feeling extra fancy. The name may change but such little bites endure as cocktail party necessities. These are super easy to make, which is exactly the idea behind this kind of roll-up pinwheel wrap.

Two 14-ounce cans unsweetened coconut milk
1 teaspoon salt
2 cups sushi rice
1 pound boneless, skinless chicken breasts
1 tablespoon vegetable oil
½ cup chicken broth
4 tablespoons Thai green curry paste
Salt
6 rectangular sheets lavash bread (like that for sandwich wraps)

Combine the coconut milk, salt, and rice in a medium saucepan. Bring to a boil over high heat. Reduce the heat to low, cover, and simmer for 20 minutes until all liquid is absorbed and the rice is tender. If the rice is dry but the moisture is gone, add a bit of water. If too much coconut milk remains, remove the lid and cook while stirring, until absorbed. Cool slightly for 5 minutes with the lid removed.

While the rice cooks, prepare the chicken filling. Cut the breasts into 1-inch cubes. Heat the oil over medium-high heat. Add the chicken. Stir and cook until thoroughly cooked through, 5 to 7 minutes. Transfer to a food processor. Puree until you get a texture best described as "fine shred." Return it to the skillet. Add the chicken broth and curry paste. Cook and blend until the paste is thoroughly mixed in. Season to taste with salt.

Lay one lavash on a work surface with the long end toward you. Using a flexible spatula, spread one-sixth of the rice on the lavash, as you might for a sushi roll. Make it thin and even and cover to each of the 4 edges. On top of the rice, spread a heaping ⅓ cup of the chicken filling in a line along the long end of the lavash. Roll up tightly, starting at the long end. Repeat with remaining 5 pieces of lavash. Using a sharp knife, cut the ragged ends off of each roll. Then cut each roll into 8 to 10 equal pieces. Arrange on a serving platter.

Makes 48 to 60 small appetizers; serves 10

In the bleak mid-winter
Frosty wind made moan,
Earth stood hard as iron,
Water like a stone;
Snow had fallen, snow on snow,
Snow on snow,
In the bleak mid-winter,
Long ago.

—Christina Rosetti

No cloud above, no earth below—
A universe of sky and snow.

—John Greenleaf Whittier

golden caviar toasts

Shiny black osetra may be the height of luxury, but golden sparkling domestic caviar, like that of Great Lakes whitefish, won't break the bank while providing the perfect glimmer to the banquet table.

12 slices white bread
Sour cream or crème fraîche
4 ounces whitefish caviar

Toast the bread, remove crusts, and cut each slice into 4 triangles. Top each with a dollop of sour cream or crème fraîche and crowning of caviar.

Makes 48 toasts

A Culinary Blizzard

As children we might have been perfectly happy with snowflakes on our tongues, but your "First Snowfall" guests will probably want a little more in their mouths. When you're looking for ways to expand the loaves and fishes beyond the time and energy you have, consider a few store-bought embellishments:

· Turkish delight laden in snowy confectioners' sugar

· an assortment of high-quality white chocolates

· big gorgeous artisan marshmallows

· strips of candied citrus peel in sparkling sugar

· potato pierogies with sour cream

· Chinese dumplings

· white cheeses like chèvre or kasseri

golden caviar toasts

Extreme Eating

This is my grandmother's recipe for my all-time favorite winter food. It's the reason I was never very good at waiting for the first snowfall. Then in the 70s we started hearing about acid rain and began to wonder if eating snow was really such a great idea. Later came a greater awareness of salmonella with raw eggs. So, while it is possibly one of my favorite foods, it comes with two caveats: go for new-fallen snow and raw eggs at your own risk. Think of it as an adventure in extreme eating but closer to home. Leave a bowl outside to catch the snow and use eggs from a trusted source, whose animal husbandry practices you know.

> 2 eggs
> ¾ cup milk
> ½ cup sugar
> 1 big bowl of snow

Whisk together eggs, milk, and sugar. Pour over snow. Eat.

But where are the snows of yesteryear?

—François Villon

vanilla cream

> ½ cup whole milk
> One ¼-ounce package unflavored gelatin
> 2 cups whipping cream
> ⅓ cup sugar
> 1 teaspoon vanilla
> 8 ounces whole milk plain yogurt

Pour ¼ cup of the milk into a small bowl. Sprinkle the gelatin over the milk and set aside to soften for 5 minutes.

In a medium saucepan, combine the remaining ¼ cup milk with the cream, sugar, and vanilla. Stir over medium heat until the sugar is dissolved and liquids are almost at a simmer. Do not boil. Remove from the heat. Add the softened gelatin and whisk until smooth. Add the yogurt and whisk until smooth. Pour into a 4- to 5-cup gelatin mold. Cover with plastic wrap, placing it directly onto the surface to prevent a "skin" from forming, and refrigerate for at least 6 hours.

To serve, dip the mold into a bowl of warm water for a few seconds and invert onto a serving plate.

Serves 8

meringues

It doesn't get any easier than this. I went through a phase in graduate school during which, cash-strapped and friend-laden, I got into the habit of bringing meringues as a birthday gift. They are easy to make, cheap, and yet everyone seems so completely amazed at how gorgeous they are. Because humidity adversely affects meringues, the dry cold days of winter are the perfect time to make them.

3 egg whites
¾ cup sugar

Preheat the oven to 200°F. Line 2 baking sheets with parchment paper.

Beat the egg whites in a large bowl of an electric mixer until medium peaks form. With the motor running, slowly add in the sugar. Beat until stiff peaks form. Drop by spoonfuls onto the prepared baking sheets. Bake for 2 hours. Turn off the oven and let the meringues cool with the oven door closed. Remove from the parchment and store in an airtight container when completely cooled.

Makes 48 meringues

Extra! Extra! Every time you make a meringue, there's one more lonely egg yolk in the world. But there are plenty of recipes that call for just the yolk to make up for it.

* Whisky Trifle (p. 129)
* Maple Custards with Whisky Cream (p. 208)
* buttercream frosting
* homemade mayonnaise or aioli
* lemon curd
* glaze for sweet breads, such as challah

The first fall of snow is not only an event, but it is a magical event. You go to bed in one kind of world and wake up to find yourself in another quite different, and if this is not enchantment, then where is it to be found?

—J. B. Priestly

I used to be Snow White...but I drifted.

—Mae West

I can never remember whether it snowed for six days and six nights when I was twelve or whether it snowed for twelve days and twelve nights when I was six.

—Dylan Thomas

11
festival of light
— frying up around the world —

MENU
Number in Party: 8 to 10 Guests

Fried Cod Fingers
Curried Potato and Pumpkin Latkes with Yogurt Sauce
Honey-Ginger Carrot and Parsnip Latkes with Crème Fraîche
Sufganiyot (Hanukkah Donuts)

Diaspora is often spoken of with lament as the division and scattering of a people. But the upside of diaspora is diversity. A diversity of cuisine from almost every corner of the globe celebrates holidays like Hanukkah. When we talk of "Jewish cuisine" too often it's limited to Eastern European Ashkenazic traditions. But there's so much more, especially in today's world of global culture. This celebration takes classics like latkes and fried doughnuts and updates them to reflect the wide range of different cultures that Jews live and work in around the world today. A tasty migration.

fried cod fingers

No need to wrap your fish up in newspapers to get a taste of Old Blighty.

1 pound cod or haddock
½ cup flour
⅛ teaspoon salt
Pinch of freshly ground black pepper
½ cup water
Vegetable oil for frying
Kosher salt
Malt vinegar

Cut the fish into 1-inch-thick strips or another size to suit you. In a medium mixing bowl, stir together the flour, ⅛ teaspoon salt, and the black pepper. Gradually whisk in the water to prevent lumps.

Pour oil to depth of ¼ inch in a large skillet and heat over medium-high heat. Dip the fish pieces in the batter and add to the hot oil, one at a time. Cook until golden brown, 4 to 5 minutes per side. Drain on paper towels. Sprinkle with kosher salt. Serve with small cups of malt vinegar for dipping.

Serves 6 to 8 as hors d'oeuvres

A Fish Tale

The origins of that definitively British pairing of fish and chips are shrouded in the mist of time, but speculation abounds. Many tie the emergence of the tradition of fried fish to nine-teenth-century Jewish immigrants in London's East End. Others point further back to the Renaissance migration of Jews from Portugal and Spain bringing fried fish traditions from the Mediterranean. Never mind that Jews spent over three centuries exiled from England and that until the 1800s there wasn't a substantial Jewish population to establish a tradition. But of course, cultural undergrounds travel in mysterious ways, so the questions remain.

curried potato and pumpkin latkes with yogurt sauce

An Indian flare is infused into a Jewish tradition. My friend Miriam Dellheim Baumel hosts a wildly popular latke party every year and serves up her own curried version with which she recommends serving mango chutney from a jar as an alternative to making a yogurt sauce. You can also substitute butternut squash for the pumpkin.

8 ounces whole milk yogurt
2 tablespoons grated red onion
1 pound pumpkin meat from a baking pumpkin (see p. 42)
1 pound waxy potatoes, such as Yukon Gold, peeled
2 eggs
6 tablespoons flour
½ teaspoon salt
2 teaspoons curry powder
Vegetable oil for frying

In a small serving dish, stir together the yogurt and onion. Add salt to taste. Refrigerate until needed.

Grate the pumpkin and potatoes on a box grater or in a food processor. Put in a dish towel and squeeze to remove water.

In a large mixing bowl, whisk together the eggs, flour, salt, and curry powder. Stir in the grated vegetables.

Pour oil to depth of ⅛ inch in a large skillet and heat over medium heat. Drop the vegetable mixture by serving-spoonfuls (about 3 tablespoons) into 3½-inch discs. Fry until golden brown, about 5 minutes per side. Drain on paper towels. Serve, passing yogurt sauce separately.

Makes 22–24 latkes

Jewish Roots

Latkes make the most of the everyday root vegetable, the potato. Revealing its eastern European origins, the word *latke* is Yiddish and comes from the Russian *látka*, or pastry.

honey–ginger carrot and parsnip latkes with crème fraîche

honey-ginger carrot and parsnip latkes with crème fraîche

In the tradition of reviving the old as new, these latkes trade in the old New World tuber—the potato—for the new Old World tuber—the parsnip.

1 pound carrots
1 pound parsnips
2 eggs
6 tablespoons flour
½ teaspoon salt
2 teaspoons ground ginger
1 tablespoon honey
Vegetable oil for frying
Crème fraîche

Grate the carrots and parsnips on a box grater or in a food processor. Put in a dish towel and squeeze to remove water.

In a large mixing bowl, whisk together the eggs, flour, salt, and ginger. Stir in the grated vegetables. Drizzle with the honey and stir to combine.

Pour oil to depth of ⅛ inch in a large skillet and heat over medium heat. Drop the vegetable mixture by serving-spoonfuls (about 3 tablespoons) into 3½-inch discs. Fry until golden brown, about 5 minutes per side. Drain on paper towels. Serve with dollops of crème fraîche on top.

Makes 22–24 latkes

The Great Fry-Up

As with every holiday, the story of Hanukkah, or the Festival of Lights, is a cultural tale with far more details and complexity than is usually told and I always hesitate to truncate it again. The key element for culinarians today is the oil and the tradition of fried foods that follows from it. In a nutshell, the 8-day holiday celebrates the Maccabees' victory over the Syrians when the temple was rededicated. Though only enough oil remained to burn for one night, the supply miraculously lasted 8 nights. Hence the tradition of the menorah and of fried foods.

Keeping It Kosher

A lot of donut recipes call for margarine and soy milk, but because this buffet doesn't have any meat you can go all the way with the donuts.

sufganiyot (hanukkah donuts)

These donuts, a favorite of my good friend Lissa McBurney, are a stellar example of the great American melting pot of flavors and celebrations. Lissa studied Judaism in college to prepare for conversion before marriage, and though she later married a Quaker instead, she continues to enjoy the culinary traditions, foods, and holidays she learned earlier. Always with her eye on the multicultural, she suggests four round-the-world fillings in the "Filling Station" sidebar, p. 113 that have you traveling from England to Mexico on your taste buds.

> 2 packages active dry yeast
> 1¼ cups whole milk
> 1¼ cups sugar
> 4 egg yolks
> 1 teaspoon lemon zest (from ½ lemon)
> 4 cups flour
> ¾ teaspoon salt
> 4 tablespoons (½ stick) unsalted butter, softened
> About 3 quarts vegetable oil for frying
> 1½ to 2 cups of filling (see "Filling Station" on facing page)

In the bowl of an electric mixer fitted with a dough hook mix the yeast, milk, and 1 tablespoon of the sugar. Let it sit until foamy on top, about 10 minutes.

With the mixer on low speed, add the egg yolks, lemon zest, and 3 tablespoons sugar. Add the flour and salt, then mix about 2 minutes. While the mixer is running, add the butter 1 tablespoon at a time, incorporating each bit of butter before the next is added. Continue to mix the dough thoroughly (see "Windows of Opportunity," on facing page).

Turn the dough out into an oiled bowl. Cover with a damp towel and allow to rise until double, 1 to 2 hours depending on room temperature.

Turn the dough out onto a lightly floured counter and roll out ½ to ¾ inch thick. (Use the minimum amount of flour necessary as excess flour will burn in the frying oil.) Using a 2-inch round cutter or juice glass, cut the dough. Reknead the scraps together and let them rise again for another 30 minutes, then reroll and cut. Cover the donuts with a dishcloth and let the donuts rise until soft and puffy, 20 to 40 minutes.

Pour 3 inches of oil into a stockpot or kettle (6 inches deep or more) and heat over medium-high heat to 360°F. It works to put the oil on as soon as the donuts start the final rise.

Once the oil is hot enough, fry the donuts in batches, 6 to 8 at a time. Fry for 90 seconds on each side, turning once. Don't crowd the pot or the oil temperature will drop, and turn the heat up to high once the donuts are in to help the temperature recover quickly. If a large bubble forms that prevents a donut from turning over, gently pierce it with a knife. The donuts will brown quickly. You're looking for a darker golden brown like an egg braid or brioche, not the anemic beige of a commercial donut!

Cool the donuts on a cooling rack set on a cookie sheet lined with paper towels. When the donuts are cool enough to handle, fill according to the suggestions at right. After filling, roll the donuts in the remaining 1 cup sugar.

These are best eaten the same day—really they are best warm when you're standing over the kitchen counter. If you need to make the donuts in advance, you can freeze them and reheat gently in the oven for 8 to 10 minutes at 300°F. Avoid the microwave, however.

Makes 30 donuts

Windows of Opportunity

Lissa warns not to underknead the dough. To test how well you're getting on, she suggests taking a small lump of dough, about the size of a golf ball, and gently stretching it into a disk; it is ready when the center is thin enough to see light through it. Well, really, almost thin enough to read a recipe through the dough. This is a "gluten window." The total mixing time should be 8 to 10 minutes, but double that if you do it by hand.

Filling Station

First choose your fillings. Some quick and easy ideas from a jar:
· black currant jelly
· lemon curd
· hot fudge
· dulce de leche

While the oil is heating, you can set up your work area for filling the donuts. You need a
· paring knife
· shallow bowl with 1 cup of sugar
· pastry bag filled with about 1 cup of your favorite filling and fitted with a #6 tip

Cut a small slit in the side of each donut, insert the pastry tip into the middle of the donut, and squeeze gently to fill with 1 to 2 teaspoons of filling. Release pressure on the bag, but hold the tip inside the donut for 3 more seconds to keep the filling from oozing back out.

12
winter solstice
—— brightening the darkest night ——

❧

MENU
Number in Party: 10 to 14 Guests

Wassail Bowl

Lambswool Punch

Yule Log Cake

❧

The winter solstice, which occurs in later December, has in many pagan traditions been greeted with great fanfare as the return of longer days and shorter nights. Today, it offers us one more reason to celebrate during the holiday season without restricting ourselves to a single day. Kick off the twelve days of Christmas just a little bit early and make this an open-house menu, inviting guests to drop in and out on their way to and from last-minute shopping.

wassail bowl

2 oranges
40 to 60 whole cloves
Two 750-ml bottles Madeira
2 cups apple cider
½ cup brandy
6 cinnamon sticks
1 cup granulated white sugar
Soft brown sugar to taste

Stick the cloves into the oranges to create a studded design. In a large stockpot, combine the Madeira, apple cider, brandy, cinnamon sticks, and granulated sugar. Bring to a simmer (do not boil) and steep over low heat for 30 minutes. Add brown sugar to suit your sweetness preference. Pour into a decorative bowl with the clove-studded oranges floating on top.

Serves 14

Punch Drunk

While the wassail bowl is perhaps the most famous hot holiday punch thanks to carols like "Here We Go A-Wassailing," there are many more versions even beyond the Lambswool Punch here. Consider expanding your repertoire of spicy warm drinks to include:

Glögg: a Scandinavian mulled wine drink sometimes spiked with brandy or vodka

Glühwein: a German version of hot spiced wine that, like Glögg, sometimes is dressed with raisins or almonds

Bowl of Bishop: a celebrated refreshment in Dickens' *A Christmas Carol* that usually starts with port and is sometimes spiked with rum

The Rebirth of the Sun

In the northern hemisphere, the winter solstice occurs on December 21 or 22. The term *solstice* derives from the Latin *solstitium*. Roughly translated, that means a stationary sun because when it reaches the point furthest from the equator on the solstice, the sun appears to stand still. With the northern hemisphere also tilted away from the sun, we experience the winter solstice as the longest night of the year but also the return of longer days as we move closer to spring. Festivities of this holiday have throughout time and across cultures celebrated the rebirth of light and the banishment of dark. The holiday roughly corresponds to the Roman Saturnalia and the mystery Mythraic religion's rites of *sol invictus* (or undefeated sun). Today local celebrations of the holiday are kept alive both by neopagans, who remind us of ancient traditions, and by scientific and environmental groups, who highlight the day with observatory tours and nature walks.

Load Your iPod with Sun Songs

Here Comes the Sun by The Beatles

(In the Evening) When the Sun Goes Down by Count Bassie

Run to the Sun by Erasure

Sun by Aztec Camera

Sun by Concrete Blonde

That Lucky Old Sun by Louis Armstrong

The Sun (String Quartet no. 4) by Joseph Hadyn

The Sun by Veruca Salt

The Sun Whose Rays are all Ablaze from *The Mikado*

Who Loves the Sun by The Velvet Underground

Why Does the Sun Shine by They Might Be Giants

You Are My Sunshine

A Fair Warning for Bad Hosts

Like Halloween, the Christmas season was once a much more public (not religious) holiday and much more about charity and hospitality. Like the option of "trick" or "treat," this old carol reminds us that good wishes and blessings for success dovetail with the possibilities of what happens when you fail to provide good hospitality:

Wassail, wassail, all over the town
Our toast it is white and our ale it is brown,
Our bowl it is made of the white maple tree,
With the wassailing bowl, we'll drink to thee.

So here is to Cherry and to his right cheek
Pray God send our master a good piece of beef
And a good piece of beef that may we all see
With the wassailing bowl, we'll drink to thee.

And here is to Dobbin and to his right eye,
Pray God send our master a good Christmas pie,
A good Christmas pie that may we all see,
With a wassailing bowl, we'll drink to thee.

And here is to Fillpail and to her left ear,
Pray God send our master a happy New Year,
A happy New Year as e'er he did see,
With a wassailing bowl, we'll drink to thee.

And here is to Colly and to her long tail,
Pray God send our master a good cask of ale,
A good cask of ale that may we all see,
With a wassailing bowl, we'll drink to thee.

Then here's to the maid in the lily-white smock,
Who tripped to the door and slipped back the lock,
Who tripped to the door and pulled back the pin,
For to let these jolly wassailers in.

Come butler, come fill us a bowl of the best,
Then I pray that your soul in heaven may rest,
But if you do bring us a bowl of the small,
May the devil take butler, bowl and all.

lambswool punch

It's the soft baked apples on top that give this drink the appearance of lambswool and thus its name. What also makes this punch a little bit quirky is that it's based on beer, rather than the usual wine of the season.

4 apples
½ cup nonalcoholic apple cider
2 tablespoons packed brown sugar
2 tablespoons unsalted butter
Four 12-ounce bottles hard cider
  (such as Woodchuck)
Four 12-ounce bottles brown ale
  (such as Newcastle Brown)
½ cup granulated sugar
6 cinnamon sticks

Preheat the oven to 350°F. Peel and core the apples and cut into 1-inch cubes. Combine the apples, nonalcoholic cider, and brown sugar in a baking dish that can hold them in a single layer. Dot with the butter. Bake for 45 minutes until very soft, stirring every 15 minutes. Remove from the oven and set aside.

In a large stockpot, combine the hard cider, brown ale, granulated sugar, and cinnamon sticks. Cover, turn heat on low, and steep for 30 minutes. Pour into a serving bowl and top with the apples. Serve in mugs or other heatproof glassware.

Serves 14

lambswool punch

yule log cake

Do not be intimidated by this cake with its many steps. The work is much easier and goes much more quickly than you expect. And when you're done, you have the sort of stunning focal point that makes everyone ooh and ahh. Best yet, this party is designed to let you indulge your inner baker without being overwhelmed by lots of other dishes. It's the perfect sort of open house get-together rounded out by two great drinks.

MERINGUE MUSHROOMS
1 large egg white, room temperature
Pinch of cream of tartar
¼ cup sugar

CAKE
¼ cup water
2 tablespoons unsalted butter
1 tablespoon plus ¼ cup plus ⅓ cup sugar
½ teaspoon salt
⅓ cup cocoa powder
6 large eggs, separated
1 teaspoon vanilla
2 tablespoons flour
½ teaspoon cream of tartar

FILLING
1 cup whipping cream
2 tablespoons sugar
1 tablespoon cocoa powder

GANACHE FROSTING
10 ounces bittersweet chocolate
1 cup whipping cream
2 tablespoons unsalted butter, softened and cut into 4 pieces
Confectioners' sugar for garnish

Preheat the oven to 200°F. Line a baking sheet with parchment paper.

To make the meringue mushrooms: In the bowl of an electric mixer, whip the egg white until foamy. Add the cream of tartar and beat until medium-stiff peaks form. With the motor running, slowly add in the sugar and beat until stiff peaks form.

Using a pastry tube fitted with a round tip, pipe mushroom caps and stems onto the parchment. I find it works best to make stems of all thicknesses and lengths by piping tiny columns of meringue up into the air. If you pipe them in lengths on the parchment surface, one side of your stem will be flat. Lengths of ¼ to 1 inch provide a nice variety.

For mushroom caps, pipe mounded discs of different shapes and sizes. Using your finger dipped in water, you can smooth the piping lines across the caps.

Keep in mind that you will have a lot of room for error, so don't be nervous. Just have fun. You'll have way more meringue than you need but because it's hard to divide an egg white, that's just how it goes.

Bake the meringues for 2 hours. Turn off the oven and let them sit inside until the oven is completely cool. Gently lift the pieces from the parchment and store in an airtight container until you're ready to decorate the cake. The meringues can be prepared three days ahead.

To make the cake: Combine the water, butter, 1 tablespoon sugar, and the salt in a small saucepan. Bring to a gentle boil over medium heat. Whisk in the cocoa powder until smooth. Set aside to cool to room temperature.

Preheat the oven to 375°F. Butter a 12 x 17-inch jelly roll pan. Line with parchment. Butter the parchment and then dust with flour.

In a large bowl of an electric mixer, beat the egg yolks on medium speed for 1 minute. With the motor running, add ¼ cup sugar and continue to beat until mixture is double in volume, thick, and light yellow. Beat in the cooled cocoa mixture and vanilla. Scrape down the sides and continue to beat for another minute. Transfer the batter to a large mixing bowl. Sift the flour over the batter and fold in gently. Set aside.

In a clean mixing bowl with the whisk attachment, beat the egg whites until foamy. Add the cream of tartar and continue to beat until soft peaks form. With the motor running, gradually add the remaining ⅓ cup sugar and continue to beat until stiff peaks form. Using a large spatula, gently fold into the chocolate batter by thirds. Spread the batter onto the prepared pan. Bake for 10 to 12 minutes until the cake springs back when gently pressed. Remove the pan from the oven, cover with a damp tea towel, and cool on a wire rack.

To make the filling: Combine the whipping cream, sugar, and cocoa powder in the mixing bowl of an electric mixer. Using the whisk attachment, whip the cream until medium-stiff peaks form. Scrape down the sides before the cream begins to thicken.

Lifting by the parchment paper, slide the cake out of the pan and onto a work surface. Spread the filling over the cake. It helps to use an offset spatula to get a flat surface. Turn so the long side faces you. Using the parchment to help, loosely roll the cake away from you. Don't try to make too tight a roll or the cake will crack and the "log" will be too thin. Cut approximately 2 inches of cake off of each end, cutting on the diagonal. Set aside to make "knots." Refrigerate the cake while you make the ganache frosting.

To make the ganache frosting: Coarsely chop the chocolate (no piece should be larger than ¼-inch). Place in a large mixing bowl.

Heat the cream until it barely simmers. Whisk it into the chopped chocolate and continue to whisk until all the chocolate is melted and no lumps remain. Set aside to cool slightly for 5 minutes. Whisk in the butter. Set the ganache aside to cool and reach a spreadable consistency, 1 to 4 hours, depending on your kitchen temperature. Stir every 20 to 30 minutes as it cools.

To assemble the cake: Position the cake on the platter on which you intend to serve it. Sometimes a cutting board is just the trick if you don't have a large enough platter. Have your small "stump" pieces ready. Spread chocolate ganache over the cut end of each and attach to the log in whatever pattern suits you. Usually I stick one on the side, allowing it to rest on the plate for support and position the other almost directly on top of the cake at the other end of the log. Gently frost the seam where the stumps attach to the cake. Refrigerate the cake for 10 to 15 minutes to solidify the ganache.

Reserve about 2 tablespoons of ganache for the mushrooms. Generously frost the rest of the cake, covering all seams and exposed cake. (Alternatively, you can leave the ends of the log exposed for a different look.) Once the cake is completely frosted, you can use your knife to create bark patterns or use the tines of a fork to create swirls on the end of each stump and down the length of the log. Refrigerate until ready to serve but let it sit at room temperature for 20 minutes before bringing to the table. Can be made 1 day ahead.

Just before serving, sift confectioners' sugar over top of cake to simulate snow. (If you do this too early, the sugar will become moist and fade into the surface of the cake.) Use bits of ganache to attach mushroom stems to mushroom caps. Position mushrooms on top of and around cake.

Serves 14

Burning the Yule Log at Both Ends

The Yule Log Cake is based on the pagan tradition of burning the Yule log, sometimes called a Yule clog, in ceremonies welcoming the sun. Such traditions carried over into Christmas and an early nineteenth-century quotation sums up the pleasures of a time "When ample Yule-clogs lent their heat and light, And all-spiced possets warm'd the Christmas night." At the same time, the literal Yule log evolved into a simulacrum in the form of a cake, in France known as the *Bûche de Noël*. By the nineteenth century, Parisian bakeries began to show off their talents for such confections and purchasing, rather than making your own, became a great middle-class tradition.

13
gathering greenery
a winter brunch

❦

MENU
Number in Party: 4 Guests

Renaissance Winter Greens Tart
Chicken with Barley and Green Sauce
Green Tea Gelatins

❦

Along with the celebration of light that is the winter solstice tradition also comes the celebration of life with decorations of greenery, brought in from the outside to lend color and life to the sometimes stale air of the winter indoors. Why stop at a few holly branches and some sprigs of mistletoe? Incorporate the theme of your entertaining with a colorful in-season menu.

renaissance winter greens tart

This tart draws on the recipes from early English cookbooks in which dried fruits often adorned savory dishes. To this day, sweet raisins and currants are often mixed with bitter spinach or greens in dishes from many European cultures, including French Provence and Scandinavia.

    1 sheet puff pastry, thawed
    1 large bunch fresh spinach (about 10 ounces,
        weighed with stems)
    1 large bunch kale (about 10 ounces)
    1 cup whole-milk cottage cheese
    2 large eggs
    3 tablespoons whole milk
    3 tablespoons dried currants
    ½ teaspoon salt
    ⅛ teaspoon freshly grated nutmeg
    Freshly ground black pepper

Place the rack in lowest position in the oven. Preheat the oven to 400°F. Roll out the puff pastry and place it in a 9-inch tart pan with a removable bottom. Roll a rolling pin over the tart pan to trim the puff pastry. Place parchment paper over the pastry in the bottom of the tart pan and fill with pie weights or dried beans. Partially bake for 20 minutes. Remove the pie weights and parchment and bake for 5 to 10 minutes more until golden brown. Remove from the oven and cool on wire rack while you prepare the filling. Maintain the oven temperature at 400°F.

Remove the stems from the spinach, place the leaves in a sink filled with water and allow the dirt to fall to the bottom. Carefully remove from the water and repeat. Drain in a colander. Remove the tough spines and thick stems of the kale. Wash in the same manner as the spinach and drain. Steam the kale until wilted, 7 to 8 minutes. Remove to the colander to drain again. Steam the spinach until wilted, 4 to 5 minutes. Remove to the colander to drain again. Press on the spinach and kale to remove most of the moisture. Coarsely chop the spinach and kale and place in a large mixing bowl.

In a food processor, combine the cottage cheese, eggs, and milk. Puree until you have a smooth custard with barely noticeable pips of cottage cheese. Pour the custard over the greens. Stir in the currants, salt, nutmeg, and pepper. Pour the filling into the prepared pie shell. Pat and smooth the filling until compact, smooth, and flat across the top. Bake until the filling is set, about 25 minutes. Cool for 5 minutes before serving.

Serves 4 as a main course or 6 as appetizers

Sweets and Tarts

Even when pies were fashioned around a capon, a bit of venison, or other nonsweets, it was the fashion in the Middle Ages and the Renaissance to flavor them with dried fruits and spices like cinnamon, nutmeg, and mace. In kitchens where the rare and expensive ingredient of sugar was found, a bit would be sprinkled atop the meaty pie or tart filling. For the grandest occasions, savory pies were even "iced" with rose water and sugar.

renaissance winter greens tart

chicken with barley and green sauce

GREEN SAUCE

3 tablespoons olive oil

4 garlic cloves, minced

¼ cup whipping cream

⅓ cup packed parsley leaves

½ cup packed cilantro leaves

Pinch of salt

¼ cup freshly grated Parmesan cheese

BARLEY AND SPROUT RISOTTO

½ cups pearl barley

2 cups chicken broth

1 cup water

½ teaspoon salt

½ pound Brussels sprouts

2 tablespoons unsalted butter

¼ cup chicken broth

CHICKEN

Salt

Freshly ground black pepper

4 chicken thighs (with bone and skin; about 2 pounds total)

About ½ cup flour for dredging

2 tablespoon olive oil

½ cup chicken broth

To make the green sauce: Heat the olive oil in a small saucepan over medium-low heat. Add the garlic and cook for 7 minutes, taking care not to let garlic burn but not turning down the heat so low that garlic doesn't soften. Remove from the heat and stir in the whipping cream. Cover and steep for 10 minutes. Combine the parsley, cilantro, and salt in a food processor. Add the warm garlic cream. Process until smooth. Add the Parmesan cheese and pulse a few times to combine. Set aside.

To make the barley and sprout risotto: Put the barley, chicken broth, water, and salt in a large saucepan. Bring to a boil. Reduce to a low simmer, cover, and cook for 30 minutes. If any liquid remains, remove the lid and cook for another 5 to 10 minutes until all liquid has evaporated. Remove from the heat and cover to keep warm.

While the barley cooks, prepare the Brussels sprouts. Cut off the ends and remove any discolored or wilted leaves. Using a large chef's knife, coarsely chop—leaves will separate on many. In a large skillet, melt the butter over medium heat. Add the Brussels sprouts and cook, stirring frequently, for about 3 minutes. Add the chicken broth, reduce the heat to medium-low and cook until sprouts are soft and all liquid is absorbed, 5 to 8 minutes. Set aside until the barley is finished. Stir the sprouts into the cooked barley.

To make the chicken: After preparing the Brussels sprouts, start the chicken while the barley cooks. Generously salt and pepper the chicken thighs. Dredge in the flour. Heat the oil over medium-high heat in a large skillet. Add the chicken thighs, skin side down, one at a time. Cook until golden brown, 7 to 10 minutes. Turn the thighs and cook for 5 minutes more. Add the chicken broth, reduce to a simmer, cover, and cook until the chicken is cooked through, 7 to 10 minutes.

Fill bowls with the barley and sprout risotto. Top with the chicken thighs. Spoon the green sauce over all.

Serves 4

Days of Rosemary and Remembrance

In addition to holly, ivy, and mistletoe, include rosemary in your winter greenery. In some climates, rosemary acts as an evergreen and lives on through winter so that you can pluck it right from the garden in January. Sometimes known as the "herb of remembrance," rosemary has long been associated with winter holidays. Several myths tell of this herb's place in the Christ story. One account tells that during the Holy Family's flight to Egypt Mary laid her cloak on a rosemary bush, thus turning its hitherto white flowers blue, the color often associated with purity and thus Mary. In another version of the same myth, it was Christ's cloak that was hung upon the rosemary bush, again with the same result of turning the plant's blossom's blue. In yet another story about rosemary and its role as holy coat rack, it gets its scent from Christ, who gives it to the plant in thanks for—what else?—holding up his clothes.

Breaking the Jell-O Taboo

I once announced on *Eat Feed* that I intended to recruit a whole army of Jell-O revolutionaries who recognize that there are a lot of delicious and gorgeous things you can do with this much denigrated ingredient. It really is just one more chemical tool in your culinary shed, like baking powder or egg whites. Unfortunately, because Jell-O is for many people associated with the 1950s, a decade of the worst culinary kitsch, we often deride foods with gelatin as somehow less sophisticated. However, the history of gelatin goes much farther back in time. Indeed, in Renaissance Europe gelatin was handmade from raw ingredients like hart's horn and came to grace the wealthiest tables, where elaborate spires and colorful wiggly tableaus served as the meal, the decoration, and the entertainment. And don't forget about fancy French aspics alive and well today. As you think about embracing this key ingredient, consider favorites like homemade marshmallows and the rolled fondant that gives cakes a smooth sheen you can't get with regular frosting. Let your creativity go wild as you invent your own new versions of jiggly good times by combining your favorite flavors—coffee, chocolate, cream—with this time-tested ingredient.

green tea gelatins

This new twist on green tea ice cream lends a sleeker, more modern look to the table.

> ¾ cup boiling water
> 4 bags green tea
> 1 cup whole milk
> Two 1-ounce packages unflavored gelatin
> ¾ cup whipping cream
> ¼ cup sugar
> 2 to 3 drops green food coloring (optional)
> Rosemary, mint, sage, or edible flowers (optional)

In a small bowl, pour the boiling water over the tea bags and steep for 15 minutes. As you remove the tea bags, press out any remaining liquid.

Pour the milk into a medium mixing bowl. Sprinkle the gelatin over the milk. Let the gelatin soften for 5 minutes while you prepare the next step.

In a medium saucepan, combine the cream and sugar. Cook until the sugar is dissolved and the mixture just begins to simmer. Whisk into the softened gelatin. Whisk in the green tea and food coloring, if desired. Divide among six ½-cup ramekins or small molds. Cool for 20 minutes. Refrigerate until firm, about 4 hours or up to 1 day.

To serve: Have a large bowl of hot water ready. Dip each ramekin in the water for 5 seconds to loosen the gelatin. Invert onto a dessert plate. If desired, garnish with herbs, leaves, sprigs, or edible flowers.

Serves 4

Edible Greens

These quick and easy add-ons are green in both senses of the word. They add hues from pale sea foam to rich emerald to the buffet table while showing your commitment to in-season food.

· drinks that do a lot with lime: mojitos, margaritas, limeade

· wedges of Derby sage cheese on oat biscuits

· sautéed beet greens with a drizzle of fruity green olive oil

· salad greens (such as wintry escarole) tossed with your favorite vinaigrette and topped with pistachios

· green endive leaves stuffed with a picadillo of ground chicken, capers, and white raisins

· smoked trout or mackerel (with mayonnaise) on baguette rounds dressed with thin slices of green apple and watercress

· thinly shaved rare lamb mounded on wheat bread and topped with a dollop of mint jelly

· Asian greens sautéed in toasted sesame oil and wrapped sushi-style with rice and deep green nori

· homemade mint ice cream stacked as mini-scoops in champagne flutes

· winter-themed cut-out cookies (such as pine trees and holly leaves) frosted with green icing

· a relish tray of large caper berries, cornichons, and pickled asparagus

· gooseberry preserves and Irish butter on warm scones

· a simple dish of salted edamame in the shell

· a classic Key lime tart

· a final sip of Chartreuse herbal liqueur as a digestive

The Meaning of Greening

As you look for in-season sprigs of just the right bit of green, consider the language and symbolism of favorite winter plants.

holly: protection and sacrifice

ivy: long life and fidelity

juniper: protection and fertility

mistletoe: love and fertility

pine: healing and care

rosemary: remembrance and fidelity

sage: health and wisdom

14
highlands hogmanay
— *a scottish new year* —

⁂

MENU
Number in Party: 6 Guests

Oat Cakes with Smoked Salmon and Salmon Caviar
Beef Rib-eyes with Whisky Sauce
Caramelized Onion Mashed Potatoes
Whisky Trifle

⁂

There are so many New Year traditions around the world that it was hard to pick just one. Perhaps it's the great name of Hogmanay (pronounced hog-muh-nay) that helped me choose Scotland.

oat cakes with smoked salmon and salmon caviar

There are lots of reasons to pull together a party with a bit of bread, a dollop of cream, and your favorite caviar. Like the Golden Caviar Toasts (see p. 104) in "The First Snowfall" menu, this is another quick and easy starter with those three key ingredients, only this time adapted to celebrate the lordly Scottish salmon.

> 8 ounces Scottish-style smoked salmon
> 24 Scottish oat biscuits, such as Walkers or Nairn's
> ¾ cup crème fraîche
> 4 ounces salmon caviar

Divide the smoked salmon among the oat biscuits. Top with 1½ teaspoons of crème fraîche, then a generous ½ teaspoon caviar.

Makes 24 hors d'oeuvres

Daft Days

Among the so-called Scottish Christmas holidays or "daft days" is Hogmanay. Simply put, Hogmanay is a Scottish celebration on the last day of the year. Its origins and etymology are a bit more complicated, though. There are strains of Anglo-Saxon customs and those of French Norman. One thing remains constant to this day: true to its winter timing and the craving for light, Hogmanay calls for fire ceremonies like bonfires and torch processions.

Steerage

If you're looking for good-quality Scottish beef in the United States, seek out small producers who raise rare-breed cattle with the best husbandry practices. One of my favorite producers is Fountain Prairie in Wisconsin (www.fountainprairie.com), whose beef is sold through the Heritage Breeds Foundation (www.heritagefoodsusa.com).

beef rib-eyes with whisky sauce

There just aren't that many different ways to cook a good steak indoors, but Mark Bittman has managed to create the perfect twist, so I'm borrowing it here. This allows you to get the necessary high heat for a good outer brown and medium-rare center without filling your kitchen with (too much) smoke. For an extra Scottish twist, be sure to use Black Angus Aberdeen beef.

> Salt
> Freshly ground black pepper
> 6 rib-eye steaks (10 to 12 ounces each)
> 1½ cups beef broth
> 1 cup whisky

Preheat the oven to 500°F. Generously salt and pepper the steaks. Heat 2 large ovenproof skillets over high heat. Add three steaks to each pan and immediately transfer the pans to the bottom floor of the oven or to a rack in the lowest position of the oven. Cook for 4 minutes. Turn the steaks, return to the oven floor, and cook for another 4 minutes. Remove the steaks to a platter and tent with foil while you prepare the sauce.

The main thing to remember here is that you will want to instinctively touch the burning hot handles of the skillets. To avoid this, place an oven mitt over each handle to remind you. Place both pans over high heat and add ¾ cup beef broth and ½ cup whisky to each pan to deglaze. Bring to a boil and boil until reduced to a generous ½ cup, about 5 minutes.

Mound Caramelized Onion Mashed Potatoes (recipe follows) on 6 dinner plates. Top each with a rib-eye. Pour the sauce over the meat and allow to pool around outer edge of the potatoes.

Serves 6

The cottar weanies glad an' gay,
Wi' pocks out owre their ahouther,
Sing at the doors for hogmanay.

—James Nicol, 1805

Come, follow me by the smell,
Here are delicate onions to sell;
I promise to use you well.
They make the blood warmer,
You'll feed like a farmer;
For this is every cook's opinion,
No savory dish without an onion;
But, lest your kissing should be spoiled,
Your onions must be thoroughly boiled:
Or else you may spare
Your mistress a share,
The secret will never be known:
She cannot discover
The breath of her lover,
But think it as sweet as her own.

—Jonathan Swift, "Onions"

A Wee Dram

If you really want to go whole-hog with this theme, you'll need a bottle or two of your favorite single malt to keep guests warm and toasty throughout the night. My favorite medium-priced whiskies: Balvenie 15-year and Aberlour 15-year. For more whisky suggestions, consult the experts at the Scotch Malt Whisky Society (www.smws.com).

Hogmanay in the Homeland

If you decide to go live rather than hosting your own Hogmanay, keep up with the whys and wherefores around Scotland at www.hogmanay.net.

A Tall Dark Stranger

"First Footing" is the Hogmanay tradition where your future is foretold by the first person to cross your threshold in the New Year. For good luck, the dark and handsome are favored over the bonny and fair. Be sure to offer this first footer a traditional tipple like *het pint*, a brew of ale and whisky spiked with nutmeg. Who knows, spike it with enough whisky and you may really get lucky.

caramelized onion mashed potatoes

Lovely, necessary, essential tatties are given a rich wintry extra with caramelized onions. Be careful not to use terribly large onions or you'll end up overpowering the steaks.

4 tablespoons unsalted butter

3 medium yellow onions, cut in half and thinly sliced

2 cups half-and-half

2 teaspoons salt

3 pounds waxy potatoes, such as Yukon Gold, peeled and cut into 1-inch cubes

Melt the butter in a large skillet over medium-low heat. Add the onions. Cook and stir for 10 minutes. Cover and cook for 10 more minutes. Uncover and cook until golden brown, another 10 minutes. In a food processor, puree onions with ½ cup half-and-half and the salt. Add another ½ cup half-and-half and process until combined.

Bring a large pot of salted water to a boil. Add the potatoes and cook until soft, about 15 minutes. Drain. Transfer to the bowl of an electric mixer. Add the pureed onion mixture and remaining 1 cup half-and-half. Using the whisk attachment of an electric mixer, whip until smooth. Transfer to a saucepan and reheat when the steaks and whisky sauce are ready.

Serves 6

whisky trifle

You can start this two days in advance, doing the custard one day, assembling the next, and then letting it steep until you plan to serve it on New Year's Eve.

CUSTARD
2 eggs
2 egg yolks
1 teaspoon cornstarch
1 cup milk
1 cup whipping cream
¼ cup sugar
1 teaspoon vanilla

LADY FINGERS
1½ cups apple cider
1½ cups Scottish whisky
30 Italian lady fingers

ROASTED FRUIT
2 apples
2 pears
1 tablespoon lemon juice
2 tablespoons unsalted butter
1 teaspoons sugar

WHIPPED CREAM
1 cup whipping cream
2 tablespoons sugar

TOASTED HONEY OATS
1 cup rolled oats
3 tablespoons honey
1 tablespoon butter, melted

To make the custard: In a medium mixing bowl, whisk together the eggs, egg yolks, and cornstarch.

In a medium saucepan, combine the milk, cream, and sugar. Heat until it barely simmers. Very slowly pour the warm liquid into the egg mixture as you constantly whisk the two together. Rinse the saucepan, leaving a thin coat of water. Pour the custard back into saucepan and continue to cook over gentle heat until thickened, 8 to 10 minutes. Stir for the first 5 minutes, but switch to a whisk for the remainder in order to prevent curdling. The consistency you're aiming for is still pourable, but thickly coating the back of a metal spoon. Keep in mind that the custard will continue to set as it cools.

When you've reached the right consistency, remove from the heat and whisk in the vanilla. Transfer to a clean bowl. Cover the surface with plastic wrap; lay the wrap directly onto the custard to prevent a "skin" from forming. Cool to room temperature and then refrigerate until completely cool, at least 4 hours, and up to a day ahead of assembling the trifle.

To make the lady fingers: Combine ½ cup cider and ½ cup whisky in a pie plate. Take enough lady fingers to line the bottom of a medium trifle bowl (about 9–12 cups), about 8. Quickly soak the lady fingers in liquid, about 10 seconds per side. Place the whisky-soaked cakes in the trifle bowl, closely packing together. Try not to leave any spaces.

Add another ½ cup cider and ½ cup whisky to the pie plate. Quickly soak 4 lady fingers in the liquid, 5 to 10 seconds per side. Because these cakes need to be sturdy enough to stand, use a slightly shorter soaking time than with the cake used on the bottom of the bowl. Line halfway around sides of the same trifle bowl by standing the fingers vertically. I find that doing about 4 fingers at a time works well. By the time you've placed the fourth one down, it's time to flip the first and so on.

Repeat with final ½ cup cider and ½ cup whisky and remaining lady fingers. Because trifle bowls vary in shape and size, you might find you need to do a few more or a few less lady fingers to cover the interior. Keep using equal parts cider and whisky and continue with the same soaking method.

Pour custard filling into center of the "shell" created by the lady fingers, cover with plastic wrap, and refrigerate to cure for 3 hours or overnight.

To make the roasted fruit: Preheat the oven to 400°F. Peel, core, and cut the apples and pears into ½-inch pieces. Toss the fruit with the lemon juice. Place the butter in a baking dish large enough to hold the fruit in a single layer. Put in the oven until it melts. Add fruit and toss to coat. Sprinkle the sugar over the fruit. Bake for 45 minutes, turning every 15 minutes. Cool to room temperature. Layer the roasted fruit over the custard just before serving.

No Trifling Matter

Yes, indeed, the name for this dessert does come from the notion of something trivial or of no importance. It makes sense given the fact that it is one of those desserts that often sends cooks into paroxysms of creativity and causes them to indulge in all sorts of frou-frou, ginger-bread, and other elaborate embellishments. The finished products are never something to be trifled with, though, and these are often individual masterpieces. In its early days, before all those wine- and whisky-soaked biscuits, trifle was a wonderfully rich cream infused with spices. Thomas Dawson has perhaps the earliest known version of trifle in print, from his 1596 *The Good Housewife's Jewel*:

Take a pint of thick cream, and season it with sugar and ginger, and rose water. So stir it as you would then have it and make it luke warm in a dish on a chafing dish and coals. And after put it into a silver piece or a bowl, and so serve it to the board.

....

Black Bun

If you can find a good Scottish baker and don't want to make your own desserts, go for the very traditional New Year dessert of black bun. And offer some shortbread with the coffee.

....

It is ordinary among some Plebeians in the South of Scotland, to go about from Door to Door upon New-Year's Eve, crying Hagmane.

—The Scotch Presbyterian Eloquence, 1693

....

To make the whipped cream: In the bowl of an electric mixer, combine the cream and sugar. Beat until medium-stiff peaks form. Layer over the fruit just before serving.

To make the toasted honey oats: Preheat the oven to 350°F. Line a heavy baking sheet with aluminum foil. Butter the foil. Spread the oats on the prepared baking sheet. Drizzle with the honey and melted butter. Stir to coat. Bake for 15 minutes until golden brown, stirring every 5 minutes. Allow to cool and harden. Break apart into brittle clumps and store in an airtight container until needed. Sprinkle over the whipped cream just before serving.

Serves 8 to 10

whisky trifle

15
sunday roast
—— *a return to the family table* ——

MENU

Number in Party: 6 Guests

Butternut Squash Soup

French Onion Pot Roast

Potatoes and Carrots for a Sunday Roast

Double Oatmeal Cookies

After all those New Year's Eve indulgences come the first-of-the-year resolutions, and hopefully you've made some space in those promises to spend more time with friends and family. What better way than with the revival of Sunday dinner, complete with a roast and other hearty winter foods to help you bear up under the pressures of the week to come.

butternut squash soup

A good friend's mother, Betsy Disharoon, has this talent of always producing the perfect soup for the occasion. I'm passionate about her cucumber mint soup for a warm summer day, but for a family get-together on a cold winter night, this is the right one.

2 cups apple cider
2 cups chicken broth
5 cups cubed butternut squash
2 tablespoons olive oil
3 garlic cloves, minced
2 tablespoons minced fresh ginger
1 teaspoon salt
¾ teaspoon freshly ground black pepper
1 cup sour cream
Sprigs of fresh dill

Combine the apple cider, chicken broth, and butternut squash in a 3-quart saucepan. Bring to a simmer and cook over medium heat until tender, about 15 minutes.

While the squash is cooking, heat the oil in a small skillet over medium heat. Add the garlic and ginger and sauté until light brown. Add to the squash. Puree the soup in batches in a blender, about 2 cups at a time, taking care not to overfill and splatter the hot liquid. Return the pureed soup to the saucepan and season with salt and pepper. Ladle into bowls, swirl with the sour cream, and garnish with fresh dill.

Serves 6

The Right Beef for the Right Job

For pot roast, you want to choose a good braising cut (see p. 21). Don't invest in an expensive sirloin or rib roast, which are much better for a dry quick oven heat and cooked to medium rare. This recipe calls for a chuck blade roast, which is the best way to go for pot roast, but if you had to, you could also substitute chuck shoulder roast or top round roast, adjusting the amounts of broth and beer to suit.

french onion pot roast

This is a bit of a twist on the traditional idea of a big chunk of roast lamb, beef, or ham for the Sunday table. It starts with a typical pot roast, but since that always seems just a bit too ordinary, I throw in some beer and cheese, the two cure-alls for any hearty comfort food needing a bit of oomph.

2- to 2½-pound beef chuck blade roast
Salt
Freshly ground black pepper
3 tablespoons vegetable oil
3 medium or 2 large onions (about 1½ pounds), cut in half and thinly sliced
¾ to 1 cup beef broth
½ cup brown ale, such as Newcastle Brown
2 teaspoons packed brown sugar
1 cup grated Gruyère cheese

Generously season the roast with salt and pepper. Heat 2 tablespoons of the vegetable oil over medium-high heat in a deep skillet or Dutch oven. Add the roast and brown, about 3 minutes per side. Remove the roast to a platter and set aside.

Turn the heat to medium. Add the remaining 1 tablespoon vegetable oil to the same pan. Add the onions and cook, stirring occasionally, for 10 minutes until soft and translucent. Add ¾ cup beef broth, the brown ale, and brown sugar, stirring to combine all ingredients. Return the roast to the pan, nestle into the onion and liquid mixture, and bring to a boil. Reduce to a simmer, cover, and cook for 30 minutes. Turn the roast and cook for another 30 minutes. Turn again and cook for another 40 to 60 minutes (shorter time for a smaller roast). If using a larger roast or the roast liquid starts to dry out, add an additional ¼ cup beef broth.

When fork-tender, remove the roast to a shallow ovenproof dish, such as a gratin pan. Remove the onions with a slotted spoon and arrange over and around the roast. Turn the heat under the juices to high and boil for 10 to 15 minutes to reduce and thicken the juices, until you have ¾ to 1 cup liquid. In the meantime, preheat the broiler. Slice the roast into ¼-inch-thick slices and slightly overlap in layers in an ovenproof dish. Pour the sauce over the beef and onions. Sprinkle the roast with the cheese. Place under the broiler until bubbling and golden brown, 3 to 5 minutes.

Serves 6

butternut squash soup

potatoes and carrots for a sunday roast

This recipe is designed to accompany the French Onion Pot Roast (see p. 133), but works equally well with any roast or simply on its own when you have a craving for roasted winter roots.

> 2 pounds Russet potatoes
> 1½ pounds carrots
> ¼ cup olive oil
> Salt
> Freshly ground black pepper

Preheat the oven to 450°F. Peel the potatoes and slice lengthwise ¼ to ½ inch thick. Cut slices into sticks ¼ to ½ inch thick. Transfer to a large mixing bowl and cover with water. Soak for 10 minutes to remove any starchiness. Drain and dry thoroughly on paper towels. Peel the carrots and cut in half. Cut thin ends in half lengthwise. Cut thick ends in quarters lengthwise. Potatoes and carrots should end up roughly the same size.

In a large roasting pan, toss the potatoes and carrots with the olive oil. Spread the vegetables into a single layer. Cook until the vegetables are tender when pierced with a fork, 45 to 60 minutes, stirring every 15 to 20 minutes to prevent sticking and burning. Season with salt and pepper and serve with a roast.

Serves 6

The Many Guises of Oats

· **quick-cooking oats:** bits and pieces of rolled oats that cook in a third of the time of rolled oats—but given how quickly rolled oats cook, it isn't really worth the loss of texture and taste.

· **rolled oats** (also called "old-fashioned oats"): no surprise, oats that have been flattened between rollers

· **steel-cut oats:** bits of crunchy oat groats that haven't been rolled. I prefer them in baked goods rather than for breakfast.

double oatmeal cookies

These cookies not only give you twice the punch of the super-food oats, they follow the advice from "Secrets of the Cold-Weather Pantry" (p. 32) to use dried fruit in delicious ways. Here you have a chance to pick and choose your favorite dried fruit and go beyond just regular old raisins.

> 1½ cups rolled oats (not quick oats)
> ⅓ cup steel-cut oats
> ¾ cup flour
> ½ teaspoon baking powder
> ½ teaspoon baking soda
> 1 teaspoon salt
> ½ cup (1 stick) unsalted butter, softened
> ⅓ cup granulated sugar
> ¼ cup packed brown sugar
> 1 egg
> 1 teaspoon vanilla
> 1 cup mixed dried fruit, such as raisins, golden raisins, and dried cranberries

Line 2 baking sheets with parchment paper. Preheat the oven to 375°F.

In a medium mixing bowl, stir together the rolled oats, steel-cut oats, flour, baking powder, baking soda, and salt. Set aside.

In the bowl of an electric mixer, combine the butter with both sugars. Cream together for 2 minutes. With the mixer running, add the egg and vanilla and mix to completely blend. Scrape down the sides of the bowl. Again with the mixer running, slowly add the oat mixture. Mix until just combined. Quickly mix in the dried fruit.

Using a dough scoop or a spoon and your fingers, shape into 1½-inch balls and place 2 to 3 inches apart on the prepared cookie sheets. Bake for 10 to 12 minutes, until golden and beginning to brown around the edges. Cool for 2 minutes on the cookie sheets before transferring to a cooling rack. (Parchment sheets can be reused for the next batch.)

Makes 32 cookies

happy hour

—— *a toast to warmth and good cheer* ——

MENU

Number in Party: 6 to 8 Guests

Chicken, Sage, and Cheddar Tart
Roast Beef Sandwiches with Pear Spread and Stilton
Parsnip Fries with Two Sauces
Bloody Sigrid
Hazelnut Milk Punch

When you are making a New Year's resolution with the previous menu to gather your family around the dinner table for a home-cooked meal, hopefully you have room for a corollary as well: spend more time entertaining friends in style. Mix a little glam with your glee by whipping up an easy and elegant Happy Hour to toast the perfect time of day.

chicken, sage, and cheddar tart

Every good party needs at least one or two good tarts. Ahem. If you don't have time to make a crust, use a puff pastry and the same method as for the Renaissance Winter Greens Tart (p. 121). Give this simple tart an artisanal touch by using a high-quality farmhouse cheddar like Neal's Yard's Isle of Mull Cheddar.

CRUST
1¼ cups flour
½ teaspoon salt
½ cup (4 ounces) cold unsalted butter
2 to 4 tablespoons ice water

FILLING
2 tablespoons unsalted butter
½ cup chopped yellow onion
1 pound boneless, skinless chicken breasts, cut into ½-inch cubes
2 tablespoons flour
1 cup whipping cream
1 tablespoon minced fresh sage
1 cup (loosely packed) shredded sharp cheddar cheese (about 2½ ounces)
½ teaspoon salt
½ teaspoon white pepper
8 whole fresh sage leaves of similar size and shape

To make the crust: Mix the flour and salt in a food processor. Add the butter and pulse until the size of marbles. Add 2 tablespoons ice water and pulse just until dough begins to clump together when you grab a handful. Add additional ice water if the dough is dry. Transfer to a bowl or countertop and press into a disc without overworking. Wrap it in plastic and chill until ready to use (1 to 24 hours).

Place the rack in lowest position in the oven. Preheat the oven to 400°F. Roll out the tart crust and place in a 9-inch tart pan with a removable bottom. Place parchment paper across the crust and fill with pie weights or dried beans. Partially bake for 20 minutes. Remove from the oven and reduce oven temperature to 375°F. Remove the pie weights and parchment and cool the crust on a wire rack while you prepare the filling.

To make the filling: Melt the butter in a large skillet over medium heat. Add the onion and sauté until soft, about 5 minutes. Turn the heat to medium-high. Add the chicken and sauté until just brown on all sides, 3 to 4 minutes. Reduce the heat to medium and sprinkle the flour over the chicken. Stir for 1 minute to coat the chicken. Slowly pour in the whipping cream, stirring constantly and scraping the bottom of the pan to prevent lumps. Stir in the minced sage. Reduce the heat to low and cook for 3 minutes, occasionally stirring. Add the cheddar cheese and stir until melted, about 2 minutes. Remove from the heat. Stir in the salt and white pepper.

Pour the filling into the prepared pie crust. Arrange the whole sage leaves in a wagon wheel design on top, equally spacing them. Bake until the filling is set and the crust is golden brown, 15 to 20 minutes. Cool for 5 to 10 minutes before serving. Slice in between the sage leaves so that one sage leaf lies in the center of each piece.

Serves 8 as hors d'oeuvres

A Pepper of a Different Color
Keep white pepper on hand because it gives you a peppery taste without the appearance of black flecks in your light-colored sauces and pies.

Let us have wine and women,
mirth and laughter,
Sermons and soda-water the day after.
—Lord Byron

To fill out the menu, revisit some
small-bite favorites from other menus:

* Cinnamon Cream Puffs (p. 57)
* Phyllo Cigars (p. 67)
* Wild Mushroom Toasts (p. 95)
* Golden Caviar Toasts (p. 104)
* Fried Cod Fingers (p. 109)
* Wassail Bowl (p. 115)
* Lambswool Punch (p. 116)
* Renaissance Winter Greens Tart (p. 121)
* Beet Fries with Blue Cheese Sauce (p. 166)
* Red Pepper Harissa with Yogurt and
  Pita (p. 175)
* Cinnamon Cookies (p. 187)

Toasts for Your Tipples

When hosting internationally, it's always polite
to have the right toast handy.

· **Britain and the United States:** Cheers!
· **Ireland:** Sláinte! (slan-cha)
· **Germany:** Prost!
· **Japan:** Kanpai!
· **Norway, Denmark, and Sweden:** Skål!
  (skawl or skole)
· **Spain:** Salud!
· **France:** A votre santé! (ah vo-tra san-tay)

Then of course there's the figurative

· Bottoms up!
· Here's mud in your eye!
· Down the hatch!
· Chin-Chin! (Anglicized from the Chinese
  greeting ts'ing-ts'ing)

Claret is the liquor for boys; port,
for men; but he who aspires to be
a hero must drink brandy.
—**Samuel Johnson**

roast beef sandwiches with pear spread and stilton

2 tablespoons unsalted butter
2 ripe pears, peeled, cored, and cut into ¼-inch
    pieces
2 teaspoons sugar
2 tablespoons raisins
½ cup brandy
1 pound rare roast beef, sliced
8 ounces Stilton
Sliced pumpernickel bread

Melt the butter in a medium saucepan over medium heat. Add the pears and sugar and sauté for
4 minutes until the pears start to soften and release
their juices. Stir in the raisins and brandy. Turn the
heat to low, cover, and simmer for 25 minutes until
pears are completely soft. Remove the lid and cook
and stir another 5 minutes until almost all the liquid
is absorbed. Mash with a potato masher.

Make sandwiches by layering beef, cheese, and
pear spread on the bread. Cut in half and serve.

Serves 6 as hors d'oeuvres

roast beef sandwiches with pear spread and stilton

A man may surely be allowed to take a glass of wine by his own fireside.

—Richard Sheridan, reportedly while drinking a glass of wine in the street and watching his theater, the Drury Lane, burn down

I pray you, do not fall in love with me,
For I am falser than vows made in wine.

—William Shakespeare, *As You Like It*

parsnip fries with two sauces

In place of the hackneyed potato, dig up another root vegetable for fries with a bit more flair and slather with sauces that make the most of the sweet roasted parsnip. Honey, a classic accompaniment for parsnips, is partnered with the tang of vinegar in one. And in the other, British Wensleydale cheese acknowledges the popularity of the parsnip across the Atlantic, but if you don't have access to a good cheese seller, you can substitute a medium cheddar or dry jack instead.

2 pounds parsnips
2 tablespoon olive oil
Kosher salt

CHEESE SAUCE
1 tablespoon unsalted butter
2 teaspoons flour
½ cup milk
½ cup shredded Wensleydale cheese

HONEY VINAIGRETTE
¼ cup apple cider vinegar
2 teaspoons Dijon mustard
2 tablespoons honey
½ teaspoon freshly ground pepper
½ cup olive oil

Preheat the oven to 400°F. Cut the parsnips into sticks about 2 inches by 1 inch. Toss the parsnips with the olive oil on a rimmed baking sheet. Bake for 30 minutes, stirring every 10 minutes. Sprinkle with kosher salt and serve with sauces.

To make the cheese sauce: Melt the butter in a small saucepan over medium heat until it foams. Whisk in the flour and continue to cook and stir for another 2 minutes. Slowly pour in the milk, whisking constantly as you do so as to prevent lumps. Whisk in the cheese and heat until completely melted.

To make the honey vinaigrette: Stir together the vinegar, mustard, honey, and pepper. Whisk in the olive oil.

Serves 6 to 8 as hors d'oeuvres

bloody sigrid

This Scandinavian take on a traditional Bloody Mary replaces ordinary vodka with the spicy Nordic spirit aquavit (p. 216). Save your celery for a summer sipper and garnish instead with dill and lemon, both of which are infused into many styles of aquavit. For the flavors to properly come through, be sure to start with thoroughly chilled ingredients, and for an extra icy look to the glasses, rim them with glistening coarse sea salt.

> 4 cups (32 ounces) vegetable juice, such as V-8 or R. W. Knudsen
> 1¼ cups aquavit
> 2 tablespoons Worcestershire sauce
> 2 tablespoons lemon juice
> 1 teaspoon Tabasco sauce
> Salt
> Freshly ground black pepper
> Lemon slices
> Dill sprigs

In a large pitcher, stir together the vegetable juice, aquavit, Worcestershire sauce, lemon juice, and Tabasco. Add salt and pepper to taste. Pour into glasses and garnish with lemon slices and dill sprigs.

Serves 6

You'll have no scandal while you dine,
But honest talk and wholesome wine.

—Alfred Tennyson, "To the Reverend F. D. Maurice"

hazelnut milk punch

Flavored syrup infuses this winter classic with the taste of hazelnut. Because it is used to flavor coffee drinks and Italian sodas, you can find hazelnut syrup where coffee supplies are sold or in Italian grocery stores. Look for brands like Torani or Monin. Use the leftovers any time of day—not just at happy hour—to flavor hot chocolate or steamed milk.

> 2½ cups whole milk
> ¼ cup hazelnut syrup
> ½ cup brandy

Heat milk and hazelnut syrup to a simmer over medium heat. Remove from the heat and stir in the brandy. Divide among 6 small cups.

Serves 6

Measure for Measure

Different drinks count differently. The equivalencies for official servings:
· wine: 5 ounces
· beer: 12 ounces
· cocktail: 2 ounces

Measure for Measure, Part Two

When mixing cocktails, know the lingo:
· dash: ⅟₃₂ ounce
· pony: 1 ounce
· jigger: 1½ ounces
· pint: 16 ounces
· fifth: 25.6 ounces

Global Pub Crawl

Stock an international bar with a few beers from around the world:
· **Belgium:** Chimay
· **Canada:** Blanche De Chambly
· **China:** Tsingtao
· **Czech Republic:** Budweiser Burgerbrau
· **France:** Kronenbourg 1664
· **India:** Kingfisher
· **Italy:** Peroni
· **Jamaica:** Red Stripe
· **Japan:** Kirin
· **Mexico:** Negro Modelo
· **Singapore:** Tiger Lager
· **Thailand:** Singha

17
twelfth night
a renaissance revelry

MENU
Number in Party: 6 Guests

A Jolly Great Joint of Beef
Horseradish Cream
Yorkshire Pudding
Citrus Bacon Brussels Sprouts
Twelfth Night Cake

A Shakespeare play and an ancient custom, this menu celebrates the final day of the Twelve Days of Christmas. Though he did not actually set his play on Twelfth Night, Shakespeare likely chose the title for his comedy of the same name for the topsy-turvy mirth and revelry associated with the event.

a jolly great joint of beef

If you're going to put out a spread worthy of Merry Olde England, you'd better follow the guidelines of a proper British meat expert like Hugh Fearnley-Whittingstall. I use his high-heat sizzle (HHS) technique, which demands a good half hour at a high temperature to build a crisp crust and get the fat going.

> 6-pound prime rib roast (3 ribs)
> Salt
> Freshly ground black pepper

Preheat the oven to 425°F. Generously salt and pepper the roast all over. Place bone side down in a roasting pan. Roast for 30 minutes. Turn the heat down to 350°F and continue to roast for 10 minutes per pound for very rare meat and 15 for medium rare. Meat should check in at 120° to 125°F.

When you remove the roast from the pan, transfer to a carving board or serving platter and pour off the fat from the roasting pan. Save the drippings for Yorkshire Pudding (see p. 144). Tent the roast with foil and let it sit for at least 30 minutes. Every roasting guide tells you to do this and indeed it's very important. The resting period helps redistribute the juices and gives the roast something to do while you finish the pudding.

Increase the oven temperature to 450°F and make the Yorkshire Pudding.

Serves 6

When mighty Roast Beef
Was the Englishman's food,
It ennobled our brains
And enriched our blood.
Our soldiers were brave
And our courtiers were good
Oh the Roast Beef of Old England
And old English Roast Beef

But since we have learnt
From all-vapouring France
To eat their ragouts
As well as to dance,
We're fed up with nothing
But vain complaisance
Oh the Roast Beef of Old England
And old English Roast Beef

But now we are dwindled to,
What shall I name?
A poor sneaking race,
Half-begotten and tame,
Who sully the honours
That once shone in fame.
Oh the Roast Beef of Old England
And old English Roast Beef

In those days if fleets did
Presume on the Main,
They seldom, if ever,
Returned home again,
As witness the vaunting
Armada of Spain
Oh the Roast Beef of Old England
And old English Roast Beef

Oh then we had stomachs
To eat and to fight
And when wrongs were a-cooking
To do ourselves right.
But now we're a . . . .
I could, but goodnight!
Oh the Roast Beef of Old England
And old English Roast Beef.

—**Henry Fielding,** *The Grub Street Opera*

I am a great eater of beef, and I believe that does harm to my wit.

—*Twelfth Night*

horseradish cream

Any great roasted joint of beef would seem naked without a dressing of horseradish. For something simultaneously hearty and elegant like a rib roast, you need the strength of the pungent root mitigated by a pinch of sugar and embellished with the pomp and circumstance of the best cream.

>   1 cup whipping cream
>   1 teaspoon sugar
>   6 tablespoons prepared horseradish

In the bowl of an electric mixer, whip the cream until soft peaks form. Add the sugar and horseradish and continuing whipping until stiff peaks form.

Makes enough for 6

....

Prince Harry: O, my sweet beef, I must still be good angel to thee. The money is paid back again.
Falstaff: O, I do not like that paying back; 'tis a double labour.

—Henry IV, Part I

....

yorkshire pudding

"So, this is Yorkshire pudding. I had no idea." You will undoubtedly hear more than one guest say this to you. Mix up the batter before your roast is done and set it aside so that you are ready the moment the roast comes out of the oven.

>   3 large eggs
>   1 cup milk
>   ½ cup water
>   1¼ cups flour
>   ½ teaspoon salt
>   3 tablespoons beef drippings

Combine all ingredients in a blender and whip until smooth. Set aside while roast finishes cooking.

Preheat the oven to 450°F. Pour beef drippings into a 13 x 9-inch baking pan or equivalent oval casserole dish. Place the pan in the oven to heat for 10 minutes. Add the batter and bake for 30 minutes until pudding has puffed up and is golden brown around the edges and cooked through the center.

Serves 6

citrus bacon brussels sprouts

2 pieces bacon
⅓ cup diced shallots
⅔ cup chicken broth
⅔ cup brown ale
½ cup orange juice
Zest of 1 orange
2 tablespoons brown sugar
2 pounds Brussels sprouts, halved

Fry the bacon over medium heat until barely crisp. Using kitchen scissors, snip the bacon into ¼-inch pieces. Pour off all but 2 teaspoons fat from the pan. Add the shallots and sauté until soft. Add the chicken broth, brown ale, orange juice and zest, and brown sugar and bring to a boil. Cook for 10 minutes on medium heat. Add the bacon and sprouts and cook for 10 minutes more, stirring frequently, until sprouts are coated with a thick sauce.

Serves 6

A Blessing on the Trees

In apple-growing regions, cider was the popular potable for the New Year. In a ritual toast, revelers poured the drink on apple trees to ensure a good harvest for the coming year.

Don't Show up Empty Handed

In coming to visit, the Three Kings also came bearing gifts, so as much as Christmas, Epiphany is a time for great generosity. Charity and feeding the poor was especially important to remember on Twelfth Night. Of course, sometimes you have to be reminded to be more charitable. Too often the gentry preferred to revel it up in London, leaving their country houses cold and dark during the holiday season. Queen Elizabeth and other monarchs issued proclamations ordering them to leave the capital and return home to do their duty to those who depended on their generosity in the countryside. A popular ballad of the period lamented that Christmas is so far gone because "great men, by flockes, … there be flowne, to London-ward."

Grumio: What say you to a piece
of beef, and mustard?
Katherine: A dish that I do love
to feed upon.

—The Taming of the Shrew

Constable: And then, give them great
meals of beef, and iron and steel, they
will eat like wolves and fight like devils.

Orleans: Ay, but these English are
shrewdly out of beef.

Constable: Then shall we find
tomorrow they have only stomachs to
eat, and none to fight.

—Henry V

citrus bacon brussels sprouts

twelfth night cake

This cake is an excuse to make use of that steamed pudding mold you bought for its beauty but never quite figured out the perfect recipe for.

¼ cup cream sherry
⅓ cup currants
1½ cups flour
1½ teaspoons baking powder
½ teaspoon ground cinnamon
½ teaspoon salt
¼ teaspoon ground cloves
½ cup (1 stick) butter, softened
¾ cup sugar
1 teaspoon vanilla
Juice and zest of 1 orange
2 eggs

Butter a 5-cup mold. Heat the sherry in a small saucepan—don't even bring to a simmer. Remove from heat, add the currants. Cover and steep for 1 hour.

In a medium bowl, combine the flour, baking powder, cinnamon, salt, and cloves. Set aside. In a mixing bowl, cream together the butter and sugar. Add the vanilla and orange zest. Add the eggs and beat to combine. Add the flour mixture by the spoonful. Add the currants and soaking sherry and 2 tablespoons orange juice to the mixture. Mix until blended. Spoon into the buttered mold. Steam for 2 hours. (see "Steaming a Pudding," p. 197.)

Serves 8

Now Capons and Hens, beside Turkeys,
Geese and Ducks, besides Beef and
Mutton, must all die for the great feast,
for in twelve days a multitude of people
will not be fed with a little.

—Renaissance essayist Nicholas Breton

I ne'er drank sack in my life,
and if you give me any conserves,
give me conserves of beef.

—*The Taming of the Shrew*

Entertainments for Twelve Days

· Twelve drummers drumming
· Eleven pipers piping
· Ten lords a-leaping
· Nine ladies dancing
· Eight maids a-milking
· Seven swans a-swimming
· Six geese a-laying
· Five golden rings
· Four calling birds
· Three French hens
· Two turtle doves
· And a partridge in a pear tree!

Quick Cheat

Purchase an Italian panettone and push in a bean and a pea. Ice it all over with a mixture of confectioners' sugar and milk to hide the holes.

A World Turned Upside-Down

Twelfth Night ushers in Epiphany on January 6, a celebration of the end of the twelve days of Christmas when the Three Kings visit the lowly Christ child. This reversal of social status is mimicked in the ritual of the Twelfth Night cake. A pea and a bean were baked into the cake and whoever found them would be king and queen for the night. The King of the Bean and Queen of the Pea reigned over the Twelfth Night festivities by encouraging the assembled company in all manner of social transgressions that made the high low and the low high. With the idea of political upheaval a little too close to home, some noble households ensured in advance who would play these key roles. In the sixteenth century, the court of Mary, Queen of Scots, was for a night overseen by Mary Fleming and records from Henry VIII's royal household reveal payments for the privilege of the position.

18
citrus in season
a taste of the tropics

❧❦❧

MENU
Number in Party: 4 Guests

Chili Lime Shrimp with Rice
Coconut Black Beans
Orange Almond Cake

❧❦❧

Perhaps not where you live, but in warm climes like Italy, Spain, and Florida, citrus is ripe and ready in our coldest months. Winter is the best time to enjoy these fruits. And this quick and easy meal is as suitable for a week-night supper as for weekend entertaining.

chili lime shrimp with rice

RICE

1½ cups long-grain white rice

2¼ cups water

1 teaspoon salt

4 teaspoons olive oil

CHILI LIME SHRIMP

6 tablespoons olive oil

6 garlic cloves, minced

½ cup lime juice

2 teaspoons crushed red pepper flakes

1 teaspoon ground ancho chili powder
  (see p. 196)

2 teaspoons packed brown sugar

½ teaspoon salt

½ teaspoon freshly ground black pepper

1¼ pounds medium shrimp, shelled and deveined

To make the rice: Combine the rice, water, salt, and oil in a medium saucepan. Bring to a boil over high heat. Reduce the heat to low, cover, and simmer for 15 minutes. Remove from the heat and let it sit for another 10 minutes, covered.

To make the chili lime shrimp: Heat 3 tablespoons of the oil in a large skillet over medium-low heat. Add the garlic and sauté until soft, about 4 minutes. Stir in the lime juice, red pepper, chili powder, brown sugar, salt, and pepper. Heat to a simmer. Add the shrimp and stir and cook until pink and heated through, 4 to 5 minutes. Serve over rice.

Serves 4

coconut black beans

One 15-ounce can black beans, undrained

¼ cup unsweetened coconut

1 teaspoon ground cumin

½ teaspoon salt

In a medium saucepan, combine the black beans (with liquid from can), coconut, cumin, and salt. Heat through and serve on the side with shrimp and rice.

Serves 4

Not So Shrimpy

The size of shrimp is expressed as number per pound

· small: 51 to 60

· medium: 41 to 50

· medium-large: 36 to 40

· large: 31 to 35

· extra large: 26 to 30

Put the lime in the coconut, you drink 'em both together; Put the lime in the coconut, then you feel better.

—Harry Nilsson

> California is a fine place to live—
> if you happen to be an orange.
>
> **—Fred Allen**

> A medium dry vodka martini—
> with a slice of lemon peel.
> Shaken, not stirred.
>
> **—James Bond**

orange almond cake

¾ cup sliced blanched almonds

¾ cup plus 2 teaspoons sugar

Zest of 2 oranges

⅔ cup milk

2 eggs

1 teaspoon vanilla

½ teaspoon almond extract

1½ cups flour

1½ teaspoons baking powder

½ teaspoon baking soda

1 teaspoon salt

¾ cup (1½ sticks) unsalted butter, softened

⅓ cup fresh-squeezed orange juice

2 tablespoons orange liqueur, such as Grand Marnier

Butter and flour a 9-inch springform pan. Preheat the oven to 350°F.

Combine the almonds, ¼ cup sugar, and orange zest in a food processor. Process to a fine meal.

In a medium bowl, combine the milk, eggs, vanilla, and almond extract.

In the bowl of an electric mixer, combine the flour, baking powder, baking soda, salt, and ½ cup sugar. Stir to blend. Add the butter. Mix until ingredients are blended. On medium speed, mix for 90 seconds. The batter will be dry. Mix in the orange juice. With the mixer running on low speed, alternately add half of the almond mixture and half of the egg mixture, beating well between each addition. Repeat with the remaining mixtures.

Pour the batter into the prepared pan. Bake for 45 to 55 minutes. Cool on a rack for 10 minutes. Remove the outer pan ring. Drizzle with 1 tablespoon orange liqueur. Sprinkle with 1 teaspoon sugar. Repeat with the remaining 1 tablespoon orange liqueur and 1 teaspoon sugar. Cool to room temperature before serving.

Serves 8 to 10

chili lime shrimp with rice & coconut black beans & orange almond cake

19

feast away the winter blues

soul food for the soul

❧

MENU
Number in Party: 8 to 10 Guests

Dollars and Coins
Ham and Hot Pepper Jelly Biscuits
Cornmeal Catfish Bites
Mississippi Mud Parfaits

❧

Having lived in Chicago for so long, I feel that winter and blues sometimes go hand-in-hand. That is, just around February, you start to get a little feverish for want of sun but luckily you live in a city steeped in a musical tradition that provides you with just the right commiseration. This party solves the problem by combining the problem and the solution.

dollars and coins

Serving collard greens and black-eyed peas together is a New Year's tradition for prosperity. The collards represent "dollars" and the peas "coins." In this dish, they are rolled together in short thick cigars that look somewhat like Greek stuffed grape leaves.

> 1 large bunch collard greens (about 12 leaves total)
> One 15-ounce can black-eyed peas
> 3 pieces bacon
> ¾ cup long-grain white rice
> 1 cup chicken broth
> Salt
> Freshly ground black pepper
> Hot sauce, such as Tabasco

Cut each collard leaf in half lengthwise while removing the thick spine. Handle the leaves carefully to avoiding tearing. Prepare a deep vegetable steamer or place a steaming rack in a large Dutch oven. Stack the collard leaves in the steamer, gently folding if necessary to make them fit. Steam for 5 minutes, until thoroughly wilted. Drain on paper towels and cool while you prepare the filling.

Drain the black-eyed peas, reserving the liquid. Cook the bacon in a large skillet over medium-high heat until medium crisp. Drain on paper towels. Pour the bacon fat from pan, reserving 1 tablespoon. Chop the bacon finely.

In same skillet you used to cook bacon, combine the chopped bacon, 1 tablespoon bacon fat, ⅓ cup of liquid from the black-eyed peas, the rice, and chicken broth. Bring to a boil over high heat. Stir in the black-eyed peas. Cover, reduce to a simmer, and cook for 15 minutes. Remove from the heat and let it sit, covered, for another 10 minutes. Season to taste with salt and pepper.

To fill each halved collard leaf with rice and beans: Lay one collard leaf on a flat surface. Spread 2 tablespoons of the rice mixture across the middle of a leaf. Fold the leaf in half over the filling and press to mold. Fold over the sides of the collard leaf and continue to roll and fold over the sides as you go. Lay seam side down on your work surface. When all the leaves have been filled, transfer to the steamer and steam for another 10 minutes. Serve warm with hot sauce.

Makes 24; serves 8 as hors d'oeuvres

ham and hot pepper jelly biscuits

Hot pepper jelly comes in many colors and varieties. If you're in the South, look for a local variety. Nationwide, you'll find Tabasco brand in both red and green. Just don't confuse hot pepper jelly with sweet or red pepper jelly or jam. It should look like jelly with bits of hot pepper or hot pepper seeds in it.

> 2 cups flour
> 2 tablespoons baking powder
> ¾ teaspoon salt
> ¾ cup (1½ sticks) unsalted butter
> 1⅓ cups milk
> Hot pepper jelly
> 1 pound ham, thinly sliced

Preheat the oven to 450°F. Line a heavy baking sheet with parchment.

In a large bowl, mix together the flour, baking powder, and salt. Cut in the butter until marble-size. (You can use a food processor up to this point, but transfer the mixture to a bowl before proceeding.) Stir in the milk with a large fork. Shape with your hands until the dough holds together. Roll out to ¾ inch thick. Using a biscuit cutter or mouth of a drinking glass, cut into 3-inch circles. Place on the parchment.

Bake for 10 to 12 minutes; cool. Split each biscuit open. Spread both layers with hot pepper jelly and layer with ham.

Serves 10 as hors d'oeuvres

cornmeal catfish bites

cornmeal catfish bites

It just wouldn't be a big ol' celebration of southern foodways without some catfish, buttermilk, and cornmeal. This recipe gives you all three.

2 pounds catfish fillets
1 cup buttermilk
1½ cups cornmeal
1 tablespoon salt
Vegetable oil for frying
Hot sauce, such as Tabasco

Cut the catfish into 1- to 1½-inch cubes. In a large shallow bowl or deep pie plate, stir together the catfish cubes and buttermilk. Refrigerate for 30 minutes.

In another large shallow bowl or pie plate, stir together the cornmeal and salt. Heat the oil in a large skillet over medium-high heat. Piece by piece, dredge the catfish cubes in the cornmeal and place in the frying pan. Cook until golden brown, about 3 minutes per side. Drain on paper towels. Transfer to a large baking sheet and keep warm in a 200°F oven. When ready to pass around, top with a bamboo cocktail fork. Serve with dipping cups of hot sauce or add a splash to each bite.

Serves 8 as hors d'oeuvres

Give your iPod the Blues

Blueberry Hill by Louis Armstrong

Stone Crazy by Buddy Guy

Pretty Baby by Buddy Guy

Strange Fruit by Billie Holiday

One Bourbon, One Scotch, One Beer by John Lee Hooker

The Thrill is Gone by B. B. King

Into the Night by B. B. King

Hoochie Coochie Man by Muddy Waters

Sweet Home Chicago by Muddy Waters

Back Door Man by Howlin' Wolf

Nobody Knows You When You're Down and Out by Bessie Smith

These Blues is Killing Me by A. C. Reed

Blues After Hours by Pinetop Perkins

mississippi mud parfaits

Like the river itself, this dessert includes multiple layers and textures: a sandy delta of chocolate cookie wafer crumbs and an effluvial stream of muddy hot fudge.

8-ounce package chocolate wafer cookies (such as Newman's Own Tops and Bottoms)
¾ cup whipping cream
2 tablespoons unsalted butter
1 tablespoon plus 1 teaspoon sugar
4 ounces bittersweet or semisweet chocolate, coarsely chopped
½ gallon coffee ice cream

Using a food processor, grind the cookies into a fine sandy texture. Set aside.

To make the fudge sauce, in a small saucepan, combine the cream, butter, and sugar over medium heat. Stir until the butter melts and the cream is almost at a simmer. Remove from the heat. Whisk in the chopped chocolate until completely melted. Allow the fudge sauce cool to room temperature for 30 minutes.

How you layer and serve your parfaits is really up to you, but I recommend using wine glasses and going for something a little like this:

1. 1 tablespoon cookie crumbs in the bottom of each glass
2. 3 mini scoops of ice cream (using a 1⅜-inch metal scoop)
3. a good douse of fudge sauce
4. more cookie crumbs
5. 3 more mini scoops of ice cream
6. another current of fudge sauce
7. top with a generous sprinkling of cookie crumbs

Serves 10

20
a posh pub night
— a pint, a pie, and a pud —

❧

MENU
Number in Party: 6 Guests

Parsnip Soufflés
Beef and Brown Ale Pie
Bread Pudding

❧

Gastropubs are becoming an addictive dining habit for the way they combine classic comfort food as well as innovative seasonal specialties with the best of what's on tap. This menu brings together all the coziness of a place where everybody knows your name with a bit of British tradition and lets you enjoy great gastropub grub right at your own table.

parsnip soufflés

Try this blending of rustic good taste with haute-cuisine technique.

Dry bread crumbs
1 pound parsnips
4 tablespoons (½ stick) butter
1 cup milk
3 tablespoons flour
6 large eggs, separated
6 ounces Wensleydale cheese, grated
1½ teaspoons minced fresh rosemary
¾ teaspoon salt

Butter 6 small ramekins or ovenproof coffee cups. Dust each with bread crumbs. (This helps the soufflé to have something to "grab" onto as it rises.) Preheat the oven to 375°F.

Peel the parsnips and cut into 2-inch lengths. Cook in a large pot of boiling salted water until tender, 15 to 20 minutes. Drain thoroughly.

Transfer the parsnips to a food processor and cool slightly, about 15 minutes, with the lid of the processor removed. Add the butter, milk, and flour. Puree until smooth. Add the egg yolks, cheese, rosemary, and salt. Process to thoroughly combine. Transfer the mixture to a large mixing bowl and set aside.

In the bowl of an electric mixer, whip the egg whites until stiff. Carefully fold the whites into the parsnip mixture in 3 batches.

Divide the mixture among the prepared ramekins. Place the ramekins on a baking sheet. Bake for 30 minutes until puffed and slightly golden. Serve immediately.

Serves 6

It's in the Bag

It is a truth universally acknowledged that Britain has far more interesting flavors of potato chips, or crisps, than you find on the other side of the pond. One thing you can always be sure of in a British pub is getting a packet of crisps. One other thing is also certain: there are going to be pretty fascinating flavors. Give your party a bit of authenticity by picking up some of them at a British food specialist or import chain like World Market:

· salt and vinegar
· smoky bacon
· prawn cocktail
· roast chicken
· lamb with Moroccan spices
· Thai sweet chili
· vintage cheddar and red onion chutney

What is a Pub?

"Pub" is short for public house, a building and an institution that evolved its qualities from alehouses and taverns as well as inns, hostelries and like places where hosts opened their doors to travelers in need of food and drink – thus, making a private home a public house. FYI, a publican is the person running the pub.

I have fed purely upon ale;
I have eat my ale, drank my ale,
and I always sleep upon ale.

—George Farquhar

beef and brown ale pie

Though you can use whatever mushrooms suit your fancy, a richer brown mushroom like cremini is ideal in this savory pie. Serve with a dark English ale such as St. Peter's Porter or a local porter-style microbrew from your own neck of the woods.

> One 12-ounce bottle brown ale, such as Newcastle Brown
>
> 1 cup beef broth
>
> 2 tablespoons Worcestershire sauce
>
> 2 pounds beef chuck roast
>
> 2 tablespoons vegetable oil
>
> 1 large onion, chopped (about 1 cup)
>
> 6 tablespoons (¾ stick) unsalted butter
>
> 8 ounces mushrooms, thickly sliced
>
> 5 tablespoons flour
>
> 1 pound white potatoes, peeled and cut into ¼-inch cubes
>
> 1 sheet puff pastry, thawed

Combine the beer, beef broth, and Worcestershire sauce in a medium bowl. Set aside.

Trim the fat from the beef and cut into ½-inch cubes. Set aside.

In a large, deep skillet, heat 1 tablespoon of the oil over medium heat. Add the onion and cook until soft, about 5 minutes. Turn the heat to medium-high. Add half the beef and cook until browned on all sides, 4 to 5 minutes. Add the remaining 1 tablespoon oil and brown the rest of the beef. With a slotted spoon, remove the beef and onions to a large mixing bowl.

Reduce the heat to medium. In the same pan, melt 2 tablespoons of the butter. Sauté the mushrooms 6 to 8 minutes until browned. Remove from the heat and add to the beef onion mixture. Melt the remaining 4 tablespoons butter and whisk in the flour to create a smooth paste and cook for about 1 minute, until a nutty brown color. Very slowly pour in the broth and beer mixture, whisking constantly to prevent lumps. Once thoroughly combined, bring to a boil and continue to whisk. Add the beef mixture and stir to coat in the sauce. Bring to a simmer. Cover, reduce the heat to low, and simmer for 30 minutes. Add the potatoes and simmer for an additional 30 minutes.

Preheat the oven to 400°F while the filling cools. Pour the filling into a 9-inch deep-dish pie plate. Roll out the puff pastry and place over the filling.

Seal the edges to pie plate. Bake for 40 to 45 minutes until puff pastry is cooked through. Check the pastry after 25 minutes and cover with foil if it is browning too much. Cool for 5 minutes before serving.

Serves 6

Suggestions for British Beers

· St. Peter's Porter
· Belhaven
· Duchy Original Organic Ale
· Newcastle Brown
· Samuel Smith
· Wychwood Brewery

A Lighter Tipple

If you're entertaining family-style, have fun with some nonalcoholic British drinks for the kiddies

· Ribena
· Horlicks
· Lemon Barley Water
· Vimto
· Ginger Beer

When heaviness the mind
doth oppress,
And sorrow and grief
the heart doth assail,
No remedy quicker,
but take up your liquor,
And wash away care with a
pot of Good Ale.

--Thomas Randall

parsnip soufflés

Literary Opinions on Pudding

While Voltaire slandered an entire category of English after-dinner treats with the criticism that "The English plays are like their English puddings: nobody has any taste for them but themselves," Charles Dickens immortalized plum pudding in his *A Christmas Carol* with an image that Americans continue to romanticize.

Like-Minded Dessert Lovers

The British embrace that mysterious word that continually escapes Americans: *pudding*. Is it a cake, custard, or ice cream? Yes, yes, and yes. Many different things come under the big umbrella of pudding. There's even a club where fellow pudding fans join together at the Three Ways House Hotel in the English Cotswolds (www.puddingclub.com). The group was founded in 1985 "to prevent the demise of the traditional great British Pudding." Take a cue from them and don't stop at the traditional bread and butter pudding of this menu. Try out some of those eccentrically named puddings from the British recipe box:

· Spotted Dick
· Jam Roly-Poly
· Bedfordshire Clanger
· Hollygog
· Whim-Wham
· Knights of Windsor
· Queen Mab Pudding
· Durham Fluffin
· Cumberland Rum Nicky
· Hedgehog Pudding

bread pudding

A very traditional homey dessert without any fanfare or hoo-ha of complicated sauces and flavors, this bread pudding is more like your favorite piece of French toast than a custard. It's exactly what you want on a cold February night.

½ cup brandy
½ cup raisins
5 large eggs
2 cups whole milk
1 cup whipping cream
½ cup sugar
1 teaspoon ground cinnamon
8 cups bread cubes from a French baguette, crusts removed and cut into ½-inch pieces

Bring the brandy to a simmer in a small saucepan. Add the raisins. Cover, turn off heat, and steep for 20 minutes. Drain the brandy and reserve the raisins.

Butter a 9 x 9-inch baking pan. In a large mixing bowl, whisk together the eggs, milk, cream, sugar, and cinnamon. Stir in the raisins and bread cubes. Toss to thoroughly coat the bread. Transfer the mixture to the prepared baking pan and press down to distribute and submerge the bread cubes. Cover with plastic wrap and refridgerate one to two hours to allow the bread to soak up the egg mixture.

Preheat the oven to 325°F. Bake pudding for 45 minutes.

Serves 6

Minding Your P(ub)s and Q(ueue)s

A decade ago, anthropologists from the Social Issues Research Centre studied British pubs and pubgoers to the benefit both of natives and tourists. "Visitors to Britain are bewitched by our pubs," they argued, "but they are often bothered and bewildered by the unwritten rules of pub etiquette. This is not surprising: the variety and complexity of pub customs and rituals can be equally daunting for inexperienced British pub-goers." In their findings, they take multiple paragraphs to reveal complex skills such as how to order at the bar by understanding the invisible queue and how to finesse the social and financial subtleties of a round of drinks. Should you like to ensure your guests are on their toes at this get-together, you can drink up the benefit of this research in the book *Passport to the Pub*, which has been published online at the Centre's website: www.sirc.com.

Pubs Made Famous by the Pen

Pubs, alehouses, taverns, and inns frequently appear throughout British literature and likely many a play or novel was written, if not at least conceived, in any number of charmingly named drinking establishments dotting the literary island. Just scratching the surface:

The Tabard Inn from Geoffrey Chaucer's *Canterbury Tales*

The Boar's Head from William Shakespeare's *Henry IV* plays

The Woolsack from Thomas Dekker's *The Shoemaker's Holiday*

The Six Jolly Fellowship-Porters from Charles Dickens' *Our Mutual Friend*

The Rainbow from George Eliot's *Silas Marner*

The Green Man from Kingsley Amis' *The Green Man*

The Prancing Pony from J. R. R. Tolkien's *The Lord of the Rings*

The Three Broomsticks from J. K. Rowling's *Harry Potter* books

Few things are more pleasant than
a village graced with a good church,
a good priest and a good pub.
—John Hillaby

Say, for what were hop-yards meant,
Or why was Burton built on Trent?
Oh many a peer of England brews
Livelier liquor than the Muse,
And malt does more than Milton can
To justify God's ways to man.
—A. E. Housman

21
the frozen north
—— *local bites for winter nights* ——

❧

MENU
Number in Party: 6 Guests

Smoked Fish Cakes with Spicy Hmong Slaw
Beer-Braised Brats
Beet Fries with Blue Cheese Sauce
Cranberry Tarts

❧

Even as winter wears on, I still head farther north to colder and colder climates for fun winter sports and delicious winter food. This menu celebrates so many of the native and plentiful ingredients from one of my favorite northern states, Wisconsin.

smoked fish cakes with spicy hmong slaw

This recipe is one of those "fusion" inventions that merges two great Upper Midwestern culinary traditions. It's inspired by one of the very early podcasts with Wisconsin food expert Terese Allen, who walked listeners through the Hmong flavors of the Madison farmers' market. The slaw draws on Terese's recipe for a traditional Hmong salad, Tom Sum, that gives it a Midwestern twist with wintry roots and cabbage.

SLAW
2 cups thinly sliced green cabbage
1 cup shredded celery root
⅓ cup roasted salted peanuts, coarsely chopped

DRESSING
Juice of ½ lime
2 teaspoons Thai fish sauce (nam pla)
1 teaspoon sugar
2 Thai red chilies

FISH CAKES
8 ounces smoked whitefish
8 ounces fresh mild white fish, such as whitefish, halibut, sole, or turbot
1 egg
¼ cup dry bread crumbs
Pinch of salt
¼ teaspoon freshly ground black pepper
Vegetable oil for frying

To make the slaw: In a medium bowl, toss together the cabbage, celery root, and peanuts.

To make the dressing: In a small bowl, stir together the lime juice, fish sauce, and sugar. Thinly slice Thai chilies and add (with seeds) to the dressing. Marinate while you prepare the fish cakes.

To make the fish cakes: Remove the bones and skin from the smoked fish. Cut the fresh fish into 1-inch cubes. Combine both in a food processor and pulse a few times to blend.

In a large mixing bowl, whisk the egg. Stir in the fish and thoroughly combine. Stir in the bread crumbs, salt, and pepper. Shape the mixture into 12 fish cakes.

Pour the oil into a large skillet to a depth of ¼ inch. Heat over medium heat. Cook the fish cakes in batches until golden brown, 4 to 5 minutes per side. Drain on paper towels.

Pour the dressing over the slaw and toss to thoroughly coat. Divide the slaw among 6 plates. Top with 2 fish cakes each.

Old and New Immigrants

Minnesota and Wisconsin have long been defined by culinary traditions of nineteenth-century German and Scandinavian immigrants. Countless are the jokes about herring and hot dish. But in the 1970s, after the Vietnam War, Hmong refugees began arriving from Southeast Asia and settling in the cold climes of the Upper Midwest, introducing exotic tastes like bitter melon, lemon grass, and green papaya to a region dominated by lefse and lutefisk, bratwurst and cheese curds. The immigration continues today, and most of the 150,000 Hmong that currently live in the United States reside in the Upper Midwest, transforming and being transformed by the immigrant food traditions of earlier eras.

beet fries with blue cheese sauce

beer-braised brats

Brats are synonymous with Wisconsin. They make this an easy meal with quick work.

One 12-ounce bottle pale ale
6 bratwurst sausages
6 large buns, like hoagie rolls
Your favorite mustard

Bring the beer to a simmer in a large deep skillet. Add the bratwurst and return to a simmer. Cover and cook for 5 minutes. Turn the brats. Cover and cook for 5 more minutes. Remove the lid and cook on each side for 5 minutes again.

Preheat the broiler. Remove the brats from the beer. Slice down the middle lengthwise to split open. Place the brats, cut side up, on a baking sheet and broil until cooked through and slightly crispy, about 5 minutes. Serve on rolls with your favorite mustard.

Serves 6

Wisconsin Winter Beers

· Capital Brewing Munich Dark
· Capital Brewing Winter Skål
· Lakefront Brewery Holiday Spice Lager
· Lakefront Brewery Eastside Dark
· Leinenkugels Big Butt Dopplebock
· Leinenkugels Creamy Dark
· New Glarus Coffee Stout
· New Glarus Fat Squirrel
· Tyranena Chief Blackhawk Porter
· Viking Invader
· Viking Mørketid

Cheeseheads

Now that Maytag Blue has convinced the gourmet crowd that there are superior cheeses to be found in the Midwest, it's time to explore a little further and take advantage of all that the cheese state has to offer. For this menu, consider some great Wisconsin blue cheeses such as those recommended by Wisconsin caterer Pamilyn Hatfield: Hooks Blue cheese or Carr Valley Ba Ba Blue. I also fall for Carr Valley's Virgin Pine Native Blue.

Dairy State Delights

Just a few extra things you might want to round out this party

· cheese curds
· ice cream from Babcock Hall at the University of Wisconsin Madison
· Sheboygan rolls

Order them all at www.wisconsinmade.com.

beet fries with blue cheese sauce

Along with ginseng, beets are an intriguing crop where Wisconsin leads the nation in production. What should you serve with them to show off northern flavors? Beets and blue cheese are one of those classic culinary pairings like beer and brats, pork and apples, Fred and Ginger.

1 tablespoon unsalted butter
2 teaspoons flour
½ cup half-and-half
½ cup crumbled blue cheese
6 large beets, peeled and cut into ½-inch strips
Vegetable oil for frying

Melt the butter in a small saucepan over medium heat until it foams. Whisk in the flour and continue to cook and stir for another 2 minutes. Slowly pour in the half-and-half, whisking constantly to prevent lumps. Remove from the heat and stir in the cheese so that some melts and lends its flavor to the sauce but some crumbles remain to give it texture.

Pour oil to a depth of ½ inch in a large skillet. Heat the oil to 350°F. Cook the fries in batches until crisp, about 4 minutes per side. Drain on paper towels. Serve with the blue cheese sauce.

Serves 6

cranberry tarts

Cooking the cranberries separately in a low temperature oven means they remain gorgeously plump rather than popping and deflating to a relish.

One 6-count package frozen puff pastry shells
2 cups fresh cranberries
1 tablespoon cornstarch
½ cup plus 2 tablespoons sugar
¾ cup whipping cream

Bake the puff pastry shells according to manufacturer's directions. Reduce the oven to 275°F. Stir together the cranberries, cornstarch, and ½ cup of the sugar in a baking dish. Bake for 30 minutes. Drain off the liquid into a small saucepan. Bring the juice to a boil and cook for 3 minutes until thickened. Stir back into the cranberries. Cool to room temperature.

In the bowl of an electric mixer, combine the whipping cream and the remaining 2 tablespoons sugar. Beat until medium-stiff peaks form. Divide the cream among the prepared pastry shells. Top with the cranberries.

Serves 6

Combine your entertaining with some winter activity

· Go on a cheese and beer tour of the state with a map from the Wisconsin Dairy Council

· Watch your dinner being prepared fireside outside with a January fish boil at the White Gull Inn in Door County

· Cross-country ski by candlelight in many state parks

· Snowshoe the frozen waterfalls of Marinette County

· Snowmobile in the Northwoods

· Marvel at the wintry scenery on a horse-drawn sleigh ride through Door County cherry orchards

· Enjoy a Friday night fish fry or a Saturday night prime rib at a local supper club (preferably one with a bowling alley as well)

22
haggis and a hooley

—— a burns' night do ——

MENU
Number in Party: 6 to 8 Guests

Lamb Meat Loaf with Marmalade Glaze
Potatoes and Turnips with Bacon and Cream
Fruited Gingerbread with Butterscotch Sauce

Here's one of those more obscure holidays that I can't help but celebrate—and with the noise and excitement a Celtic "hooley" demands. Burns' Night gives you many great reasons to don a kilt, download some bagpipe music, and do a bit of a traditional Scottish ceilidh dancing.

lamb meat loaf with marmalade glaze

This is the modern answer to haggis. It saves you having to make a deal with the butcher for all those lamb entrails but still keeps up the spirit of the meal.

½ cup dry bread crumbs
½ cup whipping cream
½ cup beef broth
1 pound ground lamb
1 pound ground beef
¾ cup chopped onion
¾ cup rolled oats
1 egg
½ teaspoon ground allspice
1 teaspoon salt
½ teaspoon freshly ground black pepper
½ cup orange marmalade

Preheat the oven to 450°F.

Mix the bread crumbs, cream, and broth in a small bowl and set aside to soften for 5 minutes. In a large bowl, mix together the lamb, beef, onion, oats, egg, allspice, salt, and pepper. Stir in the softened bread crumbs and any remaining liquid. This is a good time to get your hands dirty since spoons don't always cut it in making sure all meatloaf ingredients are thoroughly mixed.

Shape the mixture into a loaf 8 to 9 inches long by 2½ to 3 inches high. Place in a 13 x 9-inch baking pan and bake for 10 minutes. Reduce oven heat to 350°F. Spread the marmalade over the top and bake for another 30 to 40 minutes, until the center registers 160°F.

Serves 6 to 8

Understanding Haggis

Like English sausage, Greek *kokoretsi*, and American chitterlings, haggis is a stuffed dish. Although there are many variations, traditional haggis usually consists of sheep's "pluck," the heart, liver, and lungs of a sheep, minced with such things as onion, suet, and various spices. This mixture is then stuffed in a sheep's stomach and boiled. Today, though, the haggis is usually stuffed in some more recognizable meat casing and, believe it or not, there are even vegetarian haggises.

Scottish Delicacies Harder to Pronounce than Eat

- **Arbroath smokies:** smoked haddock produced in Arbroath

- **atholl brose:** drink of whisky, honey, and oatmeal

- **cullen skink:** soup of milk, smoked haddock, and potatoes

- **skirlie:** savory cakes of oatmeal and onions fried in pork drippings

- **forfar bridies:** small savory beef pies

- **clootie dumpling:** sweet suet pudding with spices and dried fruit

potatoes and turnips with bacon and cream

Otherwise known as tatties and neeps, potatoes and turnips are standard fare on Burns' Night.

> 2 pounds Yukon Gold potatoes (3 to 4 medium)
> 1 pound turnips (about 3 small or 1 large)
> 4 pieces bacon
> 1 cup chicken broth
> ½ cup whipping cream
> Salt
> Freshly ground black pepper

Peel the potatoes and turnips and cut into ¼-inch dice.

Heat a large skillet over medium-high heat. Using kitchen scissors, snip off ¼-inch pieces of bacon into the skillet. Cook until nearly crisp, about 5 minutes. Drain off the fat. Add the potatoes and turnips to the bacon and sauté for about 3 minutes. Add the chicken broth, bring to a boil, cover and cook for 10 minutes until vegetables are almost tender. Remove the lid. Add the cream and cook over high heat for 10 minutes, stirring occasionally until the liquid is almost evaporated. Season to taste with salt and pepper.

Serves 6 to 8

potatoes and turnips with bacon and cream

Burns' Night

Celebrated on January 25, this festival honors poet Robert Burns' birthday. The night begins with a welcome to all present, followed by the Selkirk Grace, a thanks attributed to Burns but also known in the seventeenth century as the Galloway Grace. The words to this grace are sobering, simple, and beautiful:

Some hae meat and cannot eat.
Some cannot eat that want it:
But we hae meat and we can eat,
Sae let the Lord be thankit.

The haggis is then bagpiped in and cut open while one of the guests reads the "Address to a Haggis." As everyone begins to eat, so too they begin the "immortal memory," a recitation of Robbie Burns' poetry and life that usually culminates in the communal singing of his famed "Auld lang syne."

fruited gingerbread with butterscotch sauce

Have your cake and drink your dram, too.

GINGERBREAD
½ cup (1 stick) unsalted butter
½ cup light molasses
2¼ cups flour
2 teaspoons ground ginger
1 teaspoon ground cinnamon
¼ teaspoon ground cloves
¾ teaspoon baking soda
½ teaspoon salt
2 eggs
½ cup whole milk
½ cup buttermilk
¼ cup brown raisins
¼ cup golden raisins
2 tablespoons finely minced crystallized ginger

BUTTERSCOTCH SAUCE
3 tablespoons unsalted butter
½ cup packed brown sugar
2 tablespoons corn syrup
½ cup whipping cream
⅓ cup whisky
1 teaspoon vanilla

Preheat the oven to 350°F. Butter a 9 x 9-inch baking pan.

To make the gingerbread: In a large saucepan, combine the butter and molasses. Stir over medium heat until butter is completely melted. Set aside to cool slightly.

In a medium bowl, stir together the flour, ginger, cinnamon, cloves, baking soda, and salt.

Whisk the eggs into the molasses mixture, one at a time, blending well after each addition. Whisk in the milk until thoroughly combined. Whisk in half of the flour mixture. Whisk in the buttermilk. Fold in the remaining flour mixture, all the raisins, and ginger. Pour into the prepared pan. Bake for 30 to 40 minutes until a toothpick inserted into the center comes out clean.

To make the butterscotch sauce: Combine the butter, brown sugar, corn syrup, cream, and whisky in a small saucepan. Whisk while cooking over medium heat until the sugar is melted. Reduce the heat to a simmer and cook undisturbed for 5 more minutes over medium-low heat. Add the vanilla. Cool slightly.

Serves 9

Ode to the Meal

Mandatory reading as the main course is ushered in with bagpipe fanfare is the poet's own "Address to a Haggis" (to be read of course in your best Scots dialect):

Fair fa' your honest, sonsie face,
Great chieftain o' the puddin-race!
Aboon them a' ye tak your place,
Painch, tripe, or thairm:
Weel are ye wordy of a grace
As lang's my arm.

The groaning trencher there ye fill,
Your hurdies like a distant hill,
Your pin wad help to mend a mill
In time o' need,
While thro' your pores the dews distil
Like amber bead.

His knife see rustic Labour dight,
An' cut ye up wi' ready slight,
Trenching your gushing entrails bright,
Like onie ditch;
And then, O what a glorious sight,
Warm-reekin, rich!

Then, horn for horn, they stretch an' strive:
Deil tak the hindmost, on they drive,
Till a' their weel-swall'd kytes belyve
Are bent like drums;
Then auld Guidman, maist like to rive,
`Bethankit!' hums.

Is there that owre his French ragout,
Or olio that wad staw a sow,
Or fricassee wad mak her spew
Wi' perfect sconner,
Looks down wi' sneering, scornfu' view
On sic a dinner?

Poor devil! see him owre his trash,
As feckless as a wither'd rash,
His spindle shank a guid whip-lash,
His nieve a nit;
Thro' bluidy flood or field to dash,
O how unfit!

But mark the Rustic, haggis-fed,
The trembling earth resounds his tread,
Clap in his walie nieve a blade,
He'll make it whissle;
An' legs, an' arms, an' heads will sned
Like taps o' thrissle.
Ye Pow'rs, wha mak mankind your care,
And dish them out their bill o' fare,
Auld Scotland wants nae skinking ware,
That jaups in luggies;
But, if ye wish her gratefu' prayer,
Gie her a Haggis!

23
traveling the spice route
—— *culinary fire for a winter night* ——

❦

MENU
Number in Party: 6 Guests

Red Pepper Harissa and Yogurt with Pita Bread
North African Potato Salad
Lamb Stew with Figs and Apricots
Orange and Rose Water Ice Cream

❦

This is my answer to all the people who claim that winter food is just bland and boring. Winter is the perfect time for slow-cooked braises, and slow-cooked braises are the perfect dishes for the heat and sweet of precious spices like cumin, cayenne, and cinnamon.

red pepper harissa and yogurt with pita bread

Cold winter nights call for a nice warm fire, and harissa delivers. Turn up the temperature by adding in a third chili.

  3 tablespoons olive oil
  4 garlic cloves, minced
  2 green serrano chilies, coarsely chopped with seeds
  1 teaspoon ground cumin
  1 teaspoon ground coriander
  ¼ teaspoon caraway seeds
  One 7-ounce jar oil-packed roasted red peppers, drained
  One 7-ounce container whole milk Greek yogurt
  ⅛ teaspoon salt
  ⅛ teaspoon dried oregano
  ⅛ teaspoon dried thyme
  Olive oil for drizzling
  Pita bread

Heat the olive oil over medium-low heat. Add the garlic and sauté until soft, about 3 minutes. Add the chilies with seeds, cumin, coriander, and caraway, and cook, stirring another minute or two, until blended and chilies start to soften. Transfer to a food processor. Add the red peppers and pulse 5 to 8 times until the mixture is a coarse paste.

In a medium bowl, stir together the yogurt, a pinch of salt, oregano, and thyme. Spread around an 8-inch plate, leaving a large hole in the center. Place the pepper spread in the hole. Drizzle olive oil around the outer edge of the yogurt and over the yogurt and harissa. Serve with wedges of pita bread.

Serves 6

north african potato salad

This easy starter, like the harissa, can be made well in advance of entertaining.

  4 medium Yukon Gold potatoes, about 1 pound, peeled and cut into ¼-inch cubes
  ½ cup finely diced red onion
  1 clove garlic, minced
  ¼ cup packed minced Italian parsley leaves
  ½ cup packed minced cilantro
  ¼ cup olive oil
  2 teaspoons freshly squeezed lemon juice
  ¼ teaspoon salt
  12 oil-cured olives, pitted and halved

Cook the potatoes in boiling salted water until tender but firm, 8 to 10 minutes. Don't overcook so much that they become mushy. Drain the potatoes and run under cold water for a minute or two to speed cooling time. Cool and let dry completely while you prepare the dressing.

In a medium bowl, stir together the onion, garlic, parsley, cilantro, olive oil, lemon juice, and salt.

Transfer the potatoes to a serving bowl. Drizzle with the dressing and toss to coat. Just before serving, stir in the olives. (If the olives sit in finished salad too long, they may discolor the potatoes.)

Serves 6

Harissa

Harissa is a hot red pepper paste made with tomatoes and peppers. It is one of the most important ingredients in North African cooking and can be found in Tunisia and Algeria.

red pepper harissa and yogurt with pita bread

lamb stew with figs and apricots

Everyone should have a simple, make-ahead lamb stew in their winter repetoire. Keep the spices, canned goods, and fruit in stock throughout the season and pick up the lamb for a short notice get-together.

RAS AL-HANOUT SPICE MIXTURE

2 teaspoons ground cumin
2 teaspoons ground coriander
1½ teaspoons salt
1 teaspoon turmeric
1 teaspoon ground ginger
1 teaspoon ground cinnamon
1 teaspoon freshly ground black pepper
½ teaspoon cayenne
¼ teaspoon ground cardamom
2 pounds lamb shoulder, cut into 1-inch cubes

STEW

2 tablespoons olive oil
1 cup finely chopped yellow onion
1 garlic clove, minced
1¼ cups beef broth
One 14-ounce can diced tomatoes, undrained
One 14-ounce can garbanzo beans, drained
Zest of 1 lemon, freshly grated
1 medium rutabaga (about 12 ounces), cut into ½-inch dice
12 dried apricots
12 Turkish or Calimyrna figs, halved

To make the Ras Al-Hanout spice mixture: Mix all the ingredients well. Toss the lamb with the spice mixture until the meat is completely coated and let it sit at room temperature for 20 to 30 minutes.

To make the stew: Heat the oil in a large skillet over medium-high heat. Add the onion and garlic to the skillet and sauté until soft, about 5 minutes. Turn the heat to medium-high and add the lamb and any remaining spice powder in the bowl. Cook for about 5 minutes, turning the meat to brown on all sides. Add the broth and cook, stirring for 1 minute to scrape up any browned bits. Add the tomatoes with can juices, beans, and the lemon zest. Bring to a boil. Reduce the heat and simmer for 40 minutes. Add the rutabaga, apricots, and figs and bring back to a boil. Reduce the heat to a simmer and cook another 40 minutes, until the vegetables are tender and the sauce is slightly thickened.

Serves 6

orange and rose water ice cream

If you have an ice cream maker, just add all the ingredients and process according to the manufacturer's directions.

1 cup whipping cream
6 tablespoons sugar
One 7-ounce container Greek whole milk yogurt (such as Fage)
1 tablespoon rose water
Zest and juice of 2 oranges

In a large mixing bowl, beat the cream to soft peaks. Beat in the sugar, yogurt, and rose water until fully incorporated. Fold in the orange zest and juice. Pour into a freezer container and freeze until set, at least 6 hours.

Serves 6

Lamb Shoulder versus Lamb Leg

A lot of recipes use shoulder and leg interchangeably, which I think is a big mistake, since the fat content is significantly different and affects the texture of the meat as well as the consistency of the cooking sauce. When you're looking for a nice, rare roast, nothing does the trick like a whole lamb leg, and it's surely worth the price per pound. But when you want to stew and braise, I don't really see the point of spending more for a lamb leg when shoulder is what you really want anyway.

The fig is a very secretive fruit.
As you see it standing growing, you feel at once it is symbolic:
And it seems male.
But when you come to know it better, you agree with the Romans, it is female

—D. H. Lawrence, "Figs"

24
food of the gods
everything chocolate

❧

MENU
Number in Party: 6 Guests

Chocolate Beef Stew with Butternut Squash and Amaranth
Triple Chocolate Stuffed Mocha Cupcakes
Hot Chocolate
Sipping Chocolate

❧

Here's your chance to really indulge in a favorite food. It is the perfect way to celebrate Valentine's day, and the food so often associated with it, with a big group. Before launching into this single note menu, learn more about chocolate in "Secrets of the Cold-Weather Pantry," p. 25.

chocolate beef stew with butternut squash and amaranth

Salt

Freshly ground black pepper

2 pounds beef chuck, cut into 1-inch cubes

3 tablespoons vegetable oil

1 medium onion, diced

3 garlic cloves, minced

2 ancho chilies, seeded and snipped into 1-inch pieces

1½ cups beef broth

2 tablespoons cocoa powder

1 pound butternut squash, peeled and cut into ¾-inch cubes

1 tablespoon unsalted butter

1 cup amaranth

1½ cups chicken broth

Generously salt and pepper the beef. Heat 1 tablespoon of the oil over medium-high heat in a large stockpot. Add half the beef and cook until browned on all sides, 4 to 5 minutes. Remove to a large bowl. Add 1 tablespoon oil to the pan and brown the rest of the beef. Add to the beef in the bowl.

Heat the remaining 1 tablespoon oil to the pan over medium heat. Add the onion and garlic and sauté until soft, about 5 minutes. Add the ancho chilies, beef broth, and beef cubes and bring to a boil. Reduce to a simmer, cover, and cook for 1 hour.

Using a slotted spoon, remove the beef to a bowl. (Leave the onions in the sauce.) Puree the sauce in a blender along with cocoa powder. Return the sauce and beef to the stockpot. Add the butternut squash. Cook until the squash is tender, another 30 to 35 minutes. Stir every 10 minutes and remove the lid for the final 5 to 10 minutes of cooking to thicken the sauce slightly.

While the stew finishes cooking, prepare the amaranth. Melt the butter in a medium saucepan. Stir in the amaranth and continue to stir and cook for another 2 minutes. Add in the chicken broth and bring to a boil. Reduce the heat, cover, and simmer for 10 minutes. Remove the lid and continue to cook for another 10 minutes, stirring occasionally. Remove from the heat, cover, and let sit for 10 minutes.

Serve the stew over the amaranth.

Serves 6

Food of the Gods

In 1735 the Swedish botanist Linneas gave the genus name *Theobroma* (or "food of the gods" in Greek) to the tree from which all chocolaty goodness comes. Why this name? Perhaps Linneas had heard of the cacao tree's mythical origins: a gift to humanity from the garden paradise of the god Quetzalcoatl. Or maybe he just had a sweet tooth.

triple chocolate stuffed mocha cupcakes

These are intense little morsels for food lovers who don't like to be distracted from their chocolate by milk and sugar. As an alternative to paper cupcake liners, my number one recipe tester, Lissa McBurney, suggests buttering the muffin cups and dusting with cocoa powder, rather than flour, to get an extra chocolate kick and avoid unsightly white specs.

CUPCAKES
¾ cup boiling water
2 tablespoons instant espresso powder
1½ cups flour
⅓ cup cocoa powder
½ teaspoon baking powder
½ teaspoon baking soda
½ teaspoon salt
½ cup (1 stick) unsalted butter, softened
¾ cup sugar
2 large eggs
½ teaspoon vanilla

CHOCOLATE GANACHE
10 ounces bittersweet or semisweet chocolate
1½ cups whipping cream
⅓ cup cocoa nibs (optional)

To make the cupcakes: In a small bowl, pour the boiling water over the espresso and stir until dissolved. Cool to room temperature.

Line a 12-cup muffin tin with paper cupcake liners. Preheat the oven to 350°F.

In a medium mixing bowl, sift together the flour, cocoa powder, baking powder, baking soda, and salt. Set aside.

In the bowl of an electric mixer, combine the butter and sugar. Beat until light and fluffy, 1 to 2 minutes. Add the eggs, one at a time, blending well after each addition. Mix in the vanilla and beat for an additional minute. Scrape down the sides of the bowl. Add ½ of the flour mixture and beat for another minute. With mixer running, slowly pour in ½ of the espresso mixture and mix until completely blended; repeat. Scrape down the sides of the bowl and beat briefly to ensure everything is homogenized.

Using a ⅓-cup measure, scoop the batter into the muffin cups, dividing equally. Bake 18 to 23 minutes until a cake tester comes out clean. Cool for 10 minutes in the pan. If necessary, run a thin-blade knife around the edges to release the cupcakes from the pan; cool completely on a wire rack.

To make the ganache: While the cupcakes cool, coarsely chop the chocolate and place in a medium mixing bowl. Heat the whipping cream in a small saucepan until just beginning to bubble around the edges. Whisk the warm cream into the chopped chocolate and continue whisking until completely smooth. Cool slowly at room temperature, whisking occasionally to maintain smoothness. (Don't be tempted to rush by putting the ganache in the fridge or it will harden around the outer edges and you'll have to reheat it again to whisk the chocolate lumps back in. If you absolutely can't resist the temptation or the clock is working against you and you must resort to the fridge, just make sure to stir every 5 minutes or so.) When it reaches a spreading consistency, transfer ½ of the ganache to the bowl of an electric mixer. With the whisk attachment, whip until light and fluffy.

To fill the cupcakes, transfer the whipped ganache to a pastry bag with a plain or star metal tip. Plunge the tip into the top of each cupcake and squeeze in the filling gently. After filling, frost the cupcakes with the unwhipped ganache, making sure to cover the hole in the top from the pastry bag. If desired, sprinkle with the cocoa nibs.

Makes 12 cupcakes

Nibbly Bits

Cocoa nibs are a nifty benefit of the chocolate-making process. Cocoa seeds are fermented, roasted, and separated from the husks into cocoa nibs. Lots of creative minds have been introducing them to us as a food in their own right. But if you can't find them, you can substitute shaved chocolate for a rather different taste on top of your cupcake.

triple chocolate stuffed mocha cupcakes

Beyond Candy Bars

Eat Feed guest Martin Christy who hosts www.seventypercent.com, gives his definition of high-quality chocolate

· high percentage of cocoa solids, at least 62% or more (it's harder to hide low-quality beans at higher percentages)

· no artificial additives, no vegetable fat

· real vanilla rather than vanilla flavoring

· some consideration of the bean source: if the chocolate maker has a connection to the source, they've been to the plantation and know something of the process, what Martin calls "bean to bar" chocolate

hot chocolate

There are countless ways to concoct this number one winter warmer. This is versatile for many different palates and makes quick work of the preparation by using a blender.

> 4 cups whole milk
> ½ cup cream
> 2 tablespoons sugar
> 6 ounces bittersweet chocolate, coarsely chopped

Combine the milk, cream, and sugar in a medium saucepan and bring to a simmer. Place the chocolate in a blender. Pour the hot milk mixture over the chocolate and blend until smooth and frothy. You can also whisk the chocolate into the milk mixture on the stovetop, but you won't get the same frothy texture.

Serves 6

sipping chocolate

When drinking chocolate first made its way from the religious ceremonies of the Aztecs to the courts of Renaissance Spain, it was indeed a drink fit for kings. This ultrarich version is meant to be enjoyed slowly, sip by sip, like a fine whisky. Counter the richness with a chaser of ice-cold spring water, as hot chocolate is often served in Austrian cafés. Alternatively, give your drink a bit of Mexican spice by blending in a pinch of cinnamon and ground chiles, such as a smoky ancho or bright arbol.

- 1¼ cups whole milk
- ½ cup cream
- 5 teaspoons sugar
- 5 ounces bittersweet chocolate, coarsely chopped

Follow preparation for Hot Chocolate but serve in espresso or other small (3- to 4-ounce) cups.

Serves 6

The Evolution of Cocoa Beans

criollo: considered the descendant of the Aztec variety, very rare (some dispute that there is even a real criollo); represents about 1% of the chocolate in production

forestero: most of it originates from wild varieties; usually doesn't have the same flavor quality as criollo ; accounts for 80% of world's cocoa today

trinitario: mixture of the two, most of the fine chocolate is made from these beans today

Sourcing a Good Bean

Even though 70% of the world's chocolate comes from Africa and 100% of the African beans are forestero, there are some other places to find much better chocolate:

· Venezuela
· Papua New Guinea
· Indonesia
· Madagascar

25
fireside chat

——— a cozy dinner for two ———

MENU

Number in Party: 2 Guests

Oysters and Champagne
Pomegranate Kulfi
Cinnamon Cookies

Ou can indulge in a super easy and elegant Valentine's menu. It can double as a cozy New Year's Eve celebration or can be stretched to accommodate more, depending on just how many oysters and how much champagne you want to stock.

oysters and champagne

This quintessential romantic dinner needs no embellishments. Just choose the right bubbly and the right bivalve.

    16 fresh oysters, top shells removed
    1 lemon, cut into wedges
    1 bottle of champagne

The recipe is easy. Present the oysters on ice. Give them a fresh squeeze of lemon if you like or not if you don't. Follow with a sip of champagne.

Serves 2

Champagne Sizes

· **split:** ½ bottle

· **magnum:** 2 bottles

· **jeroboam:** 4 bottles

Pomegranates and Love Apples

Pomegranates are right at the top of the list of sexy fruits. Containing many seeds and the color of life-giving blood, these fruits have long been associated with fertility and desire.

Why, then the world's mine oyster,
Which I with sword will open.

—William Shakespeare

A cause may be inconvenient, but it's magnificent. It's like champagne or high heels, and one must be prepared to suffer for it.

—Arnold Bennett

pomegranate kulfi

Enjoy this frozen wintry homage to the love apple; in a pinch, you can just forgo the ice cream and share a fresh pomegranate.

    2 cups (16 ounces) pure pomegranate juice
    1 cup whipping cream
    One 14-ounce can sweetened condensed milk
    Seeds from ½ pomegranate

Pour the juice into a medium saucepan. Bring to a boil. Boil until reduced to 1 cup, about 20 minutes. Set aside to cool slightly and then refrigerate until slightly chilled.

In a large mixing bowl, beat the cream to soft peaks. With the motor running, slowly pour in the sweetened condensed milk. Beat on high for another minute until completely incorporated. With the motor running, slowly pour in the pomegranate juice. Whip another minute until completely incorporated. Fold in the pomegranate seeds. Pour into a freezer container and freeze until set, at least 6 hours. Serve sprinkled with pomegranate seeds.

Serves 6

oysters and champagne

cinnamon cookies

These simple little cookies seemed to open up everyone's imagination in the test kitchen. Lissa McBurney adds, "I can see these with fruit and cheese at the end of a meal or as ice cream sandwiches, or just with tea or coffee." And Sarah Marx Feldman suggests using larger-granule decorating sugar and adding these to a holiday cookie tray earlier in the season.

1½ cups flour
2 tablespoons cornstarch
1½ teaspoons ground cinnamon
¼ teaspoon baking powder
¼ teaspoon salt
½ cup (1 stick) unsalted butter, softened
½ cup sugar, plus extra for topping
1 egg
Nonstick cooking spray

Preheat the oven to 375°F. Line a heavy baking sheet with parchment paper.

In a medium mixing bowl, combine the flour, cornstarch, cinnamon, baking powder, and salt. Set aside.

In the bowl of an electric mixer, cream together the butter and sugar until light and fluffy, about 2 minutes. Add the egg and beat until incorporated. Add the flour mixture, and mix until just moistened but not yet holding together. "Knead" the dough by hand until it comes together in a ball. Do not overmix. Roll the dough into 1- to 1¼-inch balls and place on the prepared baking sheet. (I use a stainless steel scoop for this. See "The Host's Toolbox," p.45). Lightly coat the bottom of a 3-inch-diameter glass with nonstick spray, dip into a small bowl of sugar, and press down on the tops of the cookies to flatten to ⅛ inch thick. You'll need to dip the glass in sugar after each cookie and probably respray the glass after every fourth or fifth cookie as well. Bake for 12 to14 minutes, until edges are just beginning to brown.

Makes 38 cookies

The Smell of Desire

One Valentine's Day on *Eat Feed*, we took a look at the relationship between taste and smell and between smell and sexual turn-ons. My guest, Alan R. Hirsh, director of the Smell and Taste Treatment and Research Foundation in Chicago, discovered that the most arousing scent for men is a mixture of pumpkin pie and lavender. Hence the Cinnamon Cookies here. You'll just have to spritz the room to blend in the lavender. And for women? The major turn-on was the smell of Good and Plenty candy with cucumber (sorry, no recipe included).

I get no kick from champagne,
Mere alcohol doesn't thrill me at all,
So tell me why should it be true
That I get a kick out of you?
—Cole Porter

I do not weep at the world—
I am too busy
sharpening my oyster knife.
—Zora Neale Hurston

26
breakfast in bed
— fresh-squeezed for your main squeeze —

❦

MENU

Number in Party: 2 Guests

A Good Morning Squeeze

Coddled Eggs

Let's Make a Date Muffins

❦

This is the natural meal to follow the "Fireside Chat: A Cozy Dinner for Two," should evening melt into morning. Don't put all your coddled eggs in one basket, but it doesn't hurt to be prepared in advance. No matter who you're cooking for and when, I do hope this menu puts a little elegance back in the first meal of the day and spawns a revival of the word *breakfast* as a verb.

a good morning squeeze

This drinkable equivalent of a little huggin' in the a.m. makes you feel all warm and healthy.

> 2 juice oranges
> 2 blood oranges
> 2 tangerines
> Splash of champagne (optional)

Using a citrus reamer or press juicer, collect the juices of all the fruit. Divide between 2 glasses. Add a splash of champagne if you like (even if there's a slightly flat sip left over in the bottle from the night before).

Serves 2

coddled eggs

This is my absolutely favorite way to eat an egg and not just because I love the name.

> Unsalted butter
> 2 large eggs
> 2 tablespoons whipping cream
> Salt

Generously butter 2 small ramekins, heatproof coffee cups, or egg coddlers. Fill a medium saucepan or deep skillet with enough water to come a third up the side of the cups. Bring the water to a gentle boil over medium heat. Crack an egg into each buttered ramekin and place ramekins in the water. Cover the pot and cook for 2 minutes, just until the whites begin to set around the edges. Gently pour 1 tablespoon of whipping cream over each egg. Replace the cover and cook for another 2 to 3 minutes until the eggs are set but the yolk is still soft. Season with a sprinkling of salt.

Serves 2

Many Ways to Coddle

· to be overly protective
· to cook gently or stew
· to fondle or caress (as in cuddle)

A Very Versatile Egg

Should you be feeling a bit too tough for coddling, try any of the many ways this elemental ingredient loves to be treated:

· hard boiled
· soft boiled
· scrambled
· fried
· poached
· shirred

Never in her life before had she beheld half such variety on a breakfast-table.

—Jane Austen

Why, sometimes I've believed as many as six impossible things before breakfast.

—Lewis Carroll

let's make a date muffins

These muffins are inspired by a favorite dessert: sticky toffee pudding. But they are revamped for breakfast and renamed with hope that as you present your beloved with a plate of these, you'll be invited to open your Filofax and check on next Friday night.

STREUSEL TOPPING

2 tablespoons flour
3 tablespoons rolled oats
¼ cup packed brown sugar
½ cup chopped toasted pecans
2 tablespoons unsalted butter, softened

MUFFINS

9 ounces whole Medjool dates, pitted
   (about 14 dates or 2 cups)
¾ cup boiling water
2 cups flour
2½ teaspoons baking powder
½ teaspoon salt
4 tablespoons (½ stick) unsalted butter, softened
¾ cup packed dark brown sugar
2 eggs
1 teaspoon vanilla

To make the streusel topping: In a medium bowl, stir together the flour, oats, brown sugar, and pecans. Using a fork, cut in butter until well combined and mixture begins to hold together a bit. Set aside.

To make the muffins: Preheat the oven to 375°F. Butter a 12-cup muffin tin. Place the dates in a shallow bowl (in a single layer if possible), pour the boiling water over them, and soak for 15 minutes. Transfer the dates and soaking liquid to a food processor and puree until almost smooth but a few pea-sized fruit pieces remain. Set aside to cool slightly.

In a medium bowl, combine the flour, baking powder, and salt. Set aside.

In the bowl of an electric mixer, cream together the butter and brown sugar. With the motor running, mix in the eggs, one at a time. Add the vanilla. Add half of the flour mixture and mix until moistened. Follow with the date puree, and when thoroughly combined, mix in remainder of the flour mixture. Scrape down the sides and give a final stir with a spatula to make sure all ingredients are thoroughly combined. Divide the batter among the muffin cups. Top with the streusel and press down gently to adhere. Bake for 20 to 25 minutes.

Makes 12 muffins

A Date for Your Date

Regardless of your companion's age and sophistication, it's worth noting that the date in your muffin is one of the oldest cultivated fruits.

....

All happiness depends on
a leisurely breakfast.

—**John Gunther**

....

a good morning squeeze & coddled eggs & let's make a date muffins

27
party hearty
soups, stews, and microbrews

❧

MENU
Number in Party: 8 to 10 Guests

Whitefish Chowder
Rustic Winter Stew
Quick and Easy Italian Soup
Ancho Chili Soup with Sweet Potatoes and Chorizo
Chocolate Chip Steamed Pudding

❧

Cold weather means hot soups and hearty stews. And what better way to celebrate the season than with lots of both of them. This party is inspired by a show *Eat Feed* did on Soups, Stews, and Homebrews, but I thought you might like a short-cut, so it's been rebaptized.

whitefish chowder

This is one of those recipes that just sort of fell into my stockpot. In a rather *Shining* moment, my husband and I checked into a remote Wisconsin resort in the completely off season to read, write, and research in absolute quiet. We were the only guests. Just one of the many differences is that I managed to drag Daniel out each day to gather local foods, from Bea's frozen cherry pies to Charlie's Smokehouse whitefish. The best part was visiting the fish market, where you had to come after 2 when the catch was in but before 4 when it was all gone.

- ¼ pound (3 to 4 strips) applewood-smoked bacon
- 1 medium onion, chopped (about 1 cup)
- 1 pound (4 to 5 medium) Yukon Gold potatoes, cut into ½-inch cubes
- 4 cups (32 ounces) chicken broth
- 1 pound fresh Great Lakes whitefish fillets (or other white-fleshed fish such as cod, halibut, or turbot), cut into 1-inch pieces
- 1½ cups frozen corn kernels
- 1 cup whole milk
- Salt
- Freshly ground black pepper

Using scissors, snip lengths of the bacon into ¼-inch-wide pieces and place in a large stockpot or Dutch oven. Cook over medium heat for 5 minutes until fat renders. Pour off all but 1 tablespoon bacon grease. Add the onion and cook, stirring frequently, until soft, about 5 minutes more. Add the potatoes and chicken broth. Turn the heat to high. Bring to a boil, reduce heat to medium, and cook (covered) until potatoes are tender, about 10 minutes.

Remove the soup from the stove. Puree 2 to 3 cups of the soup in a blender—in batches if necessary. Return the pureed soup to the pot. Bring to a simmer over high heat. Reduce to a simmer and add the fish, frozen corn, and milk. Cook over medium heat for an additional 5 to 7 minutes, until the fish is cooked through. Season with a bit of salt and lots of freshly ground black pepper.

Serves 4 as a main course; 8 for tasting

Perfect Pairings

With fish chowder, consider a pale ale or Scottish ale. If you can get your hands on one from the Midwest (like New Glarus or Bell's), it would be great to match with the native ingredient of Great Lakes whitefish. A Bohemian-style pilsner is best with the Rustic Winter Stew, not just because they share geographical roots but also because it makes a great pairing for the difficult match of the sauerkraut. Naturally, pair a dark Mexican beer or even a German doppelbock with the Ancho Chili Soup. Both stand up to the spiciness of the ancho chilies. If you want a beer for dessert, consider a cream stout or a Belgian fruit-flavored lambic.

Bringing Home the Bacon

Bacon smoked with applewood is the absolute best for the Whitefish Chowder, and while lots of companies are springing up with their own version of applewood-smoked bacon, I still go with the original Wisconsin Nueske's because they have made applewood smoking an art and a science (see www.nueskes.com).

Greatest Thing about This Party

Everything can be made in advance and warmed up just before guests arrive.

Second Greatest Thing about This Party

You make the soup; everyone else brings the microbrews.

rustic winter stew

rustic winter stew

In the depths of winter, sauerkraut is the best "in season" vegetable going, and pairing it with pork is an Eastern European classic. Even better, in this dish, the richness of sour cream and the spark of paprika provide the perfect foil to the tang of sauerkraut. This recipe has been tweaked and transformed over the past decade from a dish in Molly O'Neill's *New York Times* magazine column. I don't know whether it's the cold Chicago winters or the grad student budget that kept bringing more tomato and sauerkraut into the mix.

1 tablespoon unsalted butter

1 medium onion, cut in half and thinly sliced

2½ pounds pork shoulder, trimmed of excess fat and cut into 1-inch cubes

3 tablespoons flour

1 tablespoon plus 1 teaspoon paprika

1 cup beef broth

1½ cups chicken broth

¾ teaspoon caraway seeds

½ cup tomato sauce

3 cups drained sauerkraut (do not rinse)

8 ounces sour cream

Salt

Freshly ground black pepper

Heat the butter in large stockpot or Dutch oven over medium heat. Add the onion and sauté until soft, about 5 minutes. Turn the heat to medium-high. Add the pork and stir to brown on all sides, about 6 minutes total. Sprinkle 2 tablespoons of the flour and all the paprika over pork and stir until coated, cooking for another minute. Slowly add the beef broth while stirring. Bring to a boil. Cover and simmer for 50 minutes.

Add the chicken broth, caraway seeds, tomato sauce, and sauerkraut. Bring back to a simmer. Cover and cook for an additional 45 minutes.

In a small bowl, whisk together the sour cream and remaining 1 tablespoon flour. Slowly stir into the stew. Simmer, uncovered, for an additional 5 minutes, until stew is the desired thickness. Add salt and pepper to taste.

Serves 6 as a main course; 10 for tasting

History of the World in One Glass

Until a few hundred years ago, making beer was usually the provenance of women. Medieval women brewed at home for their families and alewives headed cottage industries for neighborhoods and villages. The sixteenth-century poet John Skelton immortalized the alewife Elynour Rumming in doggerel verse:

She breweth noppy ale
And maketh thereof port sale
To travelers, to tinkers,
To sweaters, to swinkers
And all good ale drinkers

Save the World in One Glass

Chris O'Brien, otherwise known as the Beer Activist, has made it his mission to get others to "Drink Beer. Save the World" (see www.beeractivist.com).

I love no roast but a brown toast,
Or a crab laid in the fire.
A little bread shall do me stead,
Much bread I not desire.
Nor frost nor snow, nor wind, I trow
Can hurt me if I would,
When I am so wrapped, and
thoroughly lapped
Of jolly good ale and old.
—"Back and Side Go Bare, Go Bare,"
an early English drinking song

quick and easy italian soup

This is the little black dress of the winter cooking world. Everybody has that simple little number to throw on without much fuss, and this one not only tastes great but is packed with vitamins from kale and tomatoes. Even better, this is the easiest one in the bunch. You could do it with one spatula tied behind your back.

- 1 large bunch kale (9 to 12 ounces)
- 2 tablespoons olive oil
- 4 garlic cloves, minced
- 5 cups (40 ounces) chicken broth
- One 14-ounce can tomatoes with Italian herbs, undrained
- 1 pound spicy Italian sausage, cut into ¼-inch slices
- One 14-ounce can cannellini beans, drained
- Salt
- Freshly ground black pepper
- Red pepper flakes

Remove the thick spines from kale, discard, and coarsely chop the leaves into 2-inch pieces. In a large saucepan, heat the olive oil over medium-low heat. Sauté the garlic for about 2 minutes, until fragrant. Add the broth and tomatoes and bring to a boil over high heat. Add the sausage and kale, reduce to a simmer, and cook for 8 to 10 more minutes until meat is cooked through and vegetables are tender. Add beans and heat through. Season to taste with salt, black pepper, and red pepper flakes.

Serves 4 as a main course; 8 for tasting

A Loaf of Bread, a Bowl of Soup, and Thou

A good winter soup needs a good hearty bread. Offer a selection to match each recipe. A strong, dark bread like pumpernickel is perfect for the Rustic Winter Stew inspired by the flavors of Eastern Europe. A crusty white loaf is best for the Whitefish Chowder, and trust me on this one, even one with a bit of dried fruit, like a raisin bread, pairs perfectly with the fish. Take your choice of a big soft Cuban roll or crispy tortilla chips for the Ancho Chili Soup.

ancho chili soup with sweet potatoes and chorizo

Since the city has one of the largest Mexican populations in the nation, I think it's the Chicagoan in me that thinks the deepest nights of winter are perfect for Mexican food.

- 2 tablespoons olive oil
- 8 garlic cloves, minced
- 1 tablespoon ancho chili powder
- 5 cups (40 ounces) chicken broth
- 1 pound sweet potatoes, peeled and cut into ¼-inch cubes
- 2 fresh Mexican chorizo sausages (about ⅔ pound), sliced ¼ inch thick
- One 15.5-ounce can hominy
- Salt
- Freshly ground black pepper

Heat the oil in a large saucepan over low heat. Add the garlic and sauté until beginning to soften, about 3 minutes. Stir the ancho chili powder thoroughly into the garlic. Pour in the chicken broth, turn heat to high, and bring to a gentle boil. Add the sweet potatoes and cook until almost tender, 5 to 6 minutes. Add the sausages and hominy and simmer about 4 minutes, until the sausage is cooked through. Season to taste with salt and pepper.

Serves 4 as a main course; 8 for tasting

Spice It Up

Ancho chili powder is a real gem of an ingredient. It provides a spiciness that is more complex and way smokier than mere common cayenne. If you don't have easy access to a good supply of spices, order ancho chili powder from Penzey's Spices (www.penzeys.com).

chocolate chip steamed pudding

This is like a giant, soft, hot chocolate chip cookie. And because of the cooking techniques, you can sit and enjoy your company while the dessert stays warm and gooey up until the moment of serving. I actually developed it when I moved into my first house and the oven was broken and I needed a way to still get in my fall baking season, but it's been a favorite ever since, whether the oven is working or not.

2 cups flour
3 teaspoons baking powder
1 teaspoon salt
10 tablespoons unsalted butter, softened
½ cup packed brown sugar
½ cup granulated sugar
2 large eggs
1 teaspoon vanilla
¼ cup milk
¾ cup chocolate chips

In a medium bowl, combine the flour, baking powder, and salt. Set aside. In the bowl of an electric mixer, cream the butter and sugars. Beat in the eggs and vanilla. Mix in ½ the flour mixture. Mix in 2 tablespoons of the milk. Follow with the remaining flour mixture and then the remaining 2 tablespoons milk. Stir in the chocolate chips. Spoon into a 6-cup buttered mold. Steam for 2 hours (see "Steaming a Pudding," right.)

Serves 8

Steaming a Pudding

One of the reasons steamed puddings are hard for Americans to understand is that the British just don't have the same kind of precise directions we are used to in our desserts. The steaming method allows for culinary negligence and for you to pay attention to other things. It also allows you to use the oven for the main course while still delivering a hot dessert to the table. In its very name, steaming means that the pudding doesn't burn or dry out as it would in the oven. To steam a pudding, you need to have a large stockpot that will hold the pudding basin and a steaming rack. I place one of those metal foldable steaming baskets in the bottom of my largest soup pot and then place the pudding mold, which has its own lid, on top. Then pour boiling water halfway up the side of the pudding mold and place the lid on the stockpot. Keep the water at a simmer for the length of the cooking time. Without a pudding mold, use a pudding bowl. Butter a large piece of aluminum foil and fold to make a pleat. Cover pudding bowl and use kitchen twine to tie around the outer rim. Steam just as you would with a pudding mold.

Pudding Bowls

Choose the right one from "The Host's Toolbox" (p. 46), or get yourself a fancy pudding mold. Sure as anything, every Christmas, cookware stores trot out gorgeous and outrageously overpriced steamed pudding molds. And then just as surely they massively discount them post-holiday. I recently picked up a new nonstick one for 75% off and when another customer saw my excitement, she quizzically asked, "Are you going to actually cook with it?" Hence my crusade to get folks using and enjoying this fun and easy cooking method rather than just making such a great tool a useless gift that never sees the kitchen.

28

après ski at the swiss chalet

——— alpine tastes and traditions ———

***

MENU
Number in Party: 6 Guests

Onion Rösti

Cheese Fondue

S'mores

***

Think of all the best things you love about winter and you'll find that they are rolled into this party. This is a wonderfully quick and easy dinner you can put together on the spur of the moment to create an intimate get-together for six.

onion rösti

Rösti is just a fancy word for a potato pancake that is the ultimate Swiss accompaniment to fondue.

> 1½ pounds waxy potatoes (about 4–5 medium)
> ½ teaspoon salt
> ¼ teaspoon freshly ground black pepper
> 3 tablespoons unsalted butter
> 1 medium yellow onion, cut in half and thinly sliced (about ¾ cup)

Bring a large saucepan of salted water to a simmer. Add the whole, unpeeled potatoes and cook until tender, 15 to 20 minutes, depending on the size of the potatoes. Drain potatoes and rinse with cold water. Set aside until cool enough to handle. Peel and grate on a box grater or in a food processor with the grating attachment. Toss with salt and pepper. Set aside.

Melt 1 tablespoon butter in medium skillet over medium heat. Add the onion; sauté until soft, about 5 minutes. Set aside.

Over medium heat, melt 1 tablespoon of the butter in a 12-inch nonstick skillet. Scatter ½ of the grated potatoes across bottom of the pan. Evenly distribute all the onions on top. Add a final layer of the remaining potatoes. Press down with the spatula to compact the pancake and cook for 10 to 15 minutes.

Slide the pancake onto a plate. Invert onto a second plate. Melt remaining 1 tablespoon of butter in the same skillet. Slide the pancake back into pan, cooked side up. Cook for another 10 to 15 minutes. Slide the Rösti onto a serving platter. Cut into pie wedges to serve.

Serves 6

In a Pickle

Alas, when fondue is in season, nothing else really is. Yet you feel you have to look to your guests' health and offer something beyond a giant bowl of melted cheese. That's where people who plan ahead come in. Back when bright green asparagus spears and artichokes were in season, someone had the forethought to pickle and can them. So before you put your fondue on the table, let guests soak up some vitamins in an assortment of dilled green beans, cornichons, hearts of palm, pickled asparagus, and herbed artichoke hearts.

cheese fondue

How can you possibly introduce one of the best-known comfort foods? I think a simple "yum" will suffice.

> 2 day-old French baguettes
> 14 ounces Emmental cheese
> 14 ounces Gruyère cheese
> 2 tablespoons plus 2 teaspoons flour
> 1 garlic clove
> 2⅓ cups white wine
> 1 tablespoon Kirschwasser
> Freshly grated nutmeg

Cut the baguettes into ½- to 1-inch cubes. Place in a serving bowl. (If your baguettes are fresh and soft, cut into cubes well in advance and leave to dry a bit on a cookie sheet.)

Grate the cheeses into large mixing bowl. Sprinkle with the flour and stir to coat evenly.

Peel the garlic clove and cut in half. Thoroughly wipe the inside surface of a fondue pot with one-half. Repeat in a medium saucepan with the other half. Discard the garlic halves.

Pour the wine into the same saucepan and heat over medium heat, just until wine begins to simmer. Whisk in the cheese, ½ cup at a time, stirring until melted and smooth after each addition. After the final addition, remove the fondue from the heat. Stir in the Kirschwasser and a large pinch of nutmeg or to taste. Pour into the prepared fondue pot and set over a lit Sterno (canned fuel). Serve with large bowl of bread cubes and hand each guest a fondue fork.

Serves 6

In a Word

Fondu is the French word for "melted," whether it's butter for your lobster or molten lead. As cheese, fondue also comes in many varieties, from beer and cheddar to the Italian version with Fontina. But classic Swiss fondue needs only great aged cheese, white wine, and a tipple of Kirsch to make it perfect.

Cheesy Stories

Custom dictates that when your bread falls off your fork mid-dip, you owe a kiss to your dining companion.

The Right Fork

Just like fondue, fondue forks come in different styles. Two-pronged forks are for meat and three-pronged forks are for cheese.

A Watched Pot

Unfortunately most fondue pots readily available are totally useless. They are either too small or made from the wrong material. If you're going to make a habit of fondue, and I strongly suggest you do, hunt down a proper pot that would do Heidi proud. A fondue pot for meat fondue is often metal and has deep, sloped sides. But a cheese fondue pot is another matter altogether. It's made of pottery, is relatively shallow, and has a big wide mouth. Mine is so kitschy that it's really a mantle piece with cows painted on the bowl and metal cows riveted to the stand. It's very dairy-y, just the way I like it. For a really good fondue pot, kitschy or not, head to Roberts European Imports at www.shopswiss.com.

Why Everybody Loves a Fondue Party

· Taking less than 15 minutes to make, it's the fastest stylish meal you can set before your guests.

· Cheese! Cheese! Cheese!

· It gives you an excuse to pull out your lederhosen and show off your yodeling skills.

· It gives you an excuse to invest in a really great piece of cooking equipment.

· You know you really like the people you're having dinner with since there's no other explanation for why their forks are in your food.

· After reading the rest of this chapter, you can regale your guests with all your worldly fondue knowledge.

A Cherry of a Drink

Kirschwasser is a traditional final shot for fondue. As you shop for this clear German brandy, or *eau de vie*, be sure not to substitute any other kind of syrupy sweet cherry brandy.

s'mores

Keep the Sterno burning and let guests make their own s'mores. I'm not giving you amounts because you should feel free to serve as many or as few as you like.

> Marshmallows
> Graham crackers
> Your favorite chocolate bar

Place a square of chocolate on 1 graham cracker. Spear a marshmallow on roasting fork. Hold above lighted Sterno at a reasonable distance. Try not to set the marshmallows on fire. Turn as needed to brown evenly. Place the browned marshmallow on top of the chocolate, place another graham cracker on top of the marshmallow, squeeze together as you pull out the roasting fork. Eat.

Ganache Panache

Smarten up your s'mores with some really fine chocolate. Great ideas for the adventurous gourmand: Chocolat Bonnat Ceylan, Valrhona Palmira, or Michel Cluizel Haciendas "Los Anacones."

s'mores

29
afternoon tea
—— *late winter warmer* ——

❧❦❧

MENU
Number in Party: 4 to 8 Guests

Meyer Lemon Tea Bread
Scones with Jam and Clotted Cream
Walnut, Fig, and Goat Cheese Sandwiches

❧❦❧

Americans have always been emotionally attached to English tea. Ever since we drowned a large shipment of it in the Boston Harbor, nothing has seemed more quintessentially English to us revolutionaries. Nowadays we're much more prepared to accept it. In fact, we go far beyond mere capitulation to celebration. A new interest in tea is brewing, an interest that rivals the addiction to the fast-foodization of the other caffeine quaff by romanticizing the formalities surrounding this ritual drink. I'm a firm believer that tea is the easiest possible way to entertain and I'm always amazed how impressed guests become over simple finger sandwiches. Because I'm so much more productive in cold weather, I find that I work that much harder in winter and thus a little afternoon break is just the ticket to break up the day.

meyer lemon tea bread

2 cups flour
1 teaspoon baking powder
½ teaspoon baking soda
½ teaspoon salt
½ cup freshly squeezed Meyer lemon juice
   (4 to 5 lemons)
½ cup buttermilk
4 tablespoons (½ stick) unsalted butter, melted
1 cup sugar
Zest of 2 Meyer lemons
1 large egg

Preheat the oven to 350°F. Butter a 9 x 5-inch loaf pan.

In a medium bowl, combine the flour, baking powder, baking soda, and salt. In a small bowl, stir together lemon juice and buttermilk.

In an electric mixer, cream together the butter, sugar, and lemon zest. Beat in the egg. Add half of the lemon juice mixture, then half of flour mixture, followed by the remaining lemon juice, and then the remaining flour. Pour the batter into the prepared pan. Bake for 50 minutes, until a toothpick inserted in center comes out clean. Cool 10 minutes before removing from the pan. Cool completely before serving. This can be made 1 day ahead.

Makes 1 loaf

A Late Bloomer

Tea, and for that matter any form of caffeine, never coursed through a British bloodline until Shakespeare was long dead and the Puritans had started their migration west. Then, as trade expanded both east and west, along with coffee houses and chocolate houses, tea houses sprang up in London and other English cities in the mid-seventeenth century, creating a sober alternative to alehouses and taverns. By the eighteenth century, a light afternoon meal had developed among the wealthy to tide them over until dinner, and there are as many myths and stories to account for how this happened as there are varieties of tea leaves. By the nineteenth century, though, tea had become a firmly entrenched "event."

scones with jam and clotted cream

2 cups flour
3 tablespoons sugar
2½ teaspoons baking powder
⅛ teaspoon salt
6 tablespoons cold butter
⅔ cup milk
Jam (preferably strawberry)
Clotted cream

Preheat the oven to 425°F. Line a heavy baking sheet with parchment paper.

In a large bowl, combine the flour, sugar, baking powder, and salt. Cut the butter into the flour until pea-sized. Stir in the milk until the dough holds together. On a floured surface, roll to ¾ inch thick. Cut into 12 to14 2½-inch rounds. Transfer to the prepared baking sheet. Bake for 10 minutes. Cool slightly. Serve warm with jam and clotted cream.

Makes 12 to 14 scones

The Perfect Biscuit

To round out the menu, feel free to stock the tea tray with store-bought British biscuits available in the United States. You'll find them in gourmet shops, British themed stores, and import chains like World Market.

· McVitties Digestive Biscuits: Plain, Milk Chocolate, Dark Chocolate, Caramel

· Walkers Shortbread

· Border Biscuits

Cream of the Crop

Clotted cream is traditionally made in Devon and Cornwall. This is a seriously decadent food, weighing in at 55% butterfat—which also explains its yellowish tinge. It has a texture somewhere between soft butter and whipping cream. You can buy it at Whole Foods, specialty grocery stores, British markets, World Market, and many other places.

meyer lemon tea bread & scones with jam and clotted cream & walnut, fig, and goat cheese sandwiches

walnut, fig, and goat cheese sandwiches

¾ cup walnuts

8 dried Turkish or Calimyrna figs, cut in half

½ cup water

4 ounces chèvre (goat cheese), completely softened

2 tablespoons whipping cream

10 slices soft white bread

Preheat the oven to 350°F. Spread the walnuts on a cookie sheet. Bake for 10 minutes, turning halfway through. Cool on a baking sheet. Transfer to a food processor and coarsely chop.

Combine the figs and water in a small saucepan. Bring to a boil over high heat. Reduce to a simmer, cover, and cook for 10 minutes. Remove the lid, turn the heat to medium high, and boil until only a tablespoon of thick syrup remains, 2 to 3 minutes. Cool slightly. Add to the walnuts in the food processor. Process until you get a spreadable paste.

In a small bowl, stir together the chèvre and whipping cream.

Spread the cheese on 5 bread slices. Spread the walnut-fig paste on the remaining 5 bread slices. Put together to make sandwiches. Cut off the crusts. Cut the sandwiches in half for "fingers" or into fourths for squares.

Makes 10 to 20 sandwiches

A hardened and shameless tea-drinker, who has for twenty years diluted his meals with only the infusion of this fascinating plant; whose kettle has scarcely time to cool; who with tea amuses the evening, with tea solaces the midnight, and with tea welcomes the morning.

—Samuel Johnson

Choice British Cheeses to Round Out the Menu

· Caerphilly

· Cornish Yarg

· Double Gloucester

· Lincolnshire Poacher

· Red Leicester

· Stilton

More Finger Sandwich Flavor Ideas

· Watercress and cream cheese

· Smoked salmon and cream cheese

· Smoked trout and apple

· Prawns and mayo

· Egg salad

High Tea and Low Tea

When we refer to tea as an occasion, rather than a drink, we are really talking about two different things: afternoon tea and high tea. Unfortunately, most Americans have over the years mistakenly interpreted "high" as the indicator of the more formal event. On the contrary, high tea is more like dinner, a sort of just-off-work, early meal of energy-boosting tea and pasties, meat pies, cold cuts, cheeses, and the like. That's why the word persists in this catch-all meaning among the working classes up north. Afternoon tea, which is what emerged among the wealthy of Jane Austen's era, on the other hand, is quite often the formal affair we imagine. Typical stereotypes include the cucumber sandwiches of Oscar Wilde's *The Importance of Being Earnest*, clotted cream and scones, white linen and good silver, tiered plate racks laden with all sorts of cakes and finger sandwiches. Today, make your tea what you want it to be.

Picture you upon my knee, Just tea for two and two for tea.

—Irving Caesar

30
the last of the comfort food

—— spring eve ——

Spring is relative. Living in Chicago, I experienced it as something that didn't happen until the first week of June. But in southeastern England, May was already in full swing with garden parties where strawberries and champagne came in abundance and people came from all around to sit in the sun for the May boat races in Cambridge. Some people will be looking for a hearty winter warm-up in March and others for some early spring tastes. This final menu is just in time for the transitional period that celebrates that day in March when everyone is Irish and we honor the patron saint of the old sod, as well as the maple syrup festivities in later winter and early spring that take place once the maple trees thaw and pour forth their sap.

stout-glazed lamb chops

This time of year we see dishes with lamb and with stout, usually Guinness, proliferate. And they are almost always stews. This recipe goes a little more elegant, while still maintaining the kind of simplicity that we love in traditional Irish food.

  Salt
  Freshly ground black pepper
  4 lamb shoulder chops (6 to 8 ounces each)
  1 tablespoon olive oil
  1 cup stout, such as Guinness
  3 tablespoons packed brown sugar

Generously salt and pepper the lamb chops. Heat the oil over medium-high heat in a large skillet. Add the chops to the skillet and brown 3 minutes on each side. Remove the chops to a platter. Deglaze the pan with the stout, scraping up any browned bits. Stir in the brown sugar until it dissolves. Return the chops to the sauce. Cover and simmer for 15 minutes. Turn and cook, covered, for another 15 minutes. Remove the lid and turn the heat to medium-high. Cook the sauce and chops for a final 8-10 minutes until the sauce is thick and syrupy and the chops are tender. Turn the chops to coat in the glaze every 2 minutes or so. Serve the chops on a bed of colcannon (recipe follows) and drizzle with the sauce.

Serves 4

colcannon

This humble duet of two vegetables often associated with Ireland, potatoes and cabbage, is made perfect with a good helping of butter.

  2 pounds potatoes, peeled and cut in quarters
  6 tablespoons butter
  ½ cup warm milk
  3 cups cabbage, thinly sliced
  Salt
  White pepper

Bring a large pot of salted water to a boil. Add the potatoes and cook until soft, about 20 minutes. Drain. While the potatoes are cooking, bring a medium pot of salted water to boil and cook cabbage for 5 minutes. Drain. Mash potatoes with the butter. Stir in the milk and cabbage. Salt and pepper to taste.

Serves 4

Shouldering On

Lamb shoulder chops are becoming more popular as we look for higher-quality meats but affordable cuts. Shoulder needs to be cooked with moisture and given some good heat time to become tender enough. Lamb shoulder chops aren't served rare like more expensive rib chops, so don't confuse them. (See Braising Cuts, p. 21.)

A Rather Mutable Dish

Though colcannon is a favorite mash, often eaten at Halloween with charms buried inside (p. 85), it has made its way into March festivities to honor Ireland's patron saint as well. Colcannon comes from the Latin *caulis* "cabbage" and *ceannan* from Old Irish *ceann*, meaning "head."

maple custards with whisky cream

This dessert reveals the hybrid nature of the final meal of the season. True, maple syrup is not Ireland's national condiment. But we couldn't enter into spring without recognizing the spectacular ritual across North American maple-growing regions in late winter when the sap is gathered just as the trees start to thaw and our imaginations begin to invent all manner of new dishes with this precious liquid. Of course the whisky cream on top reminds us just a bit of an Old World favorite as well.

CUSTARD
2 whole large eggs
2 large egg yolks
¼ cup maple syrup, preferably dark amber
¾ cup whole milk
¾ cup whipping cream
Boiling water

GARNISH
½ cup whipping cream
1 tablespoon whisky
2 tablespoons sugar
Maple syrup

To make the custard: Butter four 1-cup ramekins or ovenproof coffee cups. Preheat the oven to 325°F.

In a medium mixing bowl, whisk together the eggs, egg yolks, and maple syrup. Combine the milk and whipping cream in a medium saucepan. Heat until it almost reaches a simmer. Very slowly pour the milk mixture into the egg mixture and whisk constantly as you pour. Ladle the custard into the prepared ramekins. Place the ramekins in a 13 x 9-inch pan and pour boiling water into the pan until it reaches halfway up the ramekins. Bake for 45 minutes until custard is set and only slightly wobbly in the center. Cool to room temperature. Chill thoroughly (overnight if you like).

When you are ready to serve the custards, prepare the garnish: Beat cream, whisky, and sugar together in an electric mixer until medium-stiff peaks form.

Garnish each custard with a dollop of whisky cream and drizzle with maple syrup.

Serves 4

Extra! Extra! Other things to do with maple syrup

· pour it on your waffles and pancakes, of course
· use it as an ice cream topping
· stir it into steamed milk

Maple Sugaring

While we often associate the flavor of maple with autumn desserts, maple sap is actually collected and processed just as the trees begin to thaw in March and April. When maple sap runs from maple trees, it is the consistency of water and then is boiled down to create a thick syrup.

stout-glazed lamb chops & colcannon

flurries
— more ways to eat, drink, and be merry —

❧❦❧

Celebrating the Seasons around the World
Holy Cows and Sacred Rites
As if You Needed Another Excuse ...

❧❦❧

celebrating the seasons around the world

Hospitality does not begin and end in December and there's a lot more to cold-weather entertaining than Christmas and Hanukkah. Cultures around the world have long ordered their eating and entertaining by the calendar to survive cold months and times of scarcity and pay homage to the powers that be for a good harvest and luck in the next year. I've gathered five international favorites together in a kind of cold weather cornucopia. Pick one, pick all.

Sukkot

Among Jewish autumn holidays, this is my favorite. It is both a harvest festival and a commemoration of the forty years the Israelites wandered in the desert. The important part is to build a temporary outdoor shelter called a sukkah, or booth, from materials that have grown from the earth and been cut off from it. A wonderful final opportunity to dine *al fresco* before cooler nights set in, custom dictates that you eat under the stars and be able to see the sky. What better way to enjoy the start of the autumn season?

Cheusok

This Korean Thanksgiving falls on the fifteenth day of the eighth month in the lunar calendar, which means it's on a different day of our calendar each year. As with so many other rituals and festivals during the autumn, this one too has dealings with the dead. On Cheusok you thank your ancestors for the harvest by ritually arranging food on a table so that the best and most expensive food is closest to the souls of the dead, that is, the back of the table. Typically, the food consists of fruits, spiced vegetables, fried foods, and boiled foods, in that order from front to back.

Diwali

The third day of this five-day Hindu harvest festival is called the "Festival of Lights" because people decorate their houses with candles in celebration of it. Like Cheusok, its date is determined by the lunar calendar, the fifteenth day of the new moon in the month Asvina or Kartik. For your celebration, try to make your own traditional Diwali foods, like a spicy snack of cabbage and carrot bhajia. Or, for something more substantial, whip up a chickpea and potato curry. Because the date changes each year, to keep up with the Diwali dates and happenings, check out www.diwalifestival.org.

Candlemas

The Christmas season doesn't really end until February 2. Long ago and not so far away, winter holidays in the Christian world were far more complex and long lasting than the mere Christmas and New Year's that remain with us today. Christmas was truly a season and not just a day. The calendar was punctuated with reasons to feast and didn't truly end until 40, not 12, days after Christmas, in February with the celebration of Candlemas. In Spanish-speaking countries, Candlemas is known as Candeleria, and in Mexico, Candeleria is celebrated with a big tamale party. Who makes the tamales is determined by who finds a figurine of the baby Jesus in their Epiphany king cake on Twelveth Night. What kind of tamale you serve depends on which region you favor. Some are made with corn husks and meat fillings, but closer to the coasts, banana leaves become the wrappers for fillings of fish. One of our previous guests on *Eat Feed*, Maria Laura Ricaud, insists that you not skimp on authenticity: you must use lard and accept no substitutes. Should you find yourself in Mexico for the holidays, you can learn to make authentic tamales at her cooking school (see www.traditionalmexicancooking.com).

Carnival and Lent

This pairing of plenty and want, feast and famine marks a transitional time in Christian communities around the world. It's now secularized in many places as an excuse to eat and drink and break up the long block of cold winter days before spring. Tuesday before Lent goes by many names and has many guises, but all with the same spirit: live it up now before 40 days of abstinence. There is, of course, the very familiar Mardi Gras revelries of New Orleans and the many imitations happening at local bars and restaurants in towns across the United States. But there are many more innovative ways to mark the day as well. There's Carnival in Rio with elaborate costumes and parades—and of course great Brazilian food. Or my own personal favorite, Shrove Tuesday or Pancake Day in the UK with stacks of eggy crepe-like pancakes and even pancake races. In 1600, one of Shakespeare's rival playwrights, Thomas Dekker, wrote an entire play dedicated to the glories of Pancake Day, but its roots are medieval. As flesh meats like beef and pork were restricted during Lent in the Middle Ages, so too were "whitemeats" or butter, eggs, milk, and cream. Cooking up stacks of pancakes was the perfect way to use up these forbidden ingredients before those 40 days of Lenten deprivation. Though eventually these whitemeats were allowed during Lent in the Renaissance, the tradition persisted, and Shrove Tuesday, or the day to be shriven (or forgiven) of your sins, also came to be associated with the misrule of London apprentices who attacked the brothels and theaters on the day. While we don't necessarily want to get that carried away in the twenty-first century, there's still a possibility for a bit of bawdy with our feast. So, invite some friends over and ask them to bring their favorite risqué jokes or some bawdy limericks or poetry. Find your favorite Shrove Tuesday pancake recipe on our site and have yourself a bit of the past in the present by serving up a truly medieval meal. Keep in mind that these pancakes aren't like our American flapjacks with maple syrup. They are more like a thin crepe. Quite simply, you whisk eggs, flour, and milk together to make the batter. Pour out the batter paper thin and cook evenly on both sides over medium heat. When they're done, sprinkle with lemon juice and sugar or stack between layers of parchment or wax paper and invite guests into the kitchen to choose their own toppings, from the basic sugar and lemon to jam, chocolate syrup, or whatever suits them.

holy cows and sacred rites

Once a way of ordering the Christian world, celebrations of saints' feasts still give us some intriguing vestiges of culinary rituals from days gone by. Here are a few saints of particular interest to gastronomes and the delicious reasons we have to honor them no matter where we place our faith today.

September 29, Saint Michael

Saint Michael's feast coincides with harvest duties, like settling debts and reckoning the account books, and festivities, like harvest fairs. The centerpiece of this festival is a Michaelmas goose, which given the season is leaner and milder than the sort of goose that would adorn the Christmas table. Combining all these features into one brief expression is the day's motto: "He who eats goose on Michaelmas day shan't money lack or debts to pay."

November 17, Saint Elizabeth of Hungary

To honor this patron saint of bread, what better way to welcome the return to baking than a party of bread making. You can either gather your friends together for a day of communal kneading and proofing or throw an evening party to which everyone brings their favorite homemade bread.

December 6, Saint Nicholas

That icon of Christmas is also patron saint of brewers and bakers. Of course, tradition is that children put their shoes out on this day to receive sweets and candy, but you can also go more adult for the day with another tribute to bread and that ambrosia from the grain field, beer.

December 13, Saint Lucia

Lucia of Syracuse is a complicated figure, whose legend includes ideas as diverse as that she was a witch who consorted with the devil and she was Adam's first wife. Her festival is another that celebrates the importance of light, and still today, young girls wear crowns of candles on their heads in honor of the saint. This day also provides an opportunity to bake up some Scandinavian Lussekatter, saffron buns shaped into the popular Lucia swirl or Joseph's beard. You'll also want a batch of Pepparkakor, the spicy cut-out cookies fashioned into traditional holiday shapes.

January 19, Saint Wulfstan

If you're having trouble sticking with those New Year's resolutions about eating better, turn your troubles to Saint Wulfstan, patron saint of dieters and vegetarians, whose day arrives just in time to help you stick to your New Year's resolutions. Perhaps like many of us, Wulfstan reproached himself for allowing a nearby roast goose to distract him from his duties and devotions and after that vowed never to taste meat again.

February 1, Saint Brigid of Kildare

It is said Saint Brigid, patron saint of dairymaids, poultry farmers, and cattle, comes to visit on her feast day, blessing people and livestock and bringing her white, red-eared cow with her. To welcome her, families leave an oaten cake and butter on the windowsill, as well as corn for her cow. Because her feast day is in February, when there isn't much to eat, her appearance with her bovine companion was rather miraculous.

March 1, Saint David

In the United States, come mid-March we all turn Irish and take on Ireland's Saint Patrick as our own. But for something a little more off the beaten path from green beer and other oddities of the day, turn yourself to Saint David instead. He's the patron saint of Wales and you can honor him by wearing a leek in your hat. Or, if haberdashery isn't your thing, you could cook with leeks instead. Just throw together a meal honoring this humble vegetable: think duck with braised leeks, leek and pea soup, whitefish on roasted leeks, or try making your own cawl, the leek broth that is the traditional food of Saint David's Day.

as if you needed another excuse . . .

Ten more reasons to eat and entertain rather than hibernate.

Stocking Up and Putting By

Homemade preserves are a great way to get everybody into the kitchen together. Once upon a time in order to survive the winter, you had to start getting ready for December in July by putting aside food long before you needed it. These were occasions for women to gather in one another's kitchens to cook and can and jelly—the original jam session, you might say. Start your entertaining adventure with a group trip with a few of your closest friends to a u-pick farm and then while away the afternoon making jellies, jams, and butters. Don't be daunted by this forgotten art. Even if you've never tried your hand at it, a thorough handbook like *Stocking Up* will guide you through the basics, as will the friendly people in your local community college's continuing education department. For something a bit grander, though, check out Georgeanne Brennan's classic and gorgeous *The Glass Pantry*. It is perfect for thinking about the most beautiful and tasty handmade holiday gifts for those who already have everything.

Pumpkin Carving Party

This was one of the more popular ideas from one of *Eat Feed*'s In Season programs. Listeners perked right up with lots of good feedback about why they liked this idea, so I'm including it again here. Because the pumpkin is a big part of Halloween, I think that for all its glory it really is entitled to its own special day. Which is why in preparation for October 31, I like to invite friends over for a pumpkin carving party the weekend before and serve up a buffet of great pumpkin-inspired foods. With the revival Halloween has been enjoying among adults as well as children, why not stretch it out a bit like the Christmas season and turn it into several days? For the menu, go international with an Indian-inspired pumpkin curry; elegant with a savory pumpkin soufflé; sweet with a pumpkin cake; or whimsical with some Harry Potter–inspired pumpkin pasties. Of course, it's also a good opportunity to serve the "All Hallows' Eve: It's the Great Pumpkin" menu (p. 80) if you happen to be otherwise booked on Halloween proper. Just remember to keep your cooking pumpkins and your carving pumpkins straight. The medium to large gorgeous jack o'lantern pumpkins for decorating won't do much for you in the culinary realm, though they will make for great carving. For cooking and eating, look for varieties like pie pumpkins or sugar pumpkins.

A Prize with Every Meal

This sort of event truly separates the goats from the geeks. Wear your intellectual heart on your plate with "A Nobel Dinner." Every December since 1901 when Alfred Nobel, inventor of dynamite, established the Nobel Peace Prize, there has been a Nobel dinner to go with the prize. The feast takes place at Stockholm's City Hall and is attended by Sweden's king and queen. The menu changes each year to reflect the diversity of Sweden's regional foods—lobster, potatoes, cauliflower, and turtle soup, to name a few. But one thing remains: a bombe-like ice cream parfait. Do you think everyone gets the joke?

Preseason Baking Potluck Kickoff

Get ready for the holidays and expand your baking repertoire with a recipe swap. Ask everyone to bring their favorite bit of lovin' from the oven and enough copies of the recipe to go around. Hopefully they'll be willing to share the story of the recipe as well—an immigrant grandmother's favorite cake from the Old World, the soufflé that won a wife's heart, or the Christmas cookies made every year as a child. Properly armed with tried-and-true cookies, cakes, and candies from all your favorite people, you'll never fear another office party and will face the holiday baking season with aplomb.

Old-Fashioned Skating Party

Don't let the passing of Christmas and Hanukkah force you to roll up the carpet and put out the vacation sign. There are still many more weeks in winter that want livening up, and ice provides the perfect theme. For a bit of Victorian romance, locate your nearest outdoor skating rink and gather everyone together. Even if you don't live where snow provides a reason to strap on some skis or snowshoes and head outdoors to break your cabin fever, chances are there is an indoor ice skating rink somewhere in your town. Lay on traditional old-time treats like humbugs, taffy, and toffee. Serve up a bit of nostalgia like the hot buttered rum of all those nineteenth-century novels you read in high school. Warm up with an assortment of cocoas (see p. 182-183). And, of course, don't forget the chestnuts roasting on an open fire.

A Tour on the Orient Express

Remember the wintry scenes from the film version of Agatha Christie's *Murder on the Orient Express*? The train pushes on through the coldest cities until it stalls in a snow bank and the action inside the train really heats up. Re-create the mystery and the luxury with a menu that serves up the signature cuisines of the cities that shaped the route of the Simplon Orient Express in the 1930s:

- Instanbul
- Sofia
- Belgrade
- Venice
- Milan
- Laussane
- Paris

That means putting on a spread of traditional Turkish dishes, a signature recipe from Serbia, Italian classics, some Swiss fondue perhaps, and finally your favorite Parisian specialties.

Frosty Film Festival

This is the sort of entertaining that gives a rhythm to the season as you rotate through friends' homes and hospitality each week, or each month, or however often, to set up your film fans and food friends club. Pair any of the menus in the book with one of your favorite wintry films, snuggle in with your best mates, and do it again and again throughout the season. Some suggestions for films to enhance the food (several of which, in their print versions, would fit nicely in a Cold Season Book Club as well):

- *Babette's Feast*
- *The Blair Witch Project*
- *Christmas in Connecticut*
- *The Claim*
- *Die Another Day*
- *Fargo*
- *Insomnia*
- *L'Iceberg*
- *The Lion in Winter*
- *The Polar Express*
- *The Sea*
- *The Shining*
- *Smilla's Sense of Snow*
- *Strange Brew*

Cold Season Book Club

Good winter reads with your favorite cozy food—what better way to encourage a get-together when the resorts are closed? Start early putting together a group of like-minded friends with monthly meetings of great autumn and winter books and delicious meals inspired by them. Start with some Icelandic sagas and a good translation of Beowulf for some ancient inspiration—and focus on the banquet scenes, naturally. Of course you'll also need *A Christmas Carol* for December with snacks inspired by the ghost of Christmas present, the Cratchets' holiday meal, and the punch and games of Scrooge's Christmas past. Fill out the rest of the season with a few of my personal favorites and keep your eye on the holiday book reviews for even more ideas:

- *An Enemy of the People* by Henrik Ibsen
- *Greenlanders* by Jane Smiley
- *The Golden Compass* by Philip Pullman
- *The Lion, the Witch and the Wardrobe* by C. S. Lewis
- *The Sittaford Mystery* by Agatha Christie
- *A Wild Sheep Chase* by Maruki Harukami
- *Wuthering Heights* by Emily Brontë
- *Pavel and I* by Dan Vyleta

Vikings Invade the Kitchen

This was one of the programs from the very early days of *Eat Feed* and comes completely from my fascination with Scandinavia, where they really know how to get through, and sometimes even enjoy, winter. If there's one thing that scares people off entertaining it's the idea of all the planning and the dishes. So here's a quick and easy way to overcome that and still have all the best of midwinter fun. Head to your nearest Ikea and instead of picking up another Billy bookshelf, step through to the groceries at the end of the journey. (Or, if you don't live in a town that has an Ikea or a good gourmet store, you can find these foods and other Scandinavian treats online at www.northerner.com.) Sure, lots of people load up on the butter cookies and ginger thins and chocolate bars, maybe even grab a bag of those Ikea meatballs. But look further afield and taste things you never knew existed.

· **Creamed caviar:** There are many tubes of paste in the cold section of Ikea and one of my favorites is Abba creamed caviar. I serve it on crackers for informal cocktails.

· **Elderberry:** This is a favorite flavor of northern Europeans and you'll find it at home as much in Norwegian desserts as in English garden parties. Among my favorite drinks is elderberry concentrate syrup mixed with seltzer for a nice alternative to the usual array of soft-drinks. It's also a great addition to cocktails: frappe some ice cubes, gin, sugar, and elderberry syrup for a pure white snowy winter adult slushie.

· **Lingonberries:** Great for Swedish pancakes in the morning but also just as good in your appetizer. Mia Littlejohn, *Eat Feed*'s Director of Marketing who grew up in Norway, suggests melting rich winter cheese like Tallegio on French toast rounds and topping it with a dollop of Lingonberry sauce.

· **Herring:** We can't forget herring—which in the United States is also hard to come by fresh or even smoked, when it's sold as kippers. Ikea usually sells several different varieties of pickled herring in small jars, including dill, mustard, cream sauce, and onion. Serve small pieces of herring on a dark, rich pumpernickel bread slathered with a good-quality butter.

· **Gjetost:** The name derives from the Norwegian words for goat, *gjet*, and for cheese, *ost*. These days it's quite often made with a mixture of goat's milk and cow's milk, though. Most cheeses are made by separating the whey from the curds and using the curds to make cheese. Gjetost is quite different; it's made by boiling the leftover whey of milk until the lactose caramelizes. This gives the cheese a wonderful rich brown color, a fudgelike texture, and a taste that is both sweet and tangy. Ski Queen, which comes in a bright red wrapper, is one of the most popular brands in the United States. Another popular kind, made by Tine, is Ekte, which is made from 100% pure goat's milk.

· **Aquavit:** In addition to the staples to keep on hand in the kitchen for winter cooking, keep in mind something a little off the beaten path that's becoming more and more popular for the cocktail table, reminding us that ABBA and Ikea are not the only cultural exports Scandinavia has to offer. Aquavit—a spicy, herby, bold, and biting Nordic spirit—is poised to pillage and plunder our preconceived ideas of sips you can squeeze from a few potatoes or a handful of grain. Its striking flavors, ranging from caraway and cumin to lemon and anise, remind you that "Skol" is not just a pinch between the teeth and gums but a sign that something worth toasting is at hand.

Waffle Party

There's no changing your mind on this one. I had this wonderfully frugal German grandmother, the two qualities of which combined in such things as waffles for dinner on a regular basis. These were some of my favorite childhood meals. Only later did I discover that waffle parties were popular in the 1930s, for some because they were a quick and cheap way to entertain during the tough days of the Depression and for others because they offered hostesses an opportunity to show off new electric appliances like waffle irons that were becoming all the rage in the early decades of the twentieth century. What I like about a waffle party today is that it's a sort of make-it-as-you-go dinner and can always accommodate one more guest or a late arrival. Fill out the menu with an assortment of cured and smoked meats, winter citrus fruit salads, and warm cozy drinks. Take the whole evening a step further by doing a maple syrup taste test with guests bringing their favorites to try throughout the night.

Conversion Chart

Weight Equivalents

The metric weights given in this chart are not exact equivalents, but have been rounded up or down slightly to make measuring easier.

Avoirdupois	Metric
¼ oz	7 g
½ oz	15 g
1 oz	30 g
2 oz	60 g
3 oz	90 g
4 oz	115 g
5 oz	150 g
6 oz	175 g
7 oz	200 g
8 oz (½ lb)	225 g
9 oz	250 g
10 oz	300 g
11 oz	325 g
12 oz	350 g
13 oz	375 g
14 oz	400 g
15 oz	425 g
16 oz (1 lb)	450 g
1½ lb	750 g
2 lb	900 g
2¼ lb	1 kg
3 lb	1.4 kg
4 lb	1.8 kg

Volume Equivalents

These are not exact equivalents for American cups and spoons, but have been rounded up or down slightly to make measuring easier.

American	Metric	Imperial
¼ tsp	1.2 ml	
½ tsp	2.5 ml	
1 tsp	5.0 ml	
½ Tbsp (1.5 tsp)	7.5 ml	
1 Tbsp (3 tsp)	15 ml	
¼ cup (4 Tbsp)	60 ml	2 fl oz
⅓ cup (5 Tbsp)	75 ml	2.5 fl oz
½ cup (8 Tbsp)	125 ml	4 fl oz
⅔ cup (10 Tbsp)	150 ml	5 fl oz
¾ cup (12 Tbsp)	175 ml	6 fl oz
1 cup (16 Tbsp)	250 ml	8 fl oz
1¼ cups	300 ml	10 fl oz (½ pint)
1½ cups	350 ml	12 fl oz
2 cups (1 pint)	500 ml	16 fl oz
2½ cups	625 ml	20 fl oz (1 pint)
1 quart	1 liter	32 fl oz

Oven Temperature Equivalents

Oven Mark	F	C	Gas
Very cool	250–275	130–140	1/2–1
Cool	300	150	2
Warm	325	170	3
Moderate	350	180	4
Moderately hot	375	190	5
	400	200	6
Hot	425	220	7
	450	230	8
Very hot	475	250	9

index

(Page references in *italic* refer to illustrations.)

a

Activities, winter, 163
"Address to a Haggis" (Burns), 172, 173
Afternoon Tea, 202–5, *204*
Ale, brown:
  beef and, pie, 158
  lambswool punch, 116, *117*
Allen, Fred, 150
Allen, Terese, 163
All Hallows Eve, 80–85
Almond(s), 34, 69
  cookies, 69
  orange cake, 150, *151*
Amaranth, 179
American Cookery (Simmons), 91
Ancho chili soup with sweet potatoes and chorizo, 196
Appetizers and hors d'oeuvres:
  butternut squash soup, 133, *134*
  chicken, sage, and cheddar tart, 137
  coconut rice twists, Thai, 103
  cornmeal catfish bites, *154,* 155
  curried potato and pumpkin latkes with yogurt sauce, 109
  dollars and coins, 153
  fried cod fingers, 109
  golden caviar toasts, 104, *105*
  ham and hot pepper jelly biscuits, 153
  honey-ginger carrot and parsnip latkes with crème fraîche, *110,* 111
  oat cakes with smoked salmon and salmon caviar, 127
  parsnip fries with two sauces, 140
  parsnip soufflés, 157, *159*
  phyllo cigars, *66, 67*
  potato salad, North African, 175
  red pepper harissa and yogurt with pita bread, 175, *176*
  roast beef sandwiches with pear spread and Stilton, 138, *139*
  smoked fish cakes with spicy Hmong slaw, 163
  turnip "carpaccio," 81
  wild mushroom toasts, 95
  winter greens tart, Renaissance, 121, *122*
Apple(s), 16–18, 72, 75, 79
  brandy, 79
  lambswool punch, 116, *117*
  maple tartlets, 72
  pears, and quince with paired cheeses, *78, 79*
  pork chops with brandy and, 75, *77*

and watercress salad with honey vinaigrette, 98
  see also Cider
Après Ski at the Swiss Chalet, 198–201
Aquavit, 216
  bloody Sigrid, 141
Austen, Jane, 189

b

"Back and Side Go Bare, Go Bare," 196
Bacon, 23
  citrus Brussels sprouts, 145, *146*
Baking, recipe swap and, 214
Baking pans, 45
Baklava, 65
Barley and sprout risotto, 123
Baumel, Miriam Delheim, 111
Beans, 19–20
  black, coconut, 149, *151*
  black-eyed peas, in dollars and coins, 153
  cannellini, in quick and easy Italian soup, 196
Beef, 21
  and brown ale pie, 158
  French onion pot roast, 133
  jolly great joint of, 143
  pasty pie, 87, *88*
  rib-eyes with whisky sauce, 127
  roast, sandwiches with pear spread and Stilton, 138, *139*
  stew, chocolate, with butternut squash and amaranth, 179
Beer(s), 195
  -braised brats, 165
  British, 158
  international, 141
  Soups, Stews, and Microbrews, 192–97
  stout glazed lamb chops, 207, *209*
  Wisconsin winter, 165
  see also Ale, brown
Beet(s), 37, 81
  fries with blue cheese sauce, *164,* 166
Bennett, Arnold, 185
Bierce, Ambrose, 71
Biscuits, ham and hot pepper jelly, 153
Black beans, coconut, 149, *151*
Black-eyed peas, in dollars and coins, 153
Bloody Sigrid, 141
Blue cheese sauce, *164,* 166
Blues (music), 155
Bok choi, 31
Bond, James, 150
Book clubs, 214
Bowl of bishop, 116

Braising cuts, 21
Brandy, 40
  apple and pear, 79
  kirshwasser, 200
  pork chops with apples and, 75, *77*
Brats, beer-braised, 165
Bread(s), 49
  dark, 43
  date muffins, let's make a, 190, *191*
  Meyer lemon tea, 203
  pita, red pepper harissa and yogurt with, 175, *176*
  pudding, 160
  scones with jam and clotted cream, 203, *204*
  serving with soups, 196
Breakfast in Bed, 188–90, *191*
Brennan, Georgeanne, 213
Breton, Nicholas, 147
Brigid of Kildare, Saint, 213
Bringing in the sheaves, 64–69
Browning, Robert, 56
Brown rice, 19
Brunch, 120–25
Brussels sprout(s), 31
  barley and, risotto, 123
  citrus bacon, 145, *146*
Burns, Robert, 172, 173
Burns' Night, 168–73
Burrows, Sir Fred, 95
Butter, 43
Butternut squash, 42
  chocolate beef stew with amaranth and, 179
  sauce, 82, *83*
  soup, 133, *134*
Butterscotch sauce, 172–73
Byron, George Gordon, Lord, 137

c

Cabbage, 31
  colcannon, 207, *209*
  spicy Hmong slaw, 163
Caesar, Irving, 205
Cakes (savory):
  corn, Washington's favorite, 91
  oat, with smoked salmon and salmon caviar, 127
  smoked fish, with spicy Hmong slaw, 163
  see also Latkes
Cakes (sweet):
  cheesecake with sherry sauce, 62–63
  fruited gingerbread with butterscotch sauce, 172–73
  orange almond, 150, *151*
  triple chocolate stuffed mocha cupcakes, 180, *181*
  Twelfth Night, 147

Yule log, 118–19
Candlemas, 211
Candles, 49
Cannellini beans, in quick and easy Italian soup, 196
Cardamom, 39
Carnival, 211–12
Carroll, Lewis, 189
Carrot(s), 37
    and parsnip latkes, honey-ginger, with crème fraîche, *110*, 111
    and potatoes for Sunday roast, 135
    roasted root vegetables, 98
    salad, autumn, 71
Catfish bites, cornmeal, *154*, 155
Cauliflower, 31
    Indian spiced, 56
Caviar, 49
    creamed, 216
    golden, toasts, 104, *105*
    salmon, oat cakes with smoked salmon and, 127
Celery root, 37–38
    spicy Hmong slaw, 163
Champagne, oysters and, 185, *186*
Charades, 99
Charcuterie, 22–23
Cheddar:
    chicken, and sage tart, 137
    Welsh rarebit, 71
Cheese(s), 24–25
    apples, pears, and quince with, *78*, 79
    blue, sauce, *164*, 166
    British, 205
    fondue, 199
    Gjetost, 216
    goat, walnut, and fig sandwiches, *204*, 205
    sauce, 140
    Stilton, roast beef sandwiches with pear spread and, 138, *139*
Cheesecake with sherry sauce, 62–63
Cherry(ies):
    kirshwasser, 200
    wild rice pilaf with pecans and, 76
Cheusok, 211
Chicken:
    with barley and green sauce, 123
    breasts with pumpkin seed filling and butternut sauce, 82, *83*
    sage, and cheddar tart, 137
    salad, Lincoln's inaugural, 92
    Thai coconut rice twists, 103
Chili(es), 43
    ancho, soup with sweet potatoes and chorizo, 196
    lime shrimp with rice, 149, *151*

Chocolate, 25–28, 179, 182
    beef stew with butternut squash and amaranth, 179
    chip steamed pudding, 197
    cocoa beans and, 183
    Food of the Gods, 178–83
    ganache frosting, 118, 119, 180, *180*
    hot, 182
    Mississippi mud parfaits, 155
    sipping, 183
    s'mores, 200, *201*
    triple, stuffed mocha cupcakes, 180, *181*
Chorizo, 24, 61, 62
    ancho chili soup with sweet potatoes and, 196
    Spanish pizza with peppers and, *60*, 61
Chowder, whitefish, 193
Christy, Martin, 182
Cider, 79, 145
    hard, in lambswool punch, 116, *117*
    wassail bowl, 115
Cilantro, in green sauce, 123
Cinnamon, 39, 57
    cookies, 187
    cream puffs, 57
Citron, 28
Citrus, 28–29
    bacon Brussels sprouts, 145, *146*
    peel, 33
Citrus in Season, 148–51, *151*
Clementines, 28
Clotted cream, 203
Cloves, 39
Cocoa beans, 183
Cocoa nibs, 180
Cocoa powder, 26
Coconut:
    black beans, 149, *151*
    rice twists, Thai, 103
Coddled eggs, 189, *191*
Cod fingers, fried, 109
Coffee:
    mocha cupcakes, triple chocolate stuffed, 180, *181*
    snowball, 103
Coffee cups, ovenproof, 45
Colcannon, 207, *209*
Cold Season Book Club, 214
Collard greens, 32
    dollars and coins, 153
Concord grapes, 53
Conversion charts, 217
Cookies:
    almond, 69
    cinnamon, 187
    double oatmeal, 135
Corn cakes, Washington's favorite, 91
Cornmeal catfish bites, *154*, 155
Couscous, 19
Cranberry(ies), 29–31

dried, 32–33
    -port relish, *96*, 97
    tarts, 167
    turkey and, sandwiches, Franklin's true American original, 91
Cream:
    cinnamon, puffs, 57
    clotted, 203
    horseradish, 144
    vanilla, 106
    whisky, 208
Cream cheese pumpkin squares, 84
Crucifers, 31–32
Cupcakes, triple chocolate stuffed mocha, 180, *181*
Curd, 36
Currants, 32
Curried potato and pumpkin latkes with yogurt sauce, 109
Custards, maple, with whisky cream, 208

d

Daikon radish pickles, Japanese, 35
Date(s), 33, 190
    muffins, let's make a, 190, *191*
David, Saint, 213
Dawson, Thomas, 130
Dekker, Thomas, 212
De la Mare, Walter, 98
Delicata squash, 42
Desserts:
    cinnamon cream puffs, 57
    cranberry tarts, 167
    cream cheese pumpkin squares, 84
    green tea gelatins, 124
    maple apple tartlets, 72
    maple custards with whisky cream, 208
    meringues, 107
    pears in nightshirts, 99
    s'mores, 200, *201*
    sufganiyot (Hanukkah donuts), 112–13
    vanilla cream, 106
    whisky trifle, 129–30, *131*
    see also Cakes; Cookies; Ice cream; Puddings
Dickens, Charles, 160
Dip cups, small, 48
Diwali, 211
Dollars and coins, 153
Donuts, Hanukkah (sufganiyot), 112–13
Dried fruits, 32–33, 121
Drinks:
    bloody Sigrid, 141
    British, 158
    champagne, 185
    chocolate, hot, 182

chocolate, sipping, 183
good morning squeeze, 189, *191*
hazelnut milk punch, 141
lambswool punch, 116, *117*
measurements for, 141
snowball, 103
wassail bowl, 115
Duck, 54
breasts with grapes, 54, *55*

e
Egg(s):
coddled, 189, *191*
whites. *See* Meringues
yolks, uses for, 107
Elderberry, 216
Elizabeth of Hungary, Saint, 212
English food:
fish and chips, 109
Guy Fawkes party, 86–89
A Posh Pub Night, 156–61
Renaissance winter greens tart, 121, *122*
Welsh rarebit, 71
Entrées:
brats, beer-braised, 165
cheese fondue, 199
duck breasts with grapes, 54, *55*
oysters and champagne, 185, *186*
pizza with chorizo and peppers, Spanish, *60,* 61
pork chops with apples and brandy, 75, *77*
shrimp, chili lime, with rice, 149, *151*
venison with cranberry-port relish, *96, 97*
Welsh rarebit, 71
whitefish chowder, 193
winter greens tart, Renaissance, 121, *122*
see also Beef; Chicken; Lamb; Sandwiches; Stews
Equipment, 44–49
Erd, Patty, 57

f
Fawkes, Guy, 86–89
Fearnley-Whittingstall, Hugh, 143
Feast Away the Winter Blues, 152–55
Feldman, Sarah Marx, 187
Festival of Light, 108–13
Feta, 68
olive filling, phyllo cigars with, *66, 67*
Fielding, Henry, 143
Fig(s), 33
lamb stew with apricots and, 177
walnut, and goat cheese sandwiches, *204,* 205
wheat berry and, salad, 68

"Figs" (Lawrence), 177
Film festivals, 214
Fireside Chat, 184–87
"First footing," 128
First Snowfall, The, 102–7
Fish:
catfish bites, cornmeal, *154,* 155
cod fingers, fried, 109
smoked, cakes with spicy Hmong slaw, 163
smoked and cured, 23–24
whitefish chowder, 193
Fondue, cheese, 199
Fondue pots and forks, 45, 200
Food of the Gods, 178–83
Fortune telling, 85, 128
Franklin, Benjamin, 91
French onion pot roast, 133
Fresh from the Field, 58–63
Fries:
beet, with blue cheese sauce, *164,* 166
parsnip, with two sauces, 140
Frosting, ganache, 118, 119, 180, *181*
Frosty Film Festival, 214
Frozen North, The, 162–67
Fruited gingerbread with butterscotch sauce, 172–73

g
Galloway Grace, 172
Game, 33
duck breasts with grapes, 54, *55*
venison with cranberry-port relish, *96, 97*
Ganache frosting, 118, 119, 180, *180*
Gathering Greenery, 120–25
Gelatins, green tea, 124
Gin, 40
Ginger, 39, 89
honey carrot and parsnip latkes with crème fraîche, *110,* 111
rum bonfire pudding, 89
Gingerbread, fruited, with butterscotch sauce, 172–73
Gjetost, 216
Glass Pantry, The (Brennan), 213
Glögg, 116
Glühwein, 116
Goat cheese, walnut, and fig sandwiches, *204,* 205
Golden caviar toasts, 104, *105*
Good Housewife's Jewel, The (Dawson), 130
Good morning squeeze, 189, *191*
Grains, 19–20
Grapes, 53, 54
duck breasts with, 54, *55*
Greek food, 64–69
Green foods, party with, 120–25

Greens:
collard, in dollars and coins, 153
winter, tart, Renaissance, 121, *122*
Green sauce, 123
Green tea gelatins, 124
Gunther, John, 190
Guy Fawkes party, 86–89

h
Haddock, smoked, 24
Haggis, 169
Haggis and a Hooley, 168–73
Halloween, 85
All Hallows Eve party, 80–85
Pumpkin Carving party, 213
Ham and hot pepper jelly biscuits, 153
Hanukkah, 108–13
Happy Hour, 136–41
Harissa, red pepper, and yogurt with pita bread, 175, *176*
Harvest deities, 69
Hatfield, Pamilyn, 166
Hazelnut milk punch, 141
Herring, 216
Highlands Hogmanay, 126–31
Hill, Katie, 81
Hirsh, Alan R., 187
Hmong, 167
slaw, spicy, 163
Holly, 125
Honey:
ginger carrot and parsnip latkes with crème fraîche, *110,* 111
vinaigrette, 98, 140
Hors d'oeuvres. *See* Appetizers and hors d'oeuvres
Hors d'oeuvres forks, 48
Horseradish, 43
cream, 144
Hot chocolate, 182
Hot pepper jelly and ham biscuits, 153
Hunting Party, The, 94–99
"Huntsmen, The" (de la Mare), 98
Hurston, Zora Neale, 187

i
Ice cream:
Jefferson's peanut sundaes, 92, *93*
Mississippi mud parfaits, 155
orange and rose water, 177
poire William, 76
pomegranate kulfi, 185
Ice cream makers, 45
Indian spiced cauliflower, 56
Inebriation, words for, 140
iPod speakers, 49
Italian soup, quick and easy, 196
Ivy, 125

j

Jack o'lanterns, 81
Jalapeños, 82
Jams, 36, 213
Jefferson, Thomas, 90, 91, 92
Jellies, 36, 213
Jell-O taboo, breaking, 124
Jewish food, 108–13, 211
Johnson, Samuel, 138, 205
Juniper, 125
Juniper berries, 39

k

Kale, 32
    Italian soup, quick and easy, 196
    Renaissance winter greens tart,
        121, 122
Keats, John, 53
Kimchi, 35
Kirshwasser, 200
Kulfi, pomegranate, 185

l

Lamb, 21, 177
    chops, stout-glazed, 207, 209
    meat loaf with marmalade glaze,
        169
    mint filling, phyllo cigars with,
        66, 67
    stew with figs and apricots, 177
Lambswool punch, 116, 117
Last of the Comfort Food, 206–9
Latkes, 109
    curried potato and pumpkin, with
        yogurt sauce, 109
    honey-ginger carrot and parsnip,
        with crème fraîche, 110, 111
Lavash, 48
    Thai coconut rice twists, 103
Lawrence, D. H., 177
Lemon(s), 28
    Meyer, tea bread, 203
Lent, 211–12
Lentils, 19–20
Let's make a date muffins, 190, 191
Lime(s), 28
    chili shrimp with rice, 149, 151
Lincoln, Abraham, 92
Lingonberries, 216
Littlejohn, Mia, 216
Lobster salad, Lincoln's inaugural, 92
Lucia, Saint, 212
"Lyke Wake Dirge, The," 81

m

Madeira, in wassail bowl, 115
Maple (syrup and sugar), 43, 208
    apple tartlets, 72
    custards with whisky cream, 208

Marmalade, 36
Marston, John, 72
McBurney, Lissa, 112, 113, 180, 187
Meat loaf, lamb, with marmalade
        glaze, 169
Meats:
    braising cuts, 21
    smoked and cured, 23–24
    see also specific meats
Meringue(s), 107
    mushrooms, 118
    pears in nightshirts, 99
Meyer lemon tea bread, 203
Michael, Saint, 212
Milk punch, hazelnut, 141
Mississippi mud parfaits, 155
Mistletoe, 125
Mocha cupcakes, triple chocolate
        stuffed, 180, 181
Muffins, date, let's make a, 190, 191
Muscat grapes, 53
Mushroom, wild, toasts, 95
Music:
    blues, 155
    sun songs, 115
Mustard, 43, 56

n

New Year's parties:
    Fireside Chat, 184–87
    Highlands Hogmanay, 126–31
New Year's traditions, 153
Nicholas, Saint, 212
Nicol, James, 127
Nilsson, Harry, 149
Nobel Dinner, A, 213
North African food, 174–77
Nutmeg, 39
Nuts, 34

o

Oat(meal)(s), 20, 135
    cakes with smoked salmon and
        salmon caviar, 127
    double, cookies, 135
    toasted honey, 129, 130, 131
O'Brien, Chris, 195
Old-Fashioned Skating Party, 214
Olive-feta filling, phyllo cigars with,
        66, 67
O'Neill, Molly, 195
Onion(s):
    caramelized, mashed potatoes,
        128
    pot roast, French, 133
    roasted root vegetables, 98
    rösti, 199
"Onions" (Swift), 128
Orange(s), 28–29
    almond cake, 150, 151
    good morning squeeze, 189, 191

and rose water ice cream, 177
Orchard Buffet, An, 74–79
Orient Express party, 214
Ouzo, 68
Oysters and champagne, 185, 186

p

Pancake Day, 212
Pantry, cold weather, 14–43
Parfaits, Mississippi mud, 155
Parsley, in green sauce, 123
Parsnip(s), 38
    and carrot latkes, honey-ginger,
        with crème fraîche, 110, 111
    fries with two sauces, 140
    roasted root vegetables, 98
    soufflés, 157, 159
Pastes, savory, in tubes, 48
Pasty pie, 87, 88
Peanut(s), 34
    sundaes, Jefferson's, 92, 93
Pear(s), 16, 18, 75
    apples, and quince with paired
        cheeses, 78, 79
    brandy, 79
    in nightshirts, 99
    Poire William ice cream, 76
    spread, roast beef sandwiches
        with Stilton and, 138, 139
Peas, split, 20
Pecans, 34
    wild rice pilaf with cherries and,
        76
Pepper(corns), 39, 137
Pepper(s), 59
    red, harissa and yogurt with pita
        bread, 175, 176
    Spanish pizza with chorizo and,
        60, 61
Phyllo (dough):
    cigars, 66, 67
    containers, 48
Pickles, 35, 199
Pies:
    beef and brown ale, 158
    pasty, 87, 88
Pilaf, wild rice, with cherries and
        pecans, 76
Pine, 125
Pita bread, red pepper harissa and
        yogurt with, 175, 176
Pizza with chorizo and peppers,
        Spanish, 60, 61
Poire William ice cream, 76
Politics of Food, The, 90–93
Pomegranate(s), 185
    kulfi, 185
Pork, 21
    brats, beer-braised, 165
    chops with apples and brandy,
        75, 77
    rustic winter stew, 194, 195

Port, 40
    cranberry relish, *96, 97*
Porter, Cole, 187
Posh Pub Night, A, 156–61
Potato(es), 38
    caramelized onion mashed, 128
    and carrots for Sunday roast, 135
    chips, English, 157
    colcannon, 207, *209*
    onion rösti, 199
    pasty pie, 87, *88*
    and pumpkin latkes, curried, with
      yogurt sauce, 109
    roasted root vegetables, 98
    salad, North African, 175
    and turnips with bacon and
      cream, 170, *171*
Pot roast, French onion, 133
Preseason Baking Potluck Kickoff,
    214
Preserves, 36, 213
Priestly, J. B., 104
Prosciutto, 23
Pub fare, 156–61
Pudding, Yorkshire, 144
Pudding bowls, 46
Puddings (sweet):
    bread, 160
    British, 160, 161, 197
    chocolate chip steamed, 197
    ginger rum bonfire, 89
    steaming, 197
Puff pastry, 48, 72
Pumpkin(s), 42, 81, 85
    cream cheese squares, 84
    and potato latkes, curried, with
      yogurt sauce, 109
    seed filling, chicken breasts with,
      and butternut sauce, 82, *83*
    seed oil, 71
Pumpkin Carving Party, 213
Punch:
    hazelnut milk, 141
    wassail bowl, 115

q

Quince, apples, and pears with
    paired cheeses, *78,* 79

r

Raisins, 32
Raking in the Leaves, 70–73
Reagan, Ronald, 90, 91
Red pepper harissa and yogurt with
    pita bread, 175, *176*
Renaissance Twelfth Night, 142–47
Renaissance winter greens tart, 121,
    122
Ribier grapes, 53
Ricaud, Maria Laura, 211
Rice:
    brown, 19

coconut, twists, Thai, 103
dollars and coins, 153
white, 20
see also Wild rice
Risotto, barley and sprout, 123
Roast beef sandwiches with pear
    spread and Stilton, 138, *139*
Roasted root vegetables, 98
Roasting pans, large, 46
Root vegetables, 37–38
    roasted, 98
Rosemary, 123, 125
Rosetti, Christina, 104
Rose water and orange ice cream,
    177
Rösti, onion, 199
Rum, 40
    ginger bonfire pudding, 89
Rumming, Elynour, 195
Rustic winter stew, *194, 195*
Rutabagas, in pasty pie, 87, *88*

s

Saganaki, 65
Sage, 125
    chicken, cheddar and, tart, 137
Saints' feasts, 212–13
Salads:
    carrot, autumn, 71
    chicken and lobster, Lincoln's
      inaugural, 92
    potato, North African, 175
    spicy Hmong slaw, 163
    tomato, 59
    watercress and apple, with honey
      vinaigrette, 98
    wheat berry and fig, 68
Salami, 23
Salmon, smoked, 23
    oat cakes with salmon caviar and,
      127
Sandwiches:
    roast beef, with pear spread and
      Stilton, 138, *139*
    turkey and cranberry, Franklin's
      true American original, 91
    walnut, fig, and goat cheese, *204,*
      205
Sauces (savory):
    blue cheese, *164,* 166
    butternut, 82, *83*
    cheese, 140
    green, 123
    honey vinaigrette, 140
    horseradish cream, 144
Sauces (sweet):
    butterscotch, 172–73
    sherry, 62–63
Sauerkraut, 35
    rustic winter stew, *194,* 195
Scandinavian food:
    bloody Sigrid, 141

Vikings Invade the Kitchen, 216
Scones with jam and clotted cream,
    203, *204*
Scoops, stainless steel, 45
Scotch Presbyterian Eloquence, 130
Scots delicacies, 170
Scottish parties:
    Haggis and a Hooley, 168–73
    Highlands Hogmanay, 126–31
Season of Mists and Mellow
    Fruitfulness, 52–57
Selkirk Grace, 172
Shakespeare, William, 140, 142–47,
    185
Sheridan, Richard, 140
Sherry, 63
    sauce, 62–63
Shrimp, chili lime, with rice, 149,
    151
Side dishes:
    amaranth, 179
    barley and sprout risotto, 123
    beet fries with blue cheese sauce,
      164, 166
    black beans, coconut, 149, *151*
    Brussels sprouts, citrus bacon,
      145, *146*
    cauliflower, Indian spiced, 56
    colcannon, 207, *209*
    corn cakes, Washington's favorite,
      91
    cranberry-port relish, *96,* 97
    onion rösti, 199
    potatoes, caramelized onion
      mashed, 128
    potatoes and carrots for Sunday
      roast, 135
    potatoes and turnips with bacon
      and cream, 170, *171*
    root vegetables, roasted, 98
    wild rice pilaf with cherries and
      pecans, 76
    Yorkshire pudding, 144
    see also Salads
Simmons, Amelia, 91
Sipping chocolate, 183
Skating parties, 214
Skelton, John, 195
Slaw, spicy Hmong, 163
Smell, sexual turn-ons and, 187
Smoked fish cakes with spicy Hmong
    slaw, 163
S'mores, 200, *201*
Snow:
    eating, 106
    homemade, with syrups or
      alcohol, 107
Snowball, 103
Snowmen, 140
Soufflés, parsnip, 157, *159*
Soups:
    ancho chili, with sweet potatoes
      and chorizo, 196